To Neil.

Laid Back Around the World in 180 Days

Richard Evans xx

Richard Evans

Illustrated by Dominic Trevett

"We don't stop playing because we grow old;
we grow old because we stop playing"
George Bernard Shaw (playwright, critic, socialist and lifelong cyclist)

In memory of my dear mum
How I wish you'd been here to enjoy the ride

To Pascale, Julia and Mark, with all my love

From the vast deserts of Kazakhstan to the Pyrenees via the monsoons of Southeast Asia, the Australian Nullarbor, the Canadian Rockies and Great Lakes, this is Richard Evans's travelogue of his six-month journey around the world by recumbent bicycle in 2014.

Averaging around 1,000 km per week, Richard shared treacherously potholed highways with speeding juggernauts, faced freezing nights and scorching days, and battled headwinds strong enough to blow him off the road. Having lost 7kg in the first seven weeks and with 19 weeks still to go, it was important to stabilise the weight loss. A cure was found in beer and dumplings.

Roads varied erratically from freshly tarmacked highways of international standard one minute to heavily rutted dirt tracks the next, where all evidence of any rideable surface had long since disappeared.

In the thermal pools of Taupo, New Zealand, he met ultra-runner Kevin Carr, who'd been running round the world at over 50 km/day for two years. Kevin's blog *Hardwayround* prompted Richard to consider renaming his own blog *Easywayround*. Because there were some easy bits too. And running is always harder.

In an American supermarket he stumbled across the gun counter, where a shop assistant apologised for not knowing much about firearms because she usually worked on fruit and veg.

Countless acts of spontaneous generosity from strangers propelled him along the way. Several times he was warned that he'd reached the edge of civilisation and to continue would be sheer folly because folk in the next town/province/country were aggressive savages. Upon arrival however he was invariably met by benevolent locals interested in where he was from, where he was going and how old he was (52½).

Richard eventually finished back where he started, at BikeFix in London, having ridden 23,000 km across 18 countries and four continents. The only aggression he'd faced had been on the roads: first from motorists, a sizeable minority of whom morph into murderous maniacs as soon as they get behind the wheel; and to a lesser extent from dogs – but Richard had his own special way of dealing with them…

All royalties from this book will go to RoadPeace, a small charity which looks after the bereaved and injured from road crashes, and campaigns for safer streets. Road crashes kill 1.3 million people worldwide every year – that's more every day than died in the Twin Towers on 9/11, and almost three times more than die from malaria.

The photos in this book (and many more) can be seen in full glorious Technicolor at tinyurl.com/hp688pk

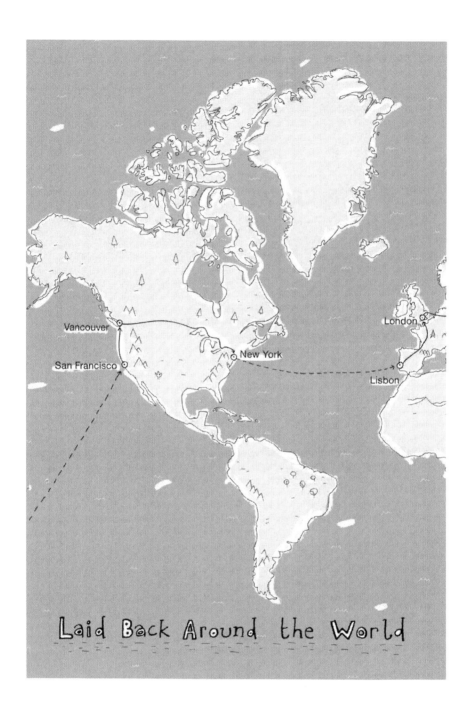

Laid Back Around the World

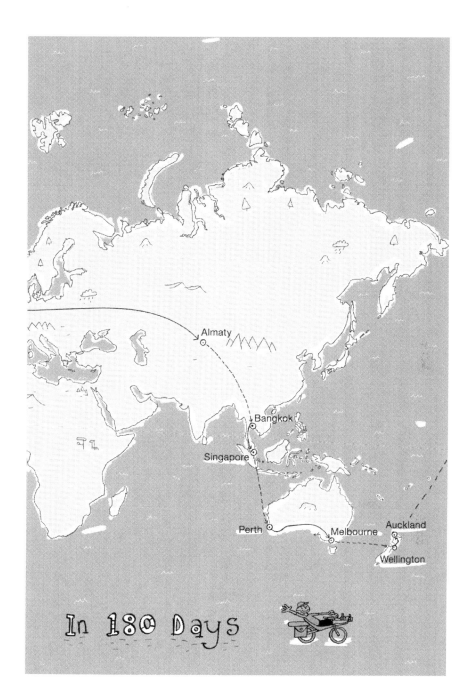

In 180 Days

CONTENTS

Acknowledgments 1

Prologue 4

London to Almaty 25

Bangkok to Singapore 85

Perth to Auckland 109

San Francisco to New York City.................................140

Lisbon to London 193

Epilogue...208

Guinness World Record..210

Vital Statistics 214

ACKNOWLEDGMENTS

Thanks are due to quite a lot of people, first and foremost to my wife Pascale for letting me go…and not changing the locks! I've lost count of the number of times I've been told what a lucky bloke I am and asked how many brownie points it took. Next to Julia and Mark for supporting and humouring their eccentric old man in all his daft endeavours and putting up with the years of background noise generated by the dreaming and planning phases – I hope you made the most of the relatively brief respite while I was actually gone. Thanks to Mum and Dad for inspiration in the early days, teaching me to enjoy the outdoor life and how to read a map (that turned out to be quite useful). My siblings: Antony for loading his eclectic CD collection on my mp3 player to keep me entertained along the way and for proof-reading this book (thus any remaining errors are his); Catherine for organising a fantastic leaving do and welcome home party; Jonathan and Philip for hosting me down under and riding with me for a few special and memorable days. Nephews, nieces and cousins too numerous to mention by name whose messages of love and support kept me going especially through the hard bits.

Thanks to colleagues at Hammersmith & Fulham Council, especially Chris and Simon for letting me go…and having me back; and to Eustace for keeping my seat warm and looking after my schools and my truckers. Andy that was an awesome leaving party!

Thanks to Dominic for the wonderful logo, book covers and maps. He tells me he's available for other commissions… www.dominictrevett.com; and to Malcolm, my second proof-reader and author of *A Virgin Discovers Long Distance Cycling: London Edinburgh London 2013*[1]

Thanks to all my friends at Audax UK who showed me how to ride a bike a long way, with special mention to Dave who shielded me from the wind all the way to Warsaw. Thanks also to fellow Kingston Wheelers and Wimbledon Common parkrunners for the wonderful send-offs, and to Stuart Dennison at Bikefix (possibly the best laid back bike shop in the world). And to warmshowers and so many other hosts, name-checked through the book, who made me so welcome me across four continents.

Thanks also to Andrew at the Environmental Transport Association for the RoadPeace introduction, Bob for choreography at the finish, Richard at Cyclecentric and John and Mark at Bacchetta (for the bike), Patrick at Ison Distribution for Rohloff (14-speed hub gear), Tim at Stanfords (maps), Lija at Scott's (visas) and Amber at Holiday Safe (travel insurance).

---

[1] http://tinyurl.com/pyb77w6

ROADPEACE

Thanks last but not least to everyone who has given so generously to my chosen charity RoadPeace, and thanks to you dear reader for buying this book and also thereby supporting RoadPeace.

All proceeds from this book will go to RoadPeace, the National Charity for Road Crash Victims. If you've managed to blag a free copy, then good for you! Please donate the cover price (and a bit more!) at https://mydonate.bt.com/fundraisers/laidbackrich

A road death is not a normal death - it is sudden, violent, unexpected, and premature. Every day, five people die on British roads, and 3,900 worldwide – that's more than died in the Twin Towers on 9/11, *every single day*. Road crashes kill 1.3m people every year – more than malaria or TB. By 2030 they will kill more than HIV/AIDS[2].

One in 75 of us is bereaved through a road crash. Losing a loved one in a crash is devastating. Lives are shattered, and some never recover from the trauma. Family breakdown, job loss, depression and even suicide are the unfortunate consequences of losing a loved one in this way.

Despite this, crashes are all too often seen as unfortunate 'accidents', instead of preventable collisions. Society tolerates road death and disability as an acceptable price to pay for increased motorisation and convenience. Crash victims do not have the same rights or support as other victims of crime or trauma.

RoadPeace[3] has been campaigning since 1992 to change this, helping the bereaved with support, a helpline, befriending, guides to investigation, prosecution, and campaigning for:

- Improved investigations;
- Effective inquests;
- Appropriate prosecution and sentencing;
- Fair compensation;
- Rights for victims;
- Safer streets, reducing road danger, tackling bad driving.

As a previous world bike rider once blogged, my ride was not for charity[4]. It was a personal challenge for pleasure, and it was self-financed. I rode around the world *because it was there*, to paraphrase an early Everest mountaineer. But unlike Mallory I wasn't the first[5]; many wheel tracks were already there to be followed. Nor would I be the fastest or oldest or any kind of superlative. In essence, as Pascale reminded me once or twice, it boiled down to a six-month holiday riding my bike. But as I prepared, one of the more frequent questions from friends and colleagues was "are you doing it for charity?" It seemed that my efforts might inspire people to give

---

[2] The Economist, Jan 25th 2014

[3] http://www.roadpeace.org/

[4] http://thisisnotforcharity.com/

[5] http://tinyurl.com/pqqye7r

away some of their hard-earned folding stuff. So I set up a fundraising page for RoadPeace[6] (using mydonate which creams off substantially less than some of the better-known sites like justgiving and virgin - there can be quite a difference[7]).

My trip was entirely self-financed: none of the money donated was syphoned off to pay for new tyres or beer, it all went to RoadPeace.

The last word here goes to a bereaved mother whose son Edward was killed during the week of Christmas 1998 when an overtaking oncoming driver hit him head on.

I campaign to highlight the inadequacies of an outdated legal system that has not evolved to address the problems caused by the increasing use and misuse of motor vehicles. I campaign because I was, and still am:

- **Devastated** that my son was killed on the road;
- **Appalled** that the driver responsible for his death was not held accountable;
- **Amazed** that the Police failed to conduct a proper investigation;
- **Saddened** that the Coroner could not deliver a verdict that reflected the manner in which he died;
- **Exhausted** trying to comprehend a legal system that regards the killing of a human being by another as irrelevant;
- **Furious** that his death was only mentioned to the Magistrates by chance – it was not considered or mentioned in the charge, and consequently not reflected in the sentence;
- **Bewildered** that the previous motoring convictions of the driver could not be taken into account by the court;
- **Disbelieving** of the level of leniency by the courts;
- **Angered** that preventable crashes are perceived as accidents and that there is no deterrent for the perpetrators;
- **Dismayed** at the apathy of politicians to address an escalating problem that affects every one of us.

Julia Wright

supporting crash victims, reducing road danger
helpline 0845 4500 355 www.roadpeace.org @roadpeace

---

[6] https://mydonate.bt.com/fundraisers/laidbackrich
[7] http://tinyurl.com/3997egn

PROLOGUE

Early Days

I blame my dad! When I was at a young and impressionable age he let slip that he had ridden a bike from London to Bristol in a day to visit his mum. I was hugely impressed, and I was the proud owner of a brand new Raleigh Wayfarer. I was ten years old and it was dad's mum, or Nanny to me, who had bought me this shiny new single speed bike – my ticket to freedom! Five years later, in that long hot summer of 1976, on a new bike with five times as many gears and in the company of best mate and neighbour, Paul Harrison, I lived my first long distance cycling dream: I rode to Bristol…and back. The liberty was intoxicating. So too were the girls – Paul was the ideal riding companion and mentor, being two years older and more experienced in these matters.

There followed an interlude of some 15 lost years when I went over to the dark side and rode motorcycles. I confess that I enjoyed them too, touring and camping on trips around Britain and Europe, though the satisfaction at the end of the day was never quite the same as the buzz when I arrive at my destination under my own steam.

In 1989 I gave up smoking and rediscovered cycling. These were the early days of mountain biking and I loved it. Around this time I also joined the *London Cycling Campaign*, and a fellow campaigner had just bought a Ross recumbent bicycle. I took it for a spin one evening after an LCC rides planning session at the Boaters pub in Kingston-on-Thames, just a few hundred yards along the towpath, and was immediately hooked. This was sublime – a deckchair on wheels, a mobile sun-lounger – I had to have one! And so in 1993 I bought a second-hand Kingcycle, a low slung racing recumbent bike that, ridden by Pat Kinch and fitted with a fairing to improve aerodynamics, held the laid-back world hour record: 75.6 km. For comparison, the hour record at the time for a "normal" bike, as defined by the UCI (*Union Cycliste Internationale*), was being swapped between Graeme Obree and Chris Boardman, rising by tiny increments to a tad over 52 km. Both records have been broken several times since and currently stand at 91.6 km on a faired recumbent in August 2011 by Francesco Russo and 54.5 km on a UCI-approved bike by Sir Brad Wiggins in June 2015.[8]

By 1999 I had discovered the Dunwich Dynamo, an annual 190 km night ride from London to the Suffolk coast, and I'd also met fellow LCC

---

[8] http://en.wikipedia.org/wiki/Hour_record

members Patrick Field, Mike Bridgeland and Charlie Lloyd fresh back from Paris recounting epic tales from a much longer bike ride – they had just completed the legendary 1,200 km Paris-Brest-Paris[9] (PBP), blue riband event of long distance cycling with a history going back to 1891, predating the Tour de France by some 12 years. PBP runs only every four years, so there was plenty of time for the seed to germinate, and in early 2003 I

Riding my Kingcycle to my first PBP, August 2003

joined Audax UK, the long distance cyclists' association, which organises PBP qualifying rides for British riders. These are four rides of increasing distance: 200 km, 300 km, 400 km and 600 km, which together constitute the "Super Randonneur" (SR) series. Time limits are generous, based on a minimum speed of just 15 km/h, but they include all stops at the "controls" where you get your "brevet card" stamped or signed, and eat (traditionally) your beans on toast. On the longer rides most riders take a short sleep break too, though some will ride through the night and finish early to get a "good finish time". Most riders are out however not to *do* a good time, but to *have* a good time. It's important to note that no one ever wins an audax event, because they are not races. The grapevine and social media both serve well to impart information about who finishes first, but every finisher is a winner.

Audax rides are a relatively undiscovered gem (and long may it remain that way!) compared to the rising numbers of commercially organised "sportive" rides available today. The principal differences as I see them are:

---

[9] http://tinyurl.com/ppae6nq

	Audax	Sportive
Typical entry fee	£5 - £20	£30 - £100
Typical size of field	10 - 100	500 - 5,000
Typical bike	Steel frame with mudguards, leather saddle, saddlebag and dynamo lights	Carbon frame with tiny seat pack, electronic gears, no lights
Typical age of rider	63	36
Route directions	Route sheet (and GPX tracks for the modernists)	GPX tracks for all, marshals and arrows at junctions
Timing chip and number on your back	No	Yes
Food and drink	Beans on toast, cups of tea, cakes, beer	Isotonic drinks, gels and power bars
Is it ok to stop at the pub en route?	Yes	No
What they say	Full of blokes pretending they're not racing	Full of blokes pretending they are racing

The most common audax distance is 200 km, probably because it's still just a day ride, but slightly longer than most rides run by other organisations where anything over 100 miles (160 km) is uncommon. At 15 km/h the time limit for 200 km is 13 hours and 20 minutes, so as long as you can average a stately 20 km/h on the bike then you have three hours and 20 minutes for controls, eating and faffing. So you most definitely do not need to be any kind of elite rider – audax is open to anyone audacious enough to give it a go!

For longer rides where you might plan to take a sleep somewhere en route, you have to save up a "time buffer", so faster riders will get a time advantage and be able to sleep for longer and recover better for the following day(s). A 600 km event will typically start at 06:00 on a Saturday, and with a time limit of 40 hours, riders must finish by 22:00 the following day. I personally like to ride hard on the Saturday while the legs are fresh and, all being well, get to something like 380 km by around midnight at which point a good event organiser will have laid on a control with mats and blankets on the floor in a village hall. Then I'll be back out on the road by about 06:00 on the Sunday with just 220 km to ride, and 16 hours in which to do it. Thus I can cruise back at a moderate pace and enjoy the scenery with ample time for tea and cake stops, aiming for the *arrivée* (audax for finish) at around 18:00, still maintaining a comfortable time buffer in case of mechanical problems, headwinds, or pubs that are just so inviting it would be rude not to stop.

My very first audax ride was a 200 km on Tuesday 11th February 2003. This was the first of the "Super Randonneur" series of four rides I would need to complete by June to qualify for PBP entry for that year. It was organised by audax legend John "Rocco" Richardson of the Willesden Cycling Club and started, rather ingloriously, from a wet, empty, desolate and windswept car park on a trading estate in Ruislip, west London – a brusque and brutal initiation into the glamour of long distance cycling. It was an x-rated event, but sadly I discovered that this did not involve any nudity. X-rated audax means a cheap entry fee, e.g. £5, in return for which you get the brevet card and a route sheet, but no beans on toast. Controls were in cafés and garages where we collected either a timed receipt or a stamp on the brevet card, and there were also two proof of passage "info controls" where we had to note the colour of a barn and the name of a pub that we passed. I left home at 04:00 to ride 30 km to the start where a dozen or so riders were standing around in the freezing rain exchanging a few words and pretending to be jolly. I introduced myself to Rocco and told him I was an audax virgin. He gave me my brevet card and some soothing words of encouragement: "You've picked a great day to start!" then set us all off on the dot of six, straight down onto the A40, in the dark, in the driving rain, and into the thickening traffic, it was horrible…and then I got a flat tyre. I had managed to stay with the other riders for all of about 10 km.

After fixing the puncture I was alone for the rest of the day. I'm happy riding alone but I had been hoping to socialise a little with seasoned riders, make one or two new friends and perhaps learn a few tricks of this new trade.

Further mechanical problems followed in short order. After leaving the A40 and getting onto quieter roads and lanes, for which I was very thankful, I stopped at a T-junction and promptly keeled over. I was still getting used to my new shoes which clipped into the pedals – you need to give a little twist to release your foot. This soon becomes second nature…but it wasn't that day. No problem, I picked the bike up, brushed myself off, and set off again, and there followed an awful grinding and crunching sound from the back wheel. My topple onto the tarmac had bent the derailleur back into the spokes which then dragged it around in the wheel, mangling it into an ex-derailleur in just a few terrible seconds. It was clearly and utterly beyond repair. I looked at the map; there was no railway station within walking distance, but there was a town – Thame – where I rather hoped there might be a bike shop, open, with a suitable replacement derailleur and mechanic with spare time on his hands. I got lucky on the first three counts...and I have never fitted a replacement derailleur so fast.

Back on the road, probably an hour behind the other riders now, but still just within the time limits, I decided to press on. So did the freezing rain, all day. The ride went out into the Cotswolds before turning back eastwards towards home. Two further punctures followed. I never could get good tyres for that Kingcycle – it had unusual size wheels: 17" (Moulton size) on the front and 24" (child bike size) on the back. I finished the ride back in Ruislip at 19:20, bang on the time limit of 13 hours and 20 minutes. With the ride home, it made 260 km for the day. I flopped into bed utterly exhausted.

The following day I had a decision to make: give up this audax lark, or carry on? The first hurdle had been so hard: I'd finished without a minute to spare, and that was just the 200. Next up was the 300. The 400 and 600 would soon follow, and even if I could manage to complete them, which now looked distinctly unlikely, I'd still only be up to half the PBP distance. It seemed almost impossible.

But, as one of life's eternal optimists, there was another way to look at this. I had survived and completed a tough ride in difficult conditions, and stayed within the time limit despite filthy weather, a major mechanical episode and a series of punctures. Surely the rides to come could not all be that bad and my luck could only improve from such an inauspicious start? The 200 had been a baptism of fire, but now the days would get longer, the weather would improve, and I would learn how to stop my bike without falling off. Furthermore I had actually ridden 260 km, so the next step up to 300 did not seem quite so great.

So I took the decision to continue, a decision that ultimately led to my world bike tour, which I'm sure I would never have contemplated without the wealth of audax experience and confidence gained since 2003. Weather conditions on the remaining three qualifying rides that year were indeed much more favourable, there were no further serious mechanicals, and I finished each ride comfortably inside the time limits. I'd qualified for PBP and I was ecstatic!

Paris-Brest-Paris is a joyous jamboree which comes round every four years, a colourful and international four-day fiesta of cycling. Around half of the 5,000-odd participants are French, and the remainder flock in from all corners of the globe. There's a 90-hour time limit, so the average minimum speed is just 13.3 km/h, allowing ample time for relaxed meal and sleep breaks. The fastest 1% of riders barely stop at all and complete in around 44 hours. Their control technique resembles a Formula One pit-stop: while they dash into the control, e.g. the town lycée, to get their cards stamped, their teams of helpers (who are only allowed to meet up with riders at official controls) will be filling their water bottles and musettes, checking and fettling the bike, replacing batteries in the lights, checking the rider is adequately dressed and prepared for the expected weather on the next stage, providing instant high calorific meals that can be swallowed in minutes, and so on. The fastest rider back to Paris in 2015 was a PBP first-timer and wrote a great account of his ride on the YACF cycling forum.[10]

Most of the other 99% of riders have no helpers and are not in such a hurry. Indeed some 80% of riders finish between 80-90 hours. We are the so-called "full-value riders", getting our money's worth: we paid for 90 hours and we are going to use them! I'm well established now in the full-value category, with finish times ranging from 71:47 to 89:22 in the four PBPs I've completed, the slowest of these giving me access to the exclusive Adrian Hands Society, open to any riders successfully finishing in over 88:55, in recognition of "those randonneurs and randonneuses who believe that every ride should be enjoyed to its fullest. Membership is not for the fleetest of foot but for those that savour every moment of the journey, often using the full allotment of allowed time".[11]

A decade of "super-randonneuring" followed that first season, earning me the Ultra-Randonneur award in 2012. Every other year there was also either the PBP in 2003/07/11, or the London-Edinburgh-London (LEL) 1,400 km event in 2005/09/13. Most years I was also riding down to the south of France for family holidays, and there were testing and spectacular 1,000 km events in Wales and Scotland too. It was during these years and those long hours in the saddle that I began wondering how much further I could go on one bike ride…

Many audax riders make lengthy notes of their rides and publish them in the Audax UK magazine Arrivée, or online at YACF (Yet Another Cycling Forum). I'm not in the habit of doing that, but made an exception for a particularly enjoyable 600 km ride in 2011, my final PBP qualifier for that year:

Notes on Kernow & South West 600 km audax, 28-9 May 2011, and an attempt to answer the question: why do we do these rides?

Train to Exeter Friday afternoon, bought a pastie in city centre and ate it on the green by the cathedral in late afternoon sun, glorious start. Then rode out past the start of the ride in Whipton to familiarise myself with its whereabouts. Then failed to find Travelodge… had looked up the postcode on google maps which sent me down a small country lane where I began to think it was an odd place for a Travelodge, usually they put them a bit nearer the motorway. So rode back to the M5 junction and there it was, exactly where I had ridden past it 30 minutes earlier. D'oh! Was this an early warning?

---

[10] http://tinyurl.com/oaovvb6

[11] http://adrianhandssociety.com/

Travelodge room was smelly... musty... not been aired perhaps for a year or so? Dead body in the wardrobe perhaps? Opened window... about an inch... that's as far as it goes – is that because the inmates in these places get suicidal? I wonder why?

Marvellous fish and chips at Harry Ramsden's, met up briefly with Greenbank. Feeling better now.

Watched HIGNFY on the telly. Even better. Then a loud knock – it's my roommate, Bianchi Boy! Talked about spokes etc. way too late then decided it would be sensible to get a spot of shut-eye.

3.30am. BB's alarm goes off. An hour too early. He's keen.

4.30am we get up. Coffee, banana, cereal bar. In a smelly Travelodge. The glamour of audax!

5am we're sat on the wall outside what looks remarkably like a church but the noticeboard reassuringly says Whipton Community Centre. BB phones Ian H at 5.15 to check we are in the right place – yes don't panic. 5.30am others begin to arrive including our host Ian, all very laid-back, no sense of urgency. Marvellous! Teas and coffees, more bananas and cereal bars, and then 6am! We're off... into the wind... for 250 km.

Easy 3h15 to the first control at Bude (80 km), just like it said on the routesheet, mainly because our little peloton of six is tightly tucked in behind Speedy Toby who will go on to complete the distance in 28 hours, smashing the KSW record by some 5 hours... Toby looked completely at ease, going off the front without trying – when he realised he would ease off a bit for us to get back on. A gent on a bike. Effortless mastery.

A full English at Bude was the order of the day. When I set off at around 10am by myself Toby had long gone, having consumed just a coke and a flapjack. How do these whippets do it? I was caught by Mike Plumstead shortly into the lumpy section to Looe and we were to remain joined practically at the hip for the rest of the ride.

At Liskeard we were peckish, I couldn't wait till Looe, so we found a marvellous sandwich shop. They had all manner of deliciously moist fillings, but Mike ordered a dry grated cheese sandwich and promptly emptied half its contents all over the pavement outside the shop. So he went back inside to ask for more cheese and, in order to demonstrate there was not much cheese left in his sandwich, he opened it and emptied the rest of the contents all over their floor. They looked somewhat askance but nonetheless obligingly re-filled his sandwich. After he had finished he went back in to ask them to refill his water bottles. Brazen. I admired more effortless mastery.

We arrived in Looe (142 km) at around 1pm I think, it was raining. Had been on and off since Bude. Cornish drizzle. And a stiff headwind, did I mention that? Got an ATM statement for control purposes, then ate fantastic home-made pasties from the local bakery while our bikes blocked the pavement and we blocked the bakery doorway as we tried to shelter from the rain... and the wind.

Mike, BB and I set off together to tackle the next bit. Another hilly wet and windy bit. The routesheet said follow signs to Polruan pedestrian and cycle ferry. Mike and I don't have GPS, so we did just that. BB has GPS (is GPS cheating? Maybe a question for another thread). A junction appears, no signpost. So Mike and I stay on the main road (well, main little lane really) while BB strikes off down even littler lane, slavishly following his GPS. Let's see who gets to the ferry first!

Mike and I arrive at Polruan 10 minutes later just in time to wave goodbye to BB as he and bike steam out across the harbour. Never mind, we can have an ice cream while we wait for the next ferry. Standing in the rain. And the wind.

The next bit was quite hilly. And windy. And wet. But great views as we passed St Michael's Mount on the left, in a brief moment of clear skies. Then, before we knew it, but in fact around 7pm, we were in Penzance (240 km) at Don's delicious diner! What a fantastic control. This is why we do these rides! Thanks Don and crew, you were brilliant. I think I ate 4 bananas, cakes, two plates of pasta, rice pudding and peaches, and quite possibly 3 eggs and beans on toast as well. Phoned dad to say happy birthday. Phoned Mike Bridgeland who's doing the Didcot 400k this w/e and is in for a shock – he thought it was going to be flat! Phoned wife to check in, as you do. She's been doing useful stuff in the garden. While I am out doing useless stuff on my bike. Top missus!

Set off at around 8pm with Mike P and Justin Chapman for the long night ride back to Bude. At last we have a tail-wind… and it's stopped raining! This is why we do these rides! We flew to Newquay by 10pm, just in time to get to the garage before it shut for the night and buy various comestibles and substantially delay the staff getting home who foolishly asked where we'd been and were going…

Mike and Justin were still strong but by around midnight I was flagging on the climbs. And it was raining again. Proper rain now, the wet stuff. Why do we do these rides? Dark thoughts. Never again! Clearly I need to refer to rule 5[12]

I got back to Bude (370 km) at bang on 1am, and by 1.02am my dinner was served and I remember exactly why I do these rides. Thanks Feline, you beauty!

Slept like log despite the drunken attempted bike theft commotion, I did not hear a thing. Gentle wake-up call from Ian at 5am, brekky and ablutions and back out on the road at 6. A long section to Taunton, but no vicious hills and good tailwind, and no rain! This is why we do these rides! Quick garage stop at Tiverton (450 km) for sandwiches, chocolate and a pint of milk, then pressed onto Taunton Deane M5 service station, oh the glamour! Arriving at around 11am (480 km). Ate burger and drank coke. I NEVER normally let such rubbish pass my lips. Needs must.

The next bit of the routesheet warned of tricky navigation on the lanes around Taunton. Mike and I got lost twice. Apparently people with GPS didn't get lost. Mike and I talked quite a lot about buying GPS. But that would be cheating. Wouldn't it? [start new thread]

We arrived at the most easterly point of the ride, a BP garage somewhere near Yeovil, at around 3pm (530 km). I bought and consumed a pint of milk, sandwiches, bananas, ginger beer and packet of Mentos. On the garage forecourt, oh the tradition! Oh the glamour! Oh the smell of petrol! This is why we do these rides!

---

[12] http://www.velominati.com/blog/the-rules/#5

Back on the road for the penultimate section, across the Blackdown Hills to Seaton. Quite a hilly bit this, and finished by the sea. Now we're riding with Andy H who has to stop behind a hedge half-way to change his bib-shorts which are rather too new to be wearing on a 600. He had nearly packed last night on account of the wind and the rain, then phoned the missus who referred him to rule 5. Top missus!

Sun's out now, and the expected headwind since we changed course and struck off southwards has not materialised. So all's good with the world, and we are but a few short km from completing the legendary KSW and getting qualified for PBP...so we can ride twice as far! Arrive Seaton at about 6pm (575 km). ATM receipt.

We had been warned about the last lumpy section, just 30 km to finish, but what spectacular scenery awaited, a veritable eye candy feast of scenery, just the ticket to finish a 600. No doubt others equipped with the latest wizardry and gadgetry can tell me to the nearest metre just how scenic this bit was, but it felt like roughly half the climbing of the entire event was squeezed into this 30 km. After we popped out onto the main road (A3052) for a few km I thought that would be an end to the hills...but it wasn't...the roller-coaster went on, top value! This is why we do these rides!

Then suddenly we're off the main road and on the lanes back into Exeter, past the airport, on a Dr Beeching cycle route (I suspect?) and back at Whipton Community Centre for 8.15pm. 610 km. And the hero's welcome that the routesheet had promised. Beans on Toast fit for heroes! And eggs. And pizza. And pasta. And rice pudding and peaches. And coffee. And 5 mugs of black tea for Mike P. And then Greenbank arrives clutching cans of beer, it's his birthday! This is why we do these rides!

Getting into shape

In 2013 I rode getting on for 16,000 km (10,774 km of bike rides and events for fun, plus around 5,000 km commuting, shopping, etc.). The average annual km since 2003 had been about half that, so it was a big step up, and a good challenging set of rides it was too. I chose the Wessex SR series, without doubt the toughest I'd taken on to date, all being (unsurprisingly) in Wessex, which turns out to be rather hilly. My yardstick for a hilly ride is 1,000m of climbing per 100 km – much more than that and it's a lumpy event in my book. If you've got the fitness the hilliest rides are the best – the rugged, remote and spectacular scenery and the tricky twisting descents can take your mind off the effort and the pain. Unfit though, you'd be too miserable to notice the stunning views. Fitness comes through riding, and can be addictive – those endorphins get flowing like a raging torrent!

Wessex rides organiser Shawn Shaw is in possession of a fine sense of humour, inherited, one presumes, from those who named him. The first laugh comes in early April – he runs the Dorset Coast 200 (2,850m climbing) and the Hard Boiled 300 (4,400m climbing) both on the same weekend, in reverse order. The 300 started at 02:00 on Saturday 6th April from Poole, where the mercury had fallen to -5°C. Our water bottles froze solid over the first stage up towards Salisbury Plain where at 05:00 the splendid Plume of Feathers pub in Shrewton was open for business not at all as usual, doing a roaring trade in full English breakfasts beside a blazing fireplace – utterly surreal.

Shortly after setting off from that first control the sun rose and things warmed up to marginally above zero for most of the day. I finished around 19:00 back in Poole, and then pedalled down to Wareham where a pub dinner and my B&B awaited. My ride notes were brief: "Toughest 300 in the calendar? 4,400m of climb mostly in the last 100 km!" Sleep quality after such a ride is simply unsurpassed, utterly sublime.

A select group of Wessex ride aficionados assembled, rather bleary-eyed, early the following day for the Dorset Coast 200, a "rollercoaster" to Devon and back according to the organiser's route sheet, an accurate description. 500 hilly kms in a weekend made for a cracking start to the season.

The Porkers 400 "pig of a ride" – it's said that only the "rasher" kind of audax riders sign up for it – involves some 5,900m of climbing and was held over the weekend of 5/6 May, providing a further opportunity to stretch the legs and almost entirely confined to delightfully quiet Wessex lanes meandering mostly up and sometimes down across four counties. I made brief ride notes before falling unconscious: "Marvellous ride in Wessex series, possibly my toughest 400 to date".

Our small group assembled for a grand finale over the weekend of 8/9 June – the Brimstone 600 (7,700m climbing). Once again blessed with fine weather, we were spoiled with a surfeit of magnificent views from the highest lanes of Dorset, Hampshire, Somerset, Wiltshire and Devon. The toughest climb of all came 390 km into the ride, a brutal wall up onto the Mendips, at around 02:00 on the Sunday. This was swiftly followed by the welcome stop chez Drew Buck, a great character of Audax UK, at his *Randonneur Heaven of the Mendips* homestead where full English breakfasts awaited and riders snuggled up close on warm floors for a spot of shut-eye till around 05:00, leaving a comfortable 16 hours or so to complete the final 210 km back to Poole.

In the first week of July I rode four events in the French Alps which make up the Trophée des Oisans, the best known being the 174 km Marmotte (named after the large ground squirrel native to the slopes of the final climb), which features no less than 5,000m scaling some of the best known cols familiar to Tour de France fans – the Glandon, Telegraph, Galibier and Alpe d'Huez. It was my fourth time at this popular event and I got a personal best and gold medal time of 08:30. The final ride of the week came on the morning after the Marmotte – a time trial up the 14 km and

1,100m of the Alpe d'Huez. I finished in 1:01, my fourth climb up the famous 21 hairpins that week. I was feeling super-fit!

A month later I was back for a third appearance at the 1,400 km London-Edinburgh-London. Including the prologue ride from central London and riding back home at the end, I notched up a tad over 1,500 km in five days, and made some brief ride notes on my new blog:

Sunday 28th July, home to Pocklington (Yorkshire), 379 km
Left home at 05:00, rode to The Mall where the Prologue started at 06:00. Royal Parks had forgotten to close the road as agreed, but TfL Road Events Supremo Gary McGowan flagged down a passing police car and the road was closed to motors five minutes later. The Queen must have overslept so there was no wave-off from the royal balcony by the time we needed to get rolling at 06:15...to the official start in Loughton, Essex. A quick breakfast and I was on the road at 08:15. Fine weather and a strong tailwind plus strong legs on the first day combined to produce a fast ride across the plains of Herts, Cambs and Lincs, over the Humber Bridge and into Yorkshire just before closing time for a pint with the hearty locals at the Red Lion in Market Weighton. Controlled at 23:44 at Lyndhurst School, followed by hot dinner, quick shower and camp bed in the gym. No trouble sleeping despite cacophonous symphony of farting and snoring from several hundred weary randonneurs.

Mon 29th July, Pocklington to Moffat (Dumfries & Galloway), 371 km
A delightfully scenic route across the Pennines via Alston where we stopped in the splendid Moody-Baker tearooms and I ate all the cakes. We made it into Scotland by around tea-time, and were with beer in Moffat before dark.

Tuesday 30th July, Moffat to Brampton (Cumbria), 227 km
An early start saw us in Edinburgh for breakfast, then we turned south - time to go home. At the Traquair control I was alarmed to discover a splitting rim on my rear wheel. Luckily there was whisky. Suitably fortified, I was given a lift into Peebles by one of the volunteer controllers where the nice man in the bike shop said he could build me a new wheel for the next day if I was in a hurry. I explained just how much of a hurry I was actually in, then went for lunch in the pub. My wheel was ready to collect just as I was finishing my lasagne and pint of heavy. I'd obviously needed a new wheel, and lunch, so no time wasted, but that did set me back three hours so I only made 227 km today back to Brampton – really did not fancy going over Yad Moss atop the Pennines in the dark, leave that for the morrow.

Wednesday 31st July, Brampton to Market Rasen (Lincs), 301 km
A grey day today in the Yorkshire drizzle. Crossed back over the Humber in the company of Stuart "Bikefix" Denison [purveyor of my RTW bike] and Dominic "Wheeler" Trevett [RTW logo designer and illustrator of this book].

Thursday 1st August, Market Rasen to home, 311 km
The final day, the party's all over too soon. Strong headwinds across the flatlands of Lincs and Cambs but got into a useful group with a couple of Yanks and made stonking progress, only interrupted by frequent visits to local hostelries in premature celebration of

our achievement. Final brevet card stamp and beautiful medal at 22:53. Dinner and beers with other medallists then rode home by around 02:30. Very deep sleep.

A Bike to Ride the World

Rewind a few months. In November 2012 I had picked up my new bike, an American Bacchetta Giro recumbent, from Stuart at BikeFix, laid-back bike specialist in central London. As recumbents go, it's quite a high bike, with 26" wheels (mountain bike size) and a Rohloff 14-speed hub gear. It was custom built to my specifications with reliability being the top requirement. Some of the bike's key features are:

- steel frame, easily repaired/welded around the world;
- 26" wheels – a common wheel size around the world so tyres would be widely available;
- Rohloff 14-speed hub gear – for ease of maintenance, never needs adjustment, and tested up to 300,000 miles;
- SON dynamo front hub – for charging the GPS and the smart phone – pedal-powered navigation and tweets;
- cable-operated disc brakes;
- Schwalbe Marathon Plus world tour tyres, the most puncture resistant on the market.

In 2013 I took this spanking new bike abroad for a couple of test rides. The first trip was a 400 km mini-break to the Netherlands, a fantastic country to ride a bike in. City riding can often be stressful, especially overseas. In Holland, however, it's an unbridled joy. Segregated and well-engineered signposted cycle routes abound. When interactions with motor traffic do occur, for instance at junctions, drivers (many of whom are also likely to ride bikes themselves on occasion and probably have family members who ride bikes) are relaxed and happy to stick to the widespread 30 km/h (18mph) limit, cheerfully giving way to the multitudes of men, women and children going about their daily business awheel with not a scrap of lycra or a helmet to be seen between them. Cycling in the Netherlands is simply the most sensible, convenient and convivial way to get around for many people's typical utility journeys. Utter joy, highly recommended!

The second test-ride, in August 2013, was a fair bit longer, indeed it was my longest ride to date: a three-week "Baltic Cruise" designed to test the bike, new kit and myself to the limits. The plan had been to ride 5,000 km right around the Baltic and the Gulf of Bothnia, averaging 250 km a day through the Netherlands, Germany, Poland, Lithuania, Latvia, Estonia, Finland, Sweden and Denmark. In the event I managed to cover just under

4,000 km, cutting out the northern loop around the Gulf of Bothnia. All had been going swimmingly and to schedule until I got to Poland and beyond, where both road surfaces and navigation got rather more challenging, giving a foretaste of what was to come on the world tour a year later. It became impossible to keep up the daily 250 km, and by the time I arrived in Helsinki, 11 days and some 2,500 km out from London, I was more than a day behind schedule and clearly wouldn't manage to complete the full itinerary north around the Gulf of Bothnia in the time available.

So I headed west across Finland to Naantali for the ferry to Sweden where roads were almost universally superb. Having cut out 1,000 km I could afford to relax the pace across Sweden and Denmark – I had nine days to ride 1,500 km – so the ride became more of a leisurely cruise than a series of dawn to midnight dashes. I enjoyed a complete day off the bike swimming and fishing on a Swedish lake with Björn, a German friend who by happy co-incidence was on holiday near the remote village of Gislaved, just off my route. I also spent a long and lazy half-day visiting the wonderfully bike-friendly city that is Copenhagen. After three weeks I was back in London having ridden 3,918 km at an average speed of 19.5 km/h and around 200 km per day. The bike had performed faultlessly apart from two broken spokes in the rear wheel which I'd replaced at the roadside. I felt confident and ready to take on the world.

One of the delights of cycle touring, especially on a funny bike, is that most places I stop local people approach, interested in what I'm doing and where I'm going. And when they find out, some of them are interested in following my adventures. In 2013 I was taking my first tentative steps into the world of blogging and tweeting, posting news and photos of my Baltic Cruise as I went, so it made sense to point curious locals I met in the direction of my posts. However, writing the blog and Twitter addresses out several times a day for people was time-consuming and laborious, and I hit upon the idea of a business card for the world tour. A business card would obviously need a logo. So I enlisted fellow Kingston Wheeler, LEL and PBP rider and graphic artist extraordinaire Dominic Trevett to design and produce the laid back logo, a commission he fulfilled splendidly and the result of which now graciously adorns the cover of this book.

The Final Countdown

The first thing to plan in detail was the route. Ideally I would have done the entire circumnavigation by surface transport, but that was ruled out early on because the world's major shipping routes did not coincide with where I was planning to ride. Furthermore, the services are intermittent and expensive, and it would have taken at least a year to complete the ride rather than the six months I had available.

For some years I'd been looking at routes chosen by other inter-continental riders and highlighting roads in the pages of an old world atlas. The master plan for the first stage, after the ferry to Den Haag, was to ride from the Netherlands to Singapore via Germany, Poland, Ukraine, Russia, Kazakhstan, China, Vietnam, Laos, Thailand and Malaysia, avoiding war zones and skirting round mountain ranges as far as possible. The rest looked more straightforward, at least in the atlas! I'd fly to Perth, ride across Australia and New Zealand; fly to California, ride up to Vancouver then across Canada and down to New York City; and finally fly back into Europe via Lisbon and ride back up to London.

Now it was time to plan out this route in greater detail, so in September 2013 I took a trip to Stanfords travel bookshop in central London, returning home with a pannier full of maps which kept me busy most evenings till Christmas. By the end of that period I had cut out strips from each of the maps containing my route and had programmed 142 GPX files into the Garmin 800 satnav device recently given to me for my 50th birthday.

I enjoyed the planning phase immensely. The technology available these days is phenomenal and the internet really did seem to have the answer to everything – it was just a case of trying to think of all the right questions to ask. I street-viewed my way across the deserts, plains and mountains of the globe, discovering invaluable advice and tips from a host of fascinating cycle touring blogs and other resources including www.warmshowers.org, a fantastic and free worldwide hospitality exchange network of touring cyclists offering accommodation and ablutions – and often much more, for instance dinner, bed and breakfast and a laundry service. Highly recommended!

I was also busy buying all sorts of bike bits and tools, clothes and kit; servicing the bike; researching the flight options for the four big ocean crossings; and doing a bike box test to see how quickly and easily my special bike would come to bits and fit into a standard cardboard bike box of the type new bikes are supplied in. I learned that it took quite a bit longer than dismantling a standard bike, and I'd need the biggest box I could get my hands on – a 29" wheeled mountain-bike box was ideal. The plan was to pick these up at low, or no cost from local bike shops near the airports I'd be flying from.

I then: set up a fundraising charity page for RoadPeace; got my business cards designed and printed; contacted warmshowers hosts and made provisional bookings as far as Almaty in Kazakhstan; opened a YouTube account; built a new back wheel (following the broken spoke misery on the Baltic ride); started organising visas and vaccinations; bought travel insurance; tried to learn some basic Chinese from websites and a weekly course at Raynes Park Library; and finally packed my panniers, weighed them, unpacked, jettisoned and repacked until the weight was halved. It was a frenetically busy period but all appeared to be going smoothly and according to a schedule which I had set out on a Gantt chart to ensure nothing essential was overlooked. OK, I know, I'm a bit of an anorak, but it seemed to be working.

Visa trouble at the 11ᵗʰ hour

The smooth and stress-free planning phase careered off the rails in early 2014. With just under three months to the off, the red tape of visa bureaucracy began to take a grip. I only needed five visas, and there had been no trouble at the Vietnamese, Russian or Kazakh embassies. Research indicated that I should be able to bag the Laos visa en route at their embassy in Hanoi. The Chinese visa however was proving more problematic. Unlike most tourists, I was not planning to fly into China, nor did I have any hotels booked. So filling out flight and hotel details on the visa application was proving a little tricky. In the absence of this information, the Chinese embassy told me I would have to obtain an authorisation letter from the China National Tourism Administration (CNTA) in Xinjiang, the district in north-west China into which I would be crossing from Kazakhstan. Without this letter of approval the embassy would not accept my visa application.

Internet research led to a Chinese webpage full of contacts, which at first glance looked hopeful, but most of my emails bounced back from bad addresses and none of the others elicited any reply. I enlisted assistance from two visa agencies in London and the China Travel Service on Euston Road, and from my MP, who actually turned out to be rather helpful.

Meanwhile, closer to home, Ukraine looked on the brink of civil war following Putin's invasion of Crimea, and the Foreign Office was advising against all but essential travel. That was not too great a problem as I could take a more northerly route and ride across Belarus instead of Ukraine – I'd chosen the latter simply because Brits didn't need a visa to get into Ukraine. So I drafted my application for a Belarusian visa, ready to submit if things didn't settle down in Ukraine over the coming weeks.

Back on the Chinese visa trail, my MP had put me in touch with a Foreign Office minister, who referred me on to a couple of useful FCO contacts in China, and after a phone call and some reassuring emails it looked very much as if I'd made the crucial breakthrough and the visa would be forthcoming – it would just be a matter of time.

The clock ticked, the days passed, and emails and further phone calls were exchanged with my new friends in China. They were confident that I would get the visa, and indeed one of them was starting to make plans to link up with me while I was in China. Questions kept coming by email, some repeatedly, but I remained patient and stayed the course, though it was becoming rather tedious. Why were they so worried about a solitary bicycle traveller?

At the end of February, with little more than a month until departure, it became clear that China was not going to let me in. Due to "special circumstances in Xinjiang" my contact in China told me he was unable to obtain the invitation letter I needed to get the visa. Furthermore, he added, if the China Tourist Service in Xinjiang was unable to obtain the letter, it was unlikely that any other agent would be able to do so, and therefore crossing the border into Xinjiang "may prove impossible at this point in time". This, I was told, "would have been a high level decision, which also means that it is unlikely that there will be a later change of heart." This came as quite a shock and threw a hefty spanner into the works of my careful planning: my intended route across China was around 6,000 km, about a fifth of the entire circumnavigation. I reeled for a few moments, and then got the maps out again. It was too late in the day to think about major route changes via perhaps India or Mongolia, so the realistic options were: a) fly from Almaty (eastern Kazakhstan) into Gansu, central China, thus avoiding the troubled province of Xinjiang – for this I'd still need a special visa and a Letter of Invitation from the Gansu official tourist bureau; or b) give up on China altogether and fly from Almaty to either Hanoi or Bangkok. Neither option was particularly palatable as they both put the kybosh on my long-cherished desire to ride overland and unimpeded from the Netherlands to Singapore.

Meanwhile in Ukraine, things were far from settling back onto an even keel. President Viktor Yanukovych and opposition leaders had signed a deal leading to an early presidential poll before the end of the year, but violence was still erupting in Kiev and other cities across the country. So I sent in my Belarusian visa application.

I'd also started on a vaccinations programme, seeing the local GP practice nurse every Friday to get the numerous jabs I needed. I was acquiring new kit at an alarming rate (mozzie net, sterile medical kit, dog whistle, money belt, stuff sacks, brake pads, zip ties, duck tape...) and wondering how and where it would all fit into my two medium-sized panniers. I also needed to keep the pedals turning and stay fit during these weeks leading up to my departure so that ramping up to consecutive 200k days would not come as too great a shock – this was fulfilled by my short daily commute to Hammersmith and either a Kingston Wheeler club run or a 200 km audax ride most weekends. I was also ploughing my way through a stack of guidebooks borrowed from libraries around London, and training up a colleague at work to keep my seat warm for me while I would be away. I was burning the midnight oil and feeling overloaded, there simply weren't enough hours in the day to get everything done; increasingly I was itching to get going and just bloody pedal!

In early March I rolled the Chinese visa dice one final time, sending a grovelling missive to my contact at the official tourist agency: *Oh no this is really terrible news! So I am not welcome or wanted at all anywhere in China? I am greatly saddened; many friends here who have visited China have told me about the wonderful welcome I can expect in your country. I wonder why the authorities are so worried about a man on a bike wanting to visit your beautiful country and discover your culture and language and food and famed hospitality. I have already invested much time and money in planning to visit your country, I have been trying to learn some basic Chinese, and I have been really looking forward to the China experience. I am a harmless tourist wanting to visit your land by the world's most eco-friendly vehicle, ubiquitous in China, the humble bicycle, so I will cause no pollution in your country. I will spend money and boost your economy, and I never drop any litter so there will be no trace of my passage other than some happy memories left with people that I will meet along the route. This is a sad day for me. Is there really nothing else that you or anyone else can do to help me realise my dream to cycle across China which I have cherished for ten years?*

The brief and unsympathetic reply was not long coming: *As I said before in Xinjiang we only can get the invitation letter from the tourism bureau for the normal tourists that we are going to receive. My partners in Gansu also say the same. So I am sorry again that I can do nothing for your visa in this case. Some people say maybe you can try the business visa. Good luck.* There was no time to explore the vanishingly small possibility of getting a business visa, so the Chinese door was finally and firmly banged shut.

A further blow was shortly to follow – the Belarus Embassy rejected my visa application because I did not have a hotel booking. So I booked a hotel. Then they rejected it again, asking for a signed letter from the hotel manager to confirm the booking. I wrote to the manager to ask for such a letter, which was duly supplied by return email, not only signed but also officially stamped! But this was still not enough. Next they wanted a letter from a travel company in Belarus accepting responsibility for me while I was in the country – the sense of déja-vu was becoming overwhelming. At least they had provided a list of official travel agencies which I could approach for the letter, so in that respect they were marginally more helpful than the Chinese had been. But with under a month to go it all looked like a huge bothersome faff with no guaranteed result in sight.

So what were the alternatives? Ukraine was by now making headlines every day and was well out of bounds to any British tourist heeding Foreign Office advice. Apart from Belarus, the only other practicable route was a lengthy northerly detour through Russia via Lithuania and Latvia, adding some 800 km overall to my trip – though on the plus side no further visas would be required, and I would get to ride through Moscow. So I planned accordingly and began looking forward pedalling across Red Square, and this was looking to be the most likely solution, until one day I received a surprise email from Michael Kuz'menchuk, Chairman of *Rucheek*, a cycling club in Brest, Belarus: *Today I spoke with the head of the consular department of the Belarusian Embassy in London – Yuri Alexandrovich Prudnikovichem. And we discussed the issue of your visa. He promised to give you a visa during the day, if there is a formal invitation from Belarus. The invitation will be the organization which I chair – "Brook" (in Russian -- "Rucheek").* It took a moment to compute this good news apparently out of the blue! Some weeks earlier, at the first sign of trouble with the Belarus visa, I had fired off a hopeful long-shot email to the European Cyclists' Federation with a brief outline of my situation, enquiring if they had any member organisations in Belarus that may be able to help. I'd not really expected a reply, indeed I'd forgotten all about it, but it now seemed that my tentative fishing expedition had reeled in a splendid late catch. A few emails later, and a quick trip to the embassy in Kensington, and bingo! My Belarusian visa was in the bag.

There was just one further relatively minor visa hassle to deal with. Now that I would be flying over China rather than cycling across it meant that I would arrive in Vietnam a month before my Vietnamese visa would be valid. So I visited their embassy one afternoon towards the end of March, where at first I was told to come back the following day because consular services were only available in the morning. As I kicked myself at the gate in the freezing rain for not having paid enough attention to the opening times on the website a few hours previously, a kindly gent of distinctly oriental features appeared and questioned my business. I related my woeful tale, his expression softened, and a moment later he opened the gate and led me up to the visa office where he entered into spirited conversation (presumably in Vietnamese) with an official-looking woman behind a glass screen – undoubtedly the woman who'd informed me a few moments earlier via the intercom that the office was closed. Their brief discussion concluded and I was handed a visa form and advised to return to the embassy with the completed form, my passport and £25 fee, upon which I would be issued with the new visa. A few days later as I emerged from the embassy with a full set of valid visas, it felt like a huge burden had been lifted – I could scarcely believe that my visa problems were finally behind me.

There was to be one further hiccup. Towards the end of March, the practice nurse at the GP surgery and I realised that we'd overlooked an essential vaccination against tick-borne encephalitis (TBE). Our focus had been on Southeast Asia which is chock-full of deadly diseases like typhoid, cholera, rabies, malaria, hepatitis A&B, Japanese encephalitis...you name it, I was inoculated against the lot! But we hadn't considered TBE, a fatal brain disease endemic much closer to home including, on my route, eastern Germany, Poland, Belarus and Russia. Much of Scandinavia is also affected, where I'd ridden and camped wild in the forests the previous summer in blissful ignorance; and TBE is so widespread in Austria that all children are routinely vaccinated, just like ours are against MMR and TB.

The TBE vaccine is given in two jabs a fortnight apart. I immediately had the first in a London travel clinic, and, after a quick online search, found a clinic in Berlin where I could get the second jab on my way through, anticipated for 9th April.

On 1st April I finally resolved a nagging problem – how would I protect myself from dog attacks? It seems that all long distance cycle tourists get chased and barked at, and sometimes attacked by dogs. Some countries are worse than others. There are various defence strategies available including high-pitched whistles and electronic dog dazers. I had already bought the former, though it did not inspire much confidence, and rejected the latter, fearing that since it would have to be ready at a moment's notice, and therefore exposed to all weathers, it might well fail just when needed. Perusing yet another intercontinental cycle-tourist's blog, I found what looked to be an ideal low-tech solution: a simple but sturdy stick mounted on one of the forks. I pottered into the garage, selected a 60cm piece of dowel from my possibly-useful-bits-of-wood pile in the corner, and spent a happy half-hour whittling one end to a fine point and fashioning a tennis-racket style handle by wrapping an old inner tube around the other end. Mounted by thick rubber band (more old inner tube) to the left fork for a quick and easy draw on the move, I went for a practice run out in the street, attracting funny looks from some of the neighbours. I now felt well prepared and was almost looking forward to the first opportunity to use it – bring on the Russian attack dogs!

By the 3rd April I had just about finished my packing and unpacking and repacking routine, and got everything to fit into two medium-sized Ortlieb panniers, a cylindrical dry bag and a seat bag, altogether weighing in at 16kg. In the bags were:

- right pannier: stuff I hoped I wouldn't need too often – bike tools/spares and medical kit/supplies;
- left pannier: maps, papers, cycling and civvy clothes, washing kit, water filter;
- cylindrical dry bag: bivi bag, sleeping bag and liner, camp mattress, all rolled up together ready for rapid deployment at the end of the day;
- seat bag: a well-stocked pantry for roadside picnics;
- hanging from seat bag: a water bag with drinking tube for easy hydration on the move;

- zip-tied to the bike frame just behind the handlebar stem: a plastic lunch box containing two cache batteries which would charge from the hub dynamo and provide power to the smart-phone and GPS.

Richard's rig, ready to roll – note the dog-stick on left fork

Friday 4th April was a day of surprising relative calm – the calm before the storm perhaps. Everything was done and packed and I was pretty much ready to leave 24 hours early. There was a strong temptation to do just that – why wait? In fact there were several good reasons why I should hang on until the next day. One was that my ferry ticket was booked for the Saturday. Another compelling reason was that a number of people were planning to see me off, first from the Wimbledon parkrun and then from the official start of my adventure at Bikefix in central London – indeed some were planning to ride with me to Harwich, and one all the way to Warsaw. My family too had planned a quiet send-off dinner for the Friday evening, so it would have been jolly bad form to up and leave a day early despite incredibly itchy feet.

In the afternoon I went for a little jog round local streets with my daughter Julia, and just as we got back home my sister Catherine was arriving. Shortly after that brother Antony arrived and the champagne flowed (six months prematurely perhaps but I kept that thought to myself). Pascale and our son Mark arrived home from work to complete the gathering and we enjoyed a convivial last supper together in a local Italian restaurant – a large plate of pasta to fuel myself up for the morrow.

LONDON to ALMATY

Harwich
The Hague
London
Berlin
Warsaw
Brest
Voronezh
Saratov
Uralsk
Aktobe
Aralsk
Chaldovar
Bishkek
Almaty

LONDON TO ALMATY

Saturday 5th April, 2014

It was an early start following a short and mostly sleepless night. I was up at 05:00 to see Pascale, Mark and Catherine off on a skiing holiday. I walked to the station with them and waved them good-bye shortly before six, nursing an empty feeling in the pit of my stomach as the train drew away from the platform. I wouldn't see them again in all likelihood for the next six months. What on earth was I doing? The day was dawning sunnier and brighter than my mood. The enormity and immediacy of the project was almost overwhelming. I jogged back home and busied myself with breakfast and bike fettling.

Antony joined me for more breakfast then took on the role of chief photographer for the day as I got my bike out of the garage and loaded on the packed panniers. We pedalled off from home at around 08:30, up to Wimbledon Common for a final parkrun – and what a terrific welcome awaited me there!

I had started doing parkrun[13] in 2008 having read about it in the local paper: a free 5 km run on the common every Saturday morning at 9am, organised and timed by a small bunch of volunteers who publish the results on the parkrun website a few hours later. It would be good cross-training for my cycle fitness, especially in the winter months when I'm a bit lazy and don't do so many long rides (there is rather less appeal in the dark and cold). The Wimbledon Common event was just a year old and, following the amazing success of the Bushey Park event which had started in 2004, only the second one to be launched in the country. Parkrun has since spread like wildfire to hundreds of British towns and cities, and indeed around the world, and founder Paul Sinton-Hewitt became a CBE in the Queen's 2014 birthday honours for 'services to grass roots sports participation'. It is a truly remarkable phenomenon which has succeeded in getting tens of thousands of people, many previously inactive and unfit, into regular exercise. Our sedentary lifestyles and most people's chronic lack of sufficient physical activity are at the root of many widespread and devastating diseases of the rich western world, including obesity, diabetes,

---

[13] http://www.parkrun.org.uk/

heart disease and cancer. The cost to the public purse runs into billions. Parkrun's contribution to the fitness, health and well-being of the nation is incalculable and for this reason alone Paul's CBE was richly deserved.

Looking back at how my passion for long distance cycling had developed, I suppose it was inevitable that I would fall in with the wrong sort of runners and end up running marathons, as well as making a whole new bunch of friends. And since I was leaving on my world tour on a Saturday, by an evening ferry departure from Harwich to Holland, setting off after a final parkrun had long been a possibility, even though (or perhaps precisely because) it seemed a bit daft. The decision was cemented following a phone call in January 2014 from Debra Bourne, the Croydon event director, who was writing a book about parkrun[14]. She had heard of my plans and thought I might be an interesting character to include in her book. And she had a crazy question for me: would I be doing parkruns wherever possible around the world? Surprisingly, perhaps, that thought had not occurred to me, and of course in any case I was not planning to take running shoes with me – shoes are heavy and bulky things. My shoe strategy had been formulated long ago and consisted of a single pair of cleated Shimano sandals. The cleats, which clip into the pedals, are recessed so that the sandals are comfortable for both cycling and walking. So no, I was not planning to do parkruns around the world. But Debra was tenacious – it would make a great side story in her book. Quick as a flash she suggested that if parkrun directors around the world knew I was coming their way, they would ensure that one of their regular runners with size 10 feet would turn up on the day with a spare pair of running shoes for me to borrow. There was nowhere to hide. I warmed to the idea. It was crazy, but then so was the whole project. So I looked at a map of parkruns around the world to see which ones were on my route, and fired off emails to the respective event directors giving the approximate dates of my planned arrivals in Warsaw, Perth, Melbourne, Wellington and Auckland.

A highlight of the Wimbledon parkrun on 5th April was a home-made cake with the laid-back logo iced onto it, baked by supersonic Lisa. This lovely gesture touched me deeply but prompted me to further question the wisdom of my project: why was I leaving such close friends behind for so long to venture off far beyond the edge of my comfort zone? At the same time I was raring to get on with it – once properly on the road I'd have a new focus and purpose: just bloody pedal!

So it was with mixed feelings that I ran a cautiously slow parkrun – it would have been pretty daft to pick up any sort of injury at this stage – then set off with Antony and half a dozen parkrunners to cycle together up to Bikefix in Lambs Conduit Street where I'd bought my bike in 2012. We

---

[14] *parkrun: much more than just a run in the park* published in December 2014

arrived at about 11:30 well in time for the publicised 12 noon start, and the quiet narrow street was already thronged with family and well-wishers who had turned out to see me off – some 40 people altogether from parkrun, the London Cycling Campaign, Kingston Wheelers, work colleagues…it was a lovely moment, in brilliant warming sunshine. We stood around chewing the fat, drinking coffees and taking photos, then there was a round of farewell hugs before finally setting off to a peel of bicycle bells at around 12:15. Around half of the crowd – some 20 riders – joined Antony and me for the ride to Harwich for the evening ferry to Hook of Holland. Among that number was PBP and LEL veteran Dave Bradshaw[15]. We'd ridden a fair few miles together over the years and he was joining me for the first week of my trip as far as Warsaw. My cunning plan was to tuck in close behind Dave in his slipstream, and he'd set a good pace and get us to the Polish capital by the end of the first week, in time to do Warsaw parkrun on Saturday 12th.

Our route out of London took us via the Olympic park and then east through the delights of Ilford and Romford. Kingston Wheeler colleague Chris Wright was heard to mutter that it was grim, and I had to agree. Progress was painfully slow through congealed Saturday shopping traffic right out as far as Harold Wood where we crossed the M25, escaped the gravity of the metropolis and found ourselves pedalling through delightful Essex lanes and villages where we could finally relax and hear ourselves speak. Some riders peeled off to get early trains home from Brentwood and Colchester, but a core group of 13 made it to the Samuel Pepys pub in Harwich at around 19:00 where my father, brother-in-law and two nieces were already installed. A second final supper ensued. After dinner, a few beers and a further round of backslapping farewells, most of the others went off to the station for the train back to London, while hardcore audax rider Alan Parkinson set off back to London on his bike.

Dave, Antony and I pootled down to Parkeston Quay, Antony took some photos as we boarded the ferry, and then it was just Dave and me. We tied up the bikes on the car deck, found our cabin, and got our heads down before the ferry even set sail. I was finally on the road – this was it! The first day had all gone like clockwork, only another 179 to go. Just how hard could it be?

149 km today (audax riders always count kilometres, never miles, because of audax's French origins).

---

[15] I made no ride notes for the first week, so thanks to Dave for sharing his, upon which this account is based, my memory not being what it was!

Sunday 6ᵗʰ April

We slept well and rose early for the splendid Stena Line buffet breakfast – a true bargain for the hungry cycle tourist because you can eat as much as you like and take away provisions for lunch. It's top quality too. I started with cereals, moved on to fresh fruit salad, pancakes and yoghurt, and finished with a full English, all washed down with several mugs of coffee. As the ship docked, we waddled down to the car deck with our back pockets stuffed full of bread and cheese rolls for later.

It was drizzling but mild as we emerged from the ferry into a silent and sleepy Sunday morning in the Hook-of-Holland. Our GPS units pointed us towards the magnificent network of smooth, sign-posted and segregated *Fietspads* which span the nation. The Dutch have been planning and building for cycling since the 1970's when a combination of the oil crisis and high numbers of children killed on the roads convinced them that towns and cities might be better planned around people rather than cars. I'm rather hoping that the UK will catch on soon...

After three peaceful hours we'd covered 70 km, it had stopped raining and we found ourselves in Utrecht where we rode past tens of thousands of double-decked parked bikes near the central station. It seemed that almost everybody moving in Utrecht was on a bicycle, mostly of utilitarian design, ideal for short urban journeys and equipped to carry substantial loads, many with racks both back and front. No-one was dressed for cycling, just as no-one would dress specifically for driving or walking or taking the bus. They were dressed in normal every day clothes: no lycra, no helmets, no body armour – cycling here is not for sport, it's for transport. Many cycle routes are segregated but plenty are not, and where we found ourselves mixing with motor traffic, drivers were much more attentive and patient than we were used to in London. This is undoubtedly due to the fact that most motorists probably also cycle; perhaps also because of Holland's strict liability laws – in the event of a crash involving a motorist and a pedestrian or cyclist, the motorist is automatically liable. How refreshingly civilised, and what a contrast with Britain where we so often and readily blame the unfortunate victim.[16]

After a pit-stop for a bowl of hot soup and some coffee, we continued to make good progress eastwards, stopping briefly at a well-known fast food outlet to avail ourselves of their toilets, wifi and eat the rolls we'd prepared earlier. By early evening we'd made it across almost the entire country to Deventer, where we shared a vast pizza in the street outside a

---

[16] Most European countries have similar liability laws. The exceptions are Romania, Cyprus, Malta, Ireland and the UK.

take-away pizzeria which we'd mistaken for a sit-down restaurant. A couple of hours later at around 22:00 we crossed the border into Germany and rode on for another hour into Schüttorf, where we found a shopping mall with a large car park. Tucked away around the back, away from the road, we found a covered area ideal for our first camp.

241 km today / 390 km since London

Monday 7th April

Our first night out under the stars was mercifully mild, and we slept well until just after 05:00 when we were disturbed by a delivery vehicle arriving to supply the supermarket we had sheltered behind. The driver was unfazed and went about his business, as did we. I slipped easily into an early morning routine that I'd tried and tested the previous year around the Baltic: get dressed, perform ablutions, deflate mattress, roll up bivi and sleeping bags and stuff them into the Ortlieb dry bag, tie it all back on the bike then tuck into a first breakfast of homemade muesli with a small pack of UHT milk. Dave was hugely impressed at this slick efficiency – well, I like to think so! He'd not practised his routine and was still faffing when I was ready and raring to go. We finally set off at 06:15.

It was another mild day and we were heading to Hanover, where we would stay overnight with Björn, the ex-work colleague I'd met up with in Sweden in 2013. Arriving at the small village of Salzbergen, we stopped at the bakery. German bakeries warrant a special mention, indeed pause for applause, they are institutions of fine beauty and fare bringing joy to the heart of the hungry cyclist. We installed ourselves on the terrace to savour our gourmet second breakfast, a variety of freshly baked pastries with coffee.

Shortly after passing through the village of Recke the route I'd planned took us onto the Mittellandkanal, which, at 326 km is the longest artificial waterway in Germany. Most of it turned out to be glorious for cycling, if not quite as fast as good tarmac. We followed the canal for a fair way on a variety of surfaces and in bright sunshine, then opted for the beautiful smooth tarmac of the L road network to pick up some speed as we wanted to arrive in Hanover in respectable time for dinner and a few beers. Later in the day the road surface deteriorated and we went back onto the canal, though that too was significantly worse than it had been in the morning. We crossed a grass field then took a muddy track, and our speed fell to around 10 km/h. And then there was a ping from my back wheel – a broken spoke. This was not good on the third day into a six-month tour.

We found some decent tarmac for a swift final run into Hanover where we arrived at around 18:30. Björn met us at the city boundary and led us to his flat where the Hanoverian beers were chilling. I replaced the broken spoke as I supped my beer, then we headed out into town for a hearty German dinner involving sausages, potatoes and cabbage. And more beer – the best recovery drink for long distance cyclists… in my opinion.

194 km today / 584 km since London

Tuesday 8th April

We left Hanover at around 08:00, and 15 minutes later it began to rain, steadily at first, building slowly up to torrential by mid-morning. Dave skidded off his bike on a wet roundabout, but thankfully neither body nor bike was damaged. The weather remained mild, and on the plus side a stiff tailwind fairly blasted us across much of Germany on the B188 towards Berlin.

Blasting across Germany in Dave's slipstream

Lunch was a variety of treats perched upon bar stools at a bakery in the small town of Gardelegen. The sun reappeared in the afternoon as we made rapid progress eastwards, and all was looking good until…another ping from the back wheel announced a second broken spoke. This was bad news indeed – two broken spokes in four days. I'd brought a dozen spare spokes so at this rate I'd use them all in under a month, as well as lose significant chunks of time replacing them every few days. Clearly the wheel needed another re-build.

We stopped for some dinner at the Netto supermarket and bakery in Rathenow, a rather grey and gloomy town well into former East Germany. My wheel problem was nagging – how could I get it fixed well and quickly? Phone a friend! I related my woes to Björn in Hanover and he swung into action, calling back an hour later with details of a bike shop in Berlin where they'd be expecting me the next day.

The temperature plummeted as the sun set so we donned all our extra layers and rode on in the dark towards the German capital. For several hours I saw red flashing lights low on the horizon – it looked as if the aliens were landing. Perhaps I was tired and hallucinating already, a common experience among sleep-deprived randonneurs. But no, Dave was seeing them as well, and he too was puzzled.

We cycled into Nauen, a small town on the outskirts of Berlin where, in a shopping centre car park, we found an empty open shed, a sign on the outside promoting its daytime use: the sale of fresh asparagus. It was tight, but we managed to squeeze ourselves and the two bikes in and tie the door shut with a bungee cord. We were tucked up by 22:30, and well placed for the busy day to follow: my second TBE vaccination, a back wheel rebuild, and another 200 km to get under the wheels.

248 km today / 832 km since London

Wednesday 9th April

We were cosy and slept well in our shed, thankful to be under cover as it had been a stormy night. After a bowl of muesli we set off, and as we rode out of town the mystery of the previous evening's flashing red lights was solved: daylight revealed them to be wind turbines. Germany, having rejected nuclear power, is an emerging world leader in Aeolian power, and there were hundreds of turbines dotted about the countryside in all directions as far as the eye could see. I know some people don't like them; I personally think they're great and they're the future.

An hour or so later we rolled into Berlin, stopping briefly at the Institute of Tropical Medicine and International Health on Spandauer Damm in Berlin where I got my second TBE jab with minimal fuss and expense. We then headed into the city centre, through the famous Brandenburg Gate and to the central station to buy some Polish zlotys, and finally on to our last port of call – the bike shop, in a shopping complex a few kms into former East Berlin.

Stadler's was the biggest bike shop I'd ever seen. It was so big that customers were test-riding the bikes inside the shop on a track running between the bike stands. I was directed over to a far corner where half a dozen mechanics were busy fixing, servicing and assembling a variety of old and new bikes. Initially I was told that the order book was full and that they wouldn't be able to rebuild my wheel that day, or even that week. I referred to the phone call they'd received from Björn and revealed my magic letter –

a brief introduction of myself and my ride in the various languages I'd need around the planet. This produced the desired effect: the chief mechanic was summoned, conferred briefly with a colleague who looked at my stricken wheel, scratched his chin and sucked his teeth, eventually suggesting that they might be able to replace the broken spoke and test the others by 13:00. This was progress, but I was perfectly capable of replacing the spoke and checking the others myself; however that approach patently wasn't solving the problem. I needed a complete wheel rebuild – a new wheel strong enough to bear myself and 40kg of bike and kit 25,000 km around the world on some much rougher and tougher roads than I'd hitherto had to contend with. Further discussions ensued between the chief mechanic and a couple of others who'd started to take an interest, having read the letter. Once they began to examine the problem more closely, I knew they were rising to the challenge. The rim, the best English speaker among them explained, was not ideally suited to the German-built 14-speed Rohloff hub, which has a substantially greater diameter than a standard hub and is therefore best laced up to a rim with offset spoke holes. They demonstrated how the current arrangement on a standard rim resulted in the spokes having to make a slight bend at the nipple end to enter the spoke holes in the middle of the rim. This induced a stress for which the spokes were not designed, and that was where they were breaking. Furthermore they could recommend the ideal rim to eliminate the problem – hurrah! But… they didn't have it in stock. It was a tense moment. The mechanics were on-side, motivated and willing to help, but stymied by the absence of the part required. One of them started phoning colleagues in other bike shops around Berlin to see if any of them had the rim we needed while I crossed my fingers. He struck lucky on his third call and the office boy was promptly despatched across the city to collect the part while my broken wheel was dismantled in preparation to be laced up to the new rim when it arrived. I was told it would be available for collection at 16:00, so Dave and I took a quick U-Bahn trip to Alexanderplatz in central Berlin to see the sights and sup beer.

At 16:00 we arrived back in the shop. The wheel was built and back in the bike ready to go. I was full of admiration for this demonstration of slick German efficiency, but much more than that, deeply touched that so many of them had teamed together to prioritise my wheel above all the other pressing jobs in their order books and help me so quickly, and furthermore all at cost price! Most importantly, I finally had a back wheel which proved to be man enough for the job. It never let me down again, running true with no further spoke breakages right round the world and back to London. They even gave us a token for a free drink as we left the shop.

By 17:00 we were back on the road, heading out of Berlin in the rush hour – not ideal timing, but German drivers are on the whole patient and courteous. It was rather stop-start for some time as we gradually headed out of the drab eastern suburbs where we passed a house obviously inhabited by an even keener bike-nut than me. The entire front wall of his (one assumes it was a man) three-storey property was bedecked with around a hundred bikes of all sizes and descriptions and quotations from three famous historical supporters of cycling:

John F Kennedy: Nothing compares to the simple pleasure of a bike ride
Albert Einstein: Life is like cycling – you must keep moving to keep your balance
Adam Opel: No other invention combines utility with pleasure, like a bicycle

Just as we emerged from the clutches of Greater Berlin and were hoping to ramp up the pace and make up some lost time, the GPS pointed us onto a trunk road which was clearly out of bounds to cyclists. We considered using it anyway and pleading ignorance if ordered to stop by the polizei, but it looked busy and unappealing with thick and fast evening commuter traffic, whereas the less direct alternative that emerged after discussions with passing locals looked quieter, and more suitable and pleasant for cycling. This was somewhat frustrating after all the time we'd already lost at the clinic and in the bike shop, but in reality there was little choice. We made reasonable ground for a few hours via Strausberg, where we stopped for kebabs, then onto Neuhardenberg and Seelow, where we were again faced with a similar choice: direct but prohibited route east to the Polish border or another lengthy detour. By now it was 23:00 and we didn't hesitate; there was barely any traffic about at this hour so we swung onto it with a vengeance, determined to get to the Polish border before calling it a day. We were passed by a speeding police car but they took no interest in us and we made quick time on the superior road surface to the border town of Kustrin-Kietz, where we hunted round for a reasonable camping spot as the forecast was for another freezing stormy night. We eventually found our way into the deserted train station which, though sadly not furnished with a heated waiting room, did sport a couple of useful platform shelters. We occupied one each and got ourselves tucked up in short order soon after midnight, pleased to have got as far as we had on a day that had included two substantial interruptions and a capital city.

153 km today / 985 km since London

Thursday 10th April

It was an icy-cold, wet and gusty night in our rather inadequate platform shelters. Hard core long distance cyclists have developed a star rating system for bus and platform shelters, also known as "audax hotels". Our hotels that night were spartan and decidedly one-star. There was little depth, a wide draughty gap at the bottom, the bench was too narrow and short to stretch out on, and the flimsy structure was fabricated from transparent perspex which amplified the sound of the rain and exposed us to full view in the middle of the floodlit platform. It warranted no bonus stars for architectural merit. We just about managed to stay dry, if not warm, in our bivi bags, but were disturbed twice in the night by noisy diesel trains shunting around, and roused at 05:10 by commuters arriving to take the first train to Berlin. We made our apologies, packed up and pedalled through the unmanned border crossing into Poland where we found a most welcome, warm filling station serving hot dogs and hot drinks with free wifi.

After thawing out and enjoying a happy hour catching up with friends and family on social media, it was time to man up and get back out into the vile weather. It stayed grey, damp and chilly all morning as we headed east on the E22/24/30, a busy, narrow, international trucking route with lorries passing fast and close. Driving standards were substantially poorer than they had been in Holland and Germany, and numerous roadside shrines testified to Poland's unenviable record for road mortality rates, among the highest in Europe. No fewer than one in five EU pedestrian fatalities is Polish.

We stopped for a second breakfast at a roadside picnic spot in the woods, shortly followed by lunch in a small village bakery – any excuse to stop and shelter! A dessert of fruit and chocolate milk from a Netto supermarket set us up for the afternoon.

The road and weather both improved after lunch with the welcome appearance of a rideable hard shoulder and a dry tailwind. Navigation was easy – we stuck on the E30 – and we began making up some of the time we'd lost in Berlin. By teatime it looked as if we were back on track to make Warsaw by Friday night if we kept our heads down and limited our stops, so we gritted our teeth, girded our loins, partook of a fast food dinner near Poznan, and set out for a final 70 km before calling it a day. This would put us within a day's ride of the Polish capital, a target I was particularly keen to meet as we had a warmshowers host arranged and a date at the Warsaw parkrun on the Saturday morning.

We set off from Poznan under clear skies, the mercury plummeting. After about 35 km we were separated as Dave, beetling on a few hundred metres ahead of me, missed a turn and didn't hear me yelling at him to stop. I dithered for a few minutes but there was no way I'd catch him, so I turned left and stayed on our planned route – he'd realise his mistake and be back with me soon enough. However, an hour later he'd still not reappeared so I stopped and tried in vain to phone him. Just as I was setting off again, feeling vaguely uneasy, he caught me. Reunited, we rode on a few more kms until a particularly well-proportioned and appointed bus shelter caught our eye at just the opportune moment – a four-star audax hotel! This was a lucky find on such a freezing night, stars being awarded for all the attributes that had been missing on the previous night except aesthetic beauty – but after nearly 250 km we were rather too tired to care.

246 km today / 1,231 km since London

Friday 11th April

We woke at 05:00 to freezing fog. The Garmin registered –2°C. After a quick icy bowl of muesli we set off into the gloom, frozen fingers crossed that our tail-lights would be bright enough to be seen by approaching lorry drivers…also fervently hoping they'd be alert enough to spot us from their warm and cosy cabs after a long night on the road. We rolled into Konin at sunrise and got a few moody and misty photos at the local cemetery, then stopped at a garage to thaw out a little and get some hot breakfast inside us.

There was still over 200 km to go to Warsaw, so it wasn't long before we were back out pedalling into the foggy half-light, but the temperature was slowly rising and the fog gradually thinned and became increasingly patchy. A headwind was not welcome, but it was not too strong and I was grateful to be able to ride up close behind Dave and shelter in his slipstream as he forged ahead on the busy E30 through Kutno and Lowicz. This would be my last chance for such a "tow" until Australia.

Afternoon excitement came in the form of a quieter alternative route for a few kms to escape the ever busier E30 on the approach to Warsaw, and also the first dog attack of the trip. Both failed: the secondary routes between farming villages were less direct and of poor quality; and the dog didn't get close enough to warrant an unsheathing of my untested but surely formidable weapon.

We partook of another fast food lunch, and stopped for tea – well, chocolate milk and sandwiches – in a supermarket car park. Such is the glamorous life of a cycle tourist in a hurry.

We had made good time thus far and had just 60 km to go. However, as with all mega cities, once we hit Warsaw's sprawling suburbs our speed fell off dramatically through a long series of traffic jams and lights. There were cycling bans in some places too, and it wasn't always clear where we should be riding, resulting in further delays – all very frustrating after the early start and largely successful effort to maintain a good pace. We'd been looking forward to an early finish and hopefully a decent meal, beer and a warm night in a central Warsaw flat with my first warmshowers host, Marek.

After what seemed an age, we finally reached the city centre towards 21:00, but found ourselves in the old historic quarter on the west bank, well above the River Wisla which we needed to cross. We could see the bridge far below but it wasn't at all obvious how to get down to it, other than by joining a fast urban motorway teeming with six lanes of fuming traffic, an option which looked suicidal. There was a long flight of steps down to the bridge – not appealing with a 40kg bike. Fortunately there were also lots of people about to ask, and we were directed to a well-hidden funicular lift which, one at a time, just about accommodated us and our bikes and deposited us at bridge level.

We eventually got to Marek's at about 21:45 and discovered that he lived in a 4th floor flat with no lift. He took our luggage while we struggled up with the bikes and locked them to the bannister outside his front door. We changed quickly into our civvy clothes and Marek dropped us at a bar that, happily for us, was still serving food and drink at this late hour. Finally, after another exhausting day and a week on the road, we were able to relax. I had found it a severe test, and I was still well inside Europe – this was supposed to be the easy bit. Had I bitten off more than I could chew?

Such gloomy thoughts faded fast as we sampled the delights of the local beers. The chef recommended a hearty local dish based on smoked sausages and cabbage, perfect comfort food and carbo-loading for the starving randonneur! After a tasty apple-based dessert the grinning chef reappeared with a bottle of dubious nature; he was obviously keen to practise his English and made an intelligent guess that drinks on the house might entice us to linger a little longer. He poured large glasses of a local brew which tasted something like port but rather stronger, and we spent a happy hour helping our host hone his language skills before Marek came to the rescue. He joined us for one further beer, and then dropped me back at the flat before heading off into the night with Dave to party with friends on the other side of town.

It was all well and good for Dave to be gadding about reliving his youth and letting his hair down – he was at the end of his tour and I think quite surprised and relieved to find himself still in one piece after some hair-raising moments of Polish traffic madness. I, on the other hand, had merely completed the first week of 26, and furthermore was planning to get up the following day, do a parkrun, and then ride 200 km. So somewhat uncharacteristically I did the sensible thing and hit the sack as early as possible, around midnight.

236 km today / 1,467 km since London

Saturday 12th April

I rose early feeling full of the joys of spring. The day was dawning bright and full of promise, and the low brilliant April sunshine bleached away the anxious feelings of the previous evening. Dave was planning to spend a day or two in Warsaw and then, determined not to stretch his luck any further on hazardous Polish roads, take the train back to Berlin from where he'd pedal back to Calais and home in time to see his son ride at the Herne Hill Velodrome Good Friday track races.

Meanwhile, far from feeling daunted about continuing alone, I was chomping at the bit. Dave's company had been great fun and his slipstream to Warsaw had been immensely useful – indeed quite possibly I wouldn't have made it in time for the parkrun without his help. Nonetheless I was ready to go solo, and would have it no other way for the bulk of the trip – it's the best way to travel if you want to meet the locals.

It was also probably best for Dave that he wasn't coming any further as his previous night out on the tiles had taken its toll. He'd asked me to wake him in time to come and spectate at parkrun, which I did at 08:00. He turned over in bed to expose a sorry and somewhat alarming sight: his face was covered in dried blood. He was a little vague about how it had happened but thought he'd probably stumbled on the stairs; our host didn't surface to confirm this theory. Dave made a sterling effort to rise from his stupor, clean himself up a bit, utter some brief words of relief that his injuries were just skin deep, and help me down the four-storey stairwell with my bike and bags.

Warsaw Praga parkrun is held in the beautiful Skaryszewski city park just across the road from Marek's flat – the chief reason I'd picked him from a wide choice of warmshowers hosts in Warsaw. A hundred or so runners and volunteers were milling about at the start area when I arrived, busy putting up the event flags, finish funnel and catching up with the week's gossip – just like parkrun back home. I pushed my funny bike into this throng and was immediately welcomed by the run director who had a few pairs of running shoes ready for me to try. I selected the most comfortable pair and did a little stretching to try and bring some relief to my Achilles tendons, which were just beginning to get sore from overuse in the first week of the trip.

After the run director had given the pre-race briefing, which I assumed was pretty much verbatim what they say at parkruns back home (a description of the 5 km route, mind out for other park users and dogs, applause for today's volunteers…) we were off and I settled into a relaxed pace towards the back of the field on account of the sore Achilles and the fact that I wanted to keep some energy in reserve for the rest of the day. It was two and a bit laps around the park, and local runner Vitaliy Sorochuk came home first in a scorching 16:50. I jogged sedately over the line some 12 minutes later to complete my slowest parkrun to date, 97th out of 114 runners, but ecstatic to have made it to Warsaw in time to run at all. Post run banter and photos were fun as usual and there was a festival of chocolate – almost all runners had brought some to share so I got a good energy boost for the exertions to follow.

I bade farewell to my new parkrun friends and to Dave at around 10:00, and set off into the eastern suburbs of Warsaw and beyond towards the Belarusian border. The sun still blazed and I felt great – a wonderful feeling of liberty that I had only myself to consider; the world really was my oyster now! The weather stayed fair and I made steady progress on the E30 out through Siedlce, stopping in a bus shelter for a picnic lunch where my phone rang: a bunch of local club cyclists were planning to meet up and ride with me into their home town of Miedzyrzec Podlaski. A little later, sure enough, two cyclists were waiting for me by the side of the road and escorted me 20 km into Miedzyrzec, where we were met by a further six club members and taken to a bar to sample the local brew. They had been notified of my arrival by their Belarusian cycling friend Michael Kuz'menchuk in Brest, who had helped me get my Belarusian visa a few weeks earlier. After a couple of beers I was escorted a further 30 km down the road to Biala Podlaska where I was met by yet more cyclists and the local press. I was beginning to feel quite the Queen Bee by this stage – what a wonderful welcome! Press interviews were conducted at around 20:00 in the town square, and an hour later I was finally shown to a hotel they'd booked for me. Exhausted again, I couldn't face going out to find dinner, so managed to get the receptionist to order me a take away pizza.

158 km today / 1,625 km since London

Sunday 13th April

A lie-in at the hotel – what luxury! Today I was in no hurry because I had until noon to get to the Belarusian border just 40 km down the road. I was due to be met there by Michael Kuz'menchuk, who, I'd gathered from recent emails, had organised quite a reception for me which would take all afternoon and evening, then I'd be his overnight guest. So I rose from a good long deep sleep at 08:00, completely refreshed, and went downstairs to the dining room for an excellent cooked breakfast of scrambled eggs, bacon, cheese, paté, tomatoes, bread (basket refilled twice), butter, honey and coffee…I scoffed the lot and felt fantastic! Three local club cyclists appeared at the hotel shortly after 09:00 to help me downstairs with my bike and bags, and led me out of town and back onto the main road where they gave me a picnic, wished me happy travels and hugged me as if we'd been best buddies for years.

A couple of hours later I arrived at the border, a little ahead of schedule, so I sat on the crash barrier at the side of the road and ate my sandwiches. At noon I proceeded to the border and soon discovered that I shouldn't have tarried   this was a proper old fashioned style border with barriers, customs sheds and armed guards. I was leaving the EU and entering the Russian Federation and it was clearly going to take some time. There were long queues of cars but needless to say no other cyclists, and I was sidelined and told to wait – I wasn't sure what for. After five minutes or so a border guard tried to tell me something but the language barrier beat us both. I waited a little longer and another guard managed to convey that cyclists were not permitted to cycle (or walk) across the no-man's-land between the exit from Poland and the entry into Belarus. It became apparent that the guards were asking motorists in larger vehicles if they had space to take the bike and me across the border. After ten minutes or so I was beckoned over to a large car towing an empty trailer – perfect! The amiable driver was happy to co-operate and helped load my bike and panniers into his trailer. I was motioned to get into the passenger seat and we joined another slow queue towards a checkpoint and barrier. Our passports were duly inspected and stamped and we were waved through the barrier into a few hundred yards of no-man's-land and over a small bridge, only to join the tail of another queue to proceed through Belarusian entry formalities. Another 15 minutes elapsed and we finally emerged into Belarus proper at 13:00. I'd spent a whole hour getting through and it had felt like crossing the Iron Curtain at the height of the cold war.

I needn't have worried as my patient hosts obviously knew that these things take a while. I was a little embarrassed at the ignominy of having to unload my bike from a car trailer – this was not how I'd envisaged my arrival! But the 15 locals lined up by the side of the road waiting to meet me were clearly familiar with the procedure. Michael, a large jovial fellow wearing a loud day-glo pink and yellow jacket with megaphone voice to match, introduced himself with a great bear hug and back-slapping routine, then introduced the rest of the welcome committee – a mix of local press and cyclists…and a television crew. It was at this point that I lost all control over what happened to the rest of my day. Everything had been scripted and planned out for me and all I had to do was follow and smile and answer simple questions from time to time.

Welcome to Belarus!

We started with a couple of interviews for the local paper and the evening TV news. Fortunately one of the cyclists was an English teacher and provided a useful interpreting service. In response to an early question I referred to my blog and gave out some of my cards, which proved an instant hit – they all wanted one, so I distributed them liberally…and a minute later they were all being handed back to be autographed. I quite enjoyed this minor celebrity status.

After 20 minutes or so we all mounted our bikes and I was led into the historic city of Brest for a sightseeing tour, TV crew following and filming from their van. We visited the ruins of the fortress where the Brest-Litovsk treaty was signed in March 1918, and where locals, clearly remembered and revered as heroes, held out for six days against the invading German army in June 1941. That was followed by a lunch of borscht and pancakes in a typical Belarusian restaurant, also filmed for the TV news clip, after which I followed Michael to his third-floor flat and was briefly introduced to his wife and son.

Then I was bustled into a large car and found myself in a diminished group of six men going shopping. We stopped at a supermarket for various comestibles and beer, then drove for about half an hour out into the suburbs and parked up by a big house where the shopping was unloaded and taken down to a large shed at the bottom of the garden. I was intrigued and mildly anxious by this stage, but they all seemed genuine and friendly so I continued to let myself be carried along with their plans, which turned out to be a sauna bath and picnic in the garden shed. The shopping bags were emptied to reveal a great spread of local specialities, a number of dark bottles of strong ale, and a bottle of vodka. We all got our kit off and went into the sauna, which was cranked up to hotter than I've ever known, and I was introduced to the "special equipment" – a hefty bunch of birch twigs and leaves used to thrash each other across the backs – all jolly good harmless fun! Incriminating photos were taken but fortunately I stayed just sober enough to protect my modesty, holding a strategically positioned felt hat in one hand and the birch whip in the other. Explaining in a subsequent slide show back at work that I was holding the "special equipment", one colleague was prompted to quip: "which hand?"

The TV item was featured on the evening news bulletin[17], lasting 2½ minutes. It must have been a slow news day in Brest.

47 km today / 1,672 km since London

Monday 14th April

A comfortable night as Michael's guest in his flat was followed by a leisurely cooked breakfast, then we were off to one final engagement before I could get back out on the road: a meeting with the Mayor of Brest. We pedalled over to the City Hall and were shown up to a rather plain office on the third floor. Tea and biscuits were served and an interpreter relayed a series of familiar questions from the Mayor on my route, daily distances, where was I sleeping, etc. When he found out about my profession he quizzed me about School Travel Plans and lamented that Brest had exactly the same problems of car dependency as London – daily traffic jams with cars full of lazy parents and overweight children who should be walking and cycling to school. He was absolutely right of course and I enjoyed the meeting of minds, but as the clock ticked on towards 11:00 I was itching to get going, acutely aware that in the last 24 hours I had ridden less than 50 kms.

I finally broke free from the almost overwhelming hospitality shortly after 11:00 and set off eastwards on the M1 and M10 under foreboding grey skies and cold rain, escorted for 75 kms by a solitary Brest cyclist to Kobryn, and then finally I was alone again. All was quiet and back to a sort

---

[17] http://tinyurl.com/papeu3r

of normality, and my head fairly span as I relived the whirlwind of events of the past 24 hours – it had all been quite surreal. I tried to make up for lost time but the road surface was very poor in places impeding swift progress, so I was pleased to get as far as Pinsk by 22:00 where I retreated from the cold wet night into a roadside motel. No English spoken, nor German, French or Spanish, so I fired up Google Translate on the smartphone and chose soup, pancakes and goulash from the limited menu. My room was adequate but austere, without WC, bathroom or even a pillow, and the towel on offer for use in the communal showers was barely larger or thicker than the hanky in my pocket. Nonetheless the room was clean and a lot warmer and more comfy than a bus shelter would have been that wild night, and the sleep, as always after a day of hard pedalling, was sublime.

176 km today / 1,848 km since London

Tuesday 15th April

My 11th day on the road since leaving London was amazingly the first I'd ridden solo all day. After a reasonable hotel breakfast I was back out on the long, flat, straight M10 highway, which traverses the entire country west to east, some 600 km from Brest to Gomel near the Russian border. The landscape was bleak, alternating between vast fields, open spaces and forests. Traffic was thankfully light, mostly trucks, and most of them giving me a safe and comfortably wide berth. The road surface was variable, and my speed varied accordingly – on the good bits a useful tailwind helped push me along at giddy speeds of up to 30 km/h. It was cold still, raining on and off all day, but nothing too heavy and my new waterproofs kept me warm and dry. Every few hours I stopped for big hearty meals at roadside cafés, most of which involved borscht and potatoes, and just before 22:00 I found a handy three-star audax hotel for the night.

197 km today / 2,045 km since London

Wednesday 16th April

After a quick bowl of muesli in the bus shelter I was back on the road at 06:30, listening to some music on the mp3 player for the first time – it would have been rude in company, and yesterday, my first day alone, had been too wet and the earphones were not waterproof. Today stayed dry but still a wind-chilled 10°C. The M10 remained featureless and straight as an arrow so I lost little time stopping to take photos. Frequent roadside shrines attested to high levels of motor-slaughter – similar numbers perish every year on Belarusian roads as ours, but they have only one sixth of the UK population. That said, my personal experience in Belarus was one of sharing the roads with patient, considerate and friendly drivers. I'm glad I had not seen a recent story on the BBC News website[18] telling of the "fake body of a dead cyclist left on the side of a dangerous stretch of road in Belarus as part of a police safety campaign…the scene was set up to look like a hit-and-run, with a mangled cycle and tyre tracks left near the dummy…officers found only nine people stopped out of 186 cars that drove past…"

At 48,000 Roubles, my lunch bill at a roadside café caused momentary alarm, but at an exchange rate of 16,000:1 that was just £3. It had been a particularly fine and nourishing meal so I tried to leave 50,000 to include a small tip. The café owner was reluctant to accept this and tried to push the change back into my hands, which I managed to deposit on a neighbouring table as I was leaving. Before I could unlock my bike however, she came dashing out with a free loaf of bread for me – extraordinary! Little did I know then, but this was just the first of many increasingly generous gifts

The reception committee at Gomel

that I was to receive from complete strangers over the coming weeks.

At 16:30 I crossed the River Dnieper, and a couple of hours later was met by 40 cyclists at the Gomel city boundary and escorted en masse into the city centre for press interviews. This had obviously been arranged by Michael in Brest, whose sphere of influence apparently ranged across the entire country. After an enjoyable hour or so with the locals I was led to a recommended hotel where I showered, washed my kit, and enjoyed a hearty dinner of borscht and potatoes.

164 km today / 2,209 km since London

Thursday 17th April

After a quick breakfast at the hotel I was away by 07:00. Today was the first properly sunny day since London, but a stiff headwind pegged my average speed back to 17.5 km/h. I stopped for a mid-morning coffee at a service station, offered free of charge with bonus chocolates once they'd read my magic letter. At 45 km I crossed the open border into Russia, where a few soldierly looking types lolled about lazily with no passport stamping duties or other formalities to perform. A friendly guard posed with me for a photo, then I was on my way, feeling pleased with myself for having cycled from London to Russia in 12 days. I was rather less pleased with Russian drivers on the M13 – there was a distinct deterioration in standards with far too many close passes and dangerous overtaking manoeuvres, so I felt highly exposed and vulnerable, acutely aware that the dangers of the road far outweighed any other threats to my survival on this trip.

Welcome to Russia!

On a brighter note there were some lovely, cosy, sheltered, roadside picnic spots in the forest, very useful as towns and villages were now few and far between. I raided my seat bag for bread, cheese, paté and fruit and made a couple of social phone calls back home to family and friends. The road surface had improved marginally since the border, and the landscape was rolling gently up and down, so despite the headwind I managed to reach my target 200 kms by 23:00, where a convenient three-star audax hotel near Pochep had my name on it. It was a relief to crawl into my sleeping bag still in one piece, and I shuddered a little as I relived some of the close passes of the day.

202 km today / 2,411 km since London

Friday 18ᵗʰ April

Up and away by 06:40 after first breakfast; another cold start and the road surface much worse than yesterday. I still had sore Achilles tendons – they'd been bugging me for a week now since Germany – and the headwind had strengthened. Traffic had thickened in both directions and international juggernauts were passing far too close. The roadside was littered with shrines to the fallen on this battlefield of a highway. Then came the first serious canine attack: a hefty mongrel managed to sink its teeth into my left pannier and almost dragged the bike down and me with it, but somehow we kept steady and I withdrew the dog stick, waving it about and shouting like a lunatic. I think that did the trick because he didn't get close enough for me to strike a direct hit, more's the pity!

The road rolled on over long climbs and descents, there was less wifi available at the café stops, and more dreadful overtaking and canine incidents followed. At one point I was fending off *juggernauts to the left of me, dogs to the right, there I was, stuck in the middle with the potholes*, to paraphrase the Stealers Wheel song. All in all there was plenty of entertainment to keep me alert and occupied.

Whenever I got off the bike for comfort breaks, snack stops, shopping, etc., walking and especially going down any steps was painful and difficult on account of the sore Achilles, though surprisingly and thankfully I could still ride well enough, if a bit more slowly. Remarkably they recovered just enough each night to allow me to keep going the following day.

Today was the first properly hard day of the ride so far, and by 21:00 I'd had enough. Arriving shattered in the town of Orel I decided I'd earned myself a night in a hotel. I came up trumps with the first place I tried. The proprietor and his wife helped me upstairs with my bike and bags to the room, and a short while later brought up a huge dinner tray of various grilled meats, chips, soup, bread and beer – I must have looked too whacked even to make it back down to the dining room, or perhaps they were fearful I'd scare off the other guests! Deep sleep followed soon thereafter.

188 km today / 2,599 km since London

Saturday 19ᵗʰ April

05:30 was too early for the hotel breakfast, so I stopped at a nearby garage for coffee and snacks, and then again after 50 km for a truly splendid meal. I'd discovered over recent days that the easiest way to choose my food was to visit the kitchen and look at what was being cooked. This was usually great fun and far less laborious for both sides than trying to explain and comprehend a menu. In reality there was not usually much choice with most places offering some or all of the following: soup, potatoes, big joints of beef or lamb, cabbage, bread and dumplings; I usually ended up having a portion of each. Sometimes the quality was high…and others not. A good feed would get me up to 100 km down the road before I needed a refill.

Triumphal Entry into Kursk

It was altogether a welcome easier day today, sunny and warm at last. I even put some sun cream on – hurrah! The dog stick was unsheathed three times but the brutes never got quite close enough to be bashed. The road surface had improved, traffic was lighter, and there was a rideable hard shoulder on the M2 highway bearing south to the city of Kursk, where a warmshowers host awaited. 35 km out from the city two cyclists were waiting for me by the side of the road. Michael's sphere of influence evidently spanned international borders – I was now well over 1,000 km east of Brest. Yuri and Alex escorted me to the city boundary where a further ten local cycling club members were lined up by the city sign proudly displaying their club flag. We trundled together into the city centre, where I was strategically positioned below a replica Arc de Triomphe for a photo-shoot. After that we all rode out into the suburbs to a big family dinner with my host Dmitri and family. I think there was vodka involved, and I remember sleeping very well.

173 km today / 2,771 km since London

Sunday 20th April, Easter Day

Dmitri provided an early big breakfast and filled my seat bag with a good variety of picnic items, then escorted me 25 km out of town to the A144 highway east towards Voronezh, a poor quality road with lots of cars, though mercifully fewer lorries than recent days. There was also a fierce headwind, and I struggled at times to make even 10 km/h. At these low speeds in the blustery conditions, and trying to steer round crater-sized potholes, I was a little wobbly on the bike, so I took refuge by riding close to the stony verge out of the traffic flow. However that proved slower still, and not without its own risks – the bike wasn't brilliant on a loose surface and I nearly skidded off more than once. This was the hardest and slowest day yet, and the hilliest too, with 1,500m of climbing. My mettle was being severely tested; on a good day I could have *run* faster!

The wind dropped, as it so often does, at sunset, by which time I'd managed to cover just 140 km. I rolled into a fantastic family welcome from Boris, Nicolai, Yulia and Marina at their transport café near Gorshechnoe where, upon sight of the magic letter, not only was my huge dinner offered free of charge, but I was also asked if I would like a free bed for the night. Such a spontaneous act of kindness and generosity from complete strangers was truly moving. I accepted the dinner but faced a dilemma over the accommodation offer as I was well short of my 200 km target and the wind had dropped, so conditions were ideal to ride on for another couple of hours. On the other hand it was 22:00, dark, and the thought of going straight to bed was not without appeal. I sought advice on Twitter and a couple of followers urged me to take the bed. To this day I really don't know why I ignored their sensible advice and opted to go back out into the dark to ride another 45 kms, finishing at a two-star bus shelter in the small village of Vyaznovatovka at 01:00.

185 km today / 2,956 km since London

Monday 21st April

Back home it was Easter Bank Holiday, but evidently not here: by 05:30 there was a fast growing queue of locals at the bus stop, presumably on their way to work. They took a keen but benevolent interest in my morning routine as I rolled up my sleeping kit and poured myself a bowl of cereal.

There followed another day into the wind, my progress further impeded by the big, congested city of Voronezh, where I stopped at a chemist's to buy some more ibuprofen for my suffering Achilles tendons. Fellow audaxer Dr Helen Vecht had responded to a plaintive tweet a few days earlier and prescribed a triple-pronged approach: take ibuprofen regularly, adjust the cleats in my sandals, and raise my feet overnight on pillows. The final suggestion caused some angst; even the four-star bus shelters to date had not featured pillows. Helen suggested a pannier would do the same job.

I emerged from Voronezh to discover that the road I'd planned to use was in fact a multi-lane motorway. So I re-routed onto the P193 heading east towards Panino and Anna on smaller roads, then missed a turn and ended up on a muddy track crossing fields just as night was falling. Soon it became unrideable, so I continued on foot, hoping I was still heading towards Anna, where I would pick up the main road again. The vegetation thickened, the going got tougher, daylight faded, and then the dogs started barking – this was all rather unnerving. In these situations the quandary is whether to cut your losses and retrace backwards, losing half a day's progress, or push on and possibly compound errors. The dogs, I reasoned, probably had owners who probably lived in a village where there was probably a road…so I decided to push on gingerly, making as little noise as possible and with all lights extinguished, which didn't make progress any easier. This logic eventually proved sound and I finally emerged onto a small road at nearly midnight, having taken over five hours to cover the last 40 kms of the day. After a few more kms on the bike I camped in woods near Anna.

152 km today / 3,107 km since London

Tuesday 22nd April

In Karachan I met schoolteacher Tatiana, who was happy to practise her English with me while I was stopped at the service station for supplies, making a pleasant highlight of what was an uneventful day until I reached Borisoglebst at 19:00. Here I pulled up outside a hotel because I rather fancied a night out of the cold, and went up the steps towards the main entrance, but the door was blocked by workmen painting and decorating the lobby. Following their gesticulated directions, I went round to the back entrance, where I left the bike and was directed down a corridor back to the lobby. I picked my way between assorted tools and across dustsheets to the front desk, which was staffed by a formidable looking lady who demanded my passport. She scrutinised it page by page for a good long while, then mumbled something and passed it to a colleague. She also examined it and then disappeared into a back office and took photocopies before striding back out and handing it back to the first lady who was evidently wearing the trousers here. She barked some questions at me, which of course I had no hope of comprehending. By this time a few other people were waiting to check in, and one stepped forward to interpret for me. Apparently my papers were not in order, he explained – there was a date error on my Belarus entry card, which I had assumed, when it was given to me back on 13th April, was just for Belarus. So I had entered my expected exit date as

18th April, allowing ample time to get across 600 km of Belarus. Now I gleaned from formidable hotel lady, via the interpreter, that this card was for my passage across the entire Russian federation – Belarus, Russia and Kazakhstan, some 5,000 km – and should therefore have been valid right through to 20th May, like my Kazakh visa. Once again I was facing visa trouble, but not this time in the comfort of my home with alternative route possibilities to be explored at the click of a mouse; now I was in the middle of Russia and facing a hostile looking formidable hotel lady. It was an anxious moment as she deliberated, having gathered the facts. Was she going to call the police? Perhaps I'd get free accommodation in a Gulag.

Eventually after much tongue clicking, further mutterings with colleagues and extended exchanges with other guests in the queue, who appeared by this stage to be quite enjoying the spectacle, I was handed my passport and a room key, and led up to a room on the first floor…which was already occupied! Despite the paucity of my Russian vocabulary, I managed to convey an air of surprise to the porter, who explained that the hotel was fully booked so guests were expected to share rooms with complete strangers. I was lost for words, and not for the first time regretted that I'd not stayed outside and found a nice bus shelter. My room-mate was a seemingly polite and kind young man who did not seem at all perturbed or surprised at the situation, and tried to make me feel welcome, offering some biscuits. I was still reeling with the shock of these unexpected circumstances when a maid appeared at the door and said that another room had now become available. I began collecting up my bags and toothbrush, but the maid made it clear that it would be the other guest moving out, not me. Happy to comply, he spent five minutes vacating the room while I sat open-mouthed and speechless, thinking that I had perhaps landed in a Russian *Fawlty Towers* sitcom.

Without further ado I showered, shaved, washed some kit, and went downstairs for dinner – quite a good dinner as it turned out, but rather spoilt by pop music blasted out at disco volume into the almost empty dining room. Appeals to turn it down were met with blank stares (and no doubt deaf ears). Then the wifi stopped working. I finally hit the sack at midnight. To my great surprise, the bed did not collapse.

154 km today / 3,262 km since London

Wednesday 23rd April

I was relieved to leave the hotel of nightmares as early as possible in the morning, not taking any chances with breakfast which I picked up at a café down the road. Today was quite an easy day for a change, sunny and with a favourable wind on the A144 towards Saratov, although some terrible road surfaces meant that I couldn't take full advantage of the tailwind. Many of the town and city signs I passed were vast elaborate structures dating back to communist days and reflecting local pride. I was pretty sure that was also the last time any money had been spent on repairing and maintaining the roads.

At 09:00 a café did me a truly excellent second breakfast spread of eggs, bread, soup, salad and coffee, putting enough energy into the tank for the next 100 km. Traffic was mercifully light and the greatest excitement of the day came as I tried to steer around a large pothole and ran into the dusty verge, where I lost control and skidded off the bike. Fortunately no harm was done to bike or body and I rolled on to Kalininsk by around 20:30, where I bought a huge borscht, bread and whole chicken dinner at the café and phoned home. The chicken proved too much for one sitting so I bagged half of it for picnics then found a nice quiet bus shelter for the night where no-one was going to give me a hard time over passport irregularities or expect me to share a room.

186 km today / 3,447 km since London

Thursday 24th April

Today was planned to be easy. I'd booked a warmshowers host in Engels just 120 km down the road, a short half-day ride so I could arrive in good time and shape to engage in the polite conversation a host might reasonably expect   and with a bit of luck get some dinner too. But that plan was scuppered by the weather, which had turned from clement to vile overnight. I woke at 05:00 to a freezing strong north wind and horizontal icy rain – pretty much the most hateful conditions imaginable for cycling. The road surface was equally appalling – all in all a horrible way to start the day. Some Russians had told me their roads are the worst in the world, and I was beginning to believe it – this was even worse than Putney Bridge for goodness sake! It took 90 minutes battling across a lunar-like surface against lashing sleet to ride 18 km to a basic service station where I shivered so much I could barely drink my coffee. A café on the other side of the road was not yet open. I couldn't face going any further without a good hot meal inside me, so I waited.

Shortly after 08:00 the café opened and I got a decent breakfast of eggs, bread and more coffee. Conditions were still horrid after I'd polished off the plate so I ordered the same again. I think I might have stayed all day consuming eggs, bread and coffee if the rain hadn't stopped, but happily after the second plateful conditions were drier if not balmy. The fierce, gusty, cold north wind continued to blow all day, a cross-wind producing highly challenging conditions for cycling and literally blowing me off the

Bumpy road ahead

road several times. There was also violent buffeting by trucks to deal with – each time one passed, the wind was momentarily cut and I would wobble towards the truck, because I had been banked over that way against the wind. Just as I was correcting the wobble, the truck would be gone and the full force of the gale would slam into me again, blowing me the other way into the verge. Progress was down to 11.5 km/h and utterly exhausting. Occasional relief was provided by avenues of trees which moderated the wind, but I was reduced to walking on the more exposed treeless stretches. The road surface looked as if it had been cluster-bombed and I was wearing pretty much every shred and layer of clothing I possessed, hooded up and looking like a polar explorer. Frankly I rather felt like that too, as if I was at some wild frontier of civilisation, certainly compared with civilisation as I knew it.

I finally arrived in the city of Saratov, then crossed a long bridge over the River Volga into Engels at around 18:00 – it had taken me 13 hours to ride less than 120 km. My warmshowers host, Maxim, met me by the bridge and led me the final 10 km to his house on the edge of town, a great, sprawling, comfortable family home. I was given a warm family welcome from his sister, father and grand-mother, who had produced a rather excellent chicken stew. Beers were cracked open and suddenly everything was perfect, almost overwhelmingly so. My contrasting fortunes in such a short space of time once again reduced me to a delicate emotional state. All day I'd battled hostile elements, then the warmshowers magic happened and I was cosseted in the bosom of a friendly family drinking beer and exchanging tales about the joys of cycle travel – surreal and very moving. Warmshowers is truly the most amazing wonderful international family community of hospitable people who like riding their bikes.

126 km today / 3,575 km since London

Friday 25th April

Maxim was up at 06:00 cooking porridge for me, and, after he and his granny had tried in vain to persuade me to stay for another night, he made me a big picnic. It was hugely tempting to stay and rest after the recent long hard days, but I was already 400 km behind schedule and didn't want to fall a further 200 km behind. The immediately pressing concern was to not outstay my Russian visa. Beyond Russia sprawled the vast expanse of Kazakhstan, where roads might be even worse, and my visa would expire on 20th May. There was therefore an inexorable pressure to keep on the move. Furthermore it was the most gloriously sunny day, and although still cold and breezy, the wind was going my way for a change!

So I got going as early as was politely possible, at around 07:30, and was soon cruising along nicely at 30 km/h on good bits of road. But in between the good bits there were long stretches of poor bits where I was not able to take full advantage of the favourable wind and my speed fell back to below 20 km/h. Nonetheless I made reasonable progress overall for the day, stopping in Ershov for an excellent beef stew at 18:00 with 170 km on the clock. After dinner the weather and wind were still good, so I got back out on the road for the night shift, hoping to push well past 200 km. But annoyingly as night fell so did the road quality. Pothole dodging in the dark is a tiring and stressful business, and it was almost impossible to avoid them all, so now and again the bike took an almighty shock and I emerged from the crater thankful that I was still aboard and we were both still in one piece. After a couple of such close calls I decided it was too risky, so cut my losses and stopped for an early night camp by the roadside.

191 km today / 3,765 km since London

Saturday 26th April

It was a cold night, down to 3°C, so I had zipped myself right up inside the bivi bag. At 03:00 I woke suddenly, alarmed to be breathing deeply and with great difficulty. For a moment I could not work out what the problem was. I was having to use the full capacity of my lungs to draw in enough oxygen, like riding a time trial up the Alpe d'Huez, yet I'd been asleep for hours – why on earth was I so breathless? It occurred to me that I might be slowly asphyxiating myself in the sealed bivi bag! I opened the zip an inch and inhaled some desperately needed lungfuls of cold but oxygenated air, and my breathing gradually returned to normal. I made a mental note to ask for my money back, the sales blurb for this bivi bag having described it as breathable.

Following that scare, I was up at dawn, 05:00, and soon back on road, but the surface, or lack of surface, meant slow going again. It was just 100 km to Kazakhstan now and I desperately hoped for better roads there. Facilities were now sparse too. I found a roadside café in Dergachi at 07:30; advertised opening time was 08:00. Fortunately there was also a warm garage next door where I could wait, drink bad coffee, and buy three litres of water for the journey to the border and beyond, as the map showed few signs of civilisation until Uralsk over 200 km away. The café opened at 08:15 and I got a decent breakfast of eggs, bread, soup, salad and coffee, but no wifi – that was also becoming increasingly rare.

Harsh conditions persisted all day in the form of a cold north wind and continuing bad roads, but happily no rain. It was good to meet a team of men dressed in hi-vis looking as if they were there to mend the road, even if they were mostly standing around smoking and chewing the fat with plenty of time to down tools and pose for photos. It took nearly ten hours to do 100 km to Ozinki, the last village in Russia, where I arrived at 15:00 and found a general store to re-stock the seat bag with essential supplies, and a café for a welcome bowl of hot soup. Still no wifi.

An hour of climbing later I arrived at the border, a little nervous about the entry and exit dates on my papers following my recent encounter with formidable hotel lady in Borisoglebst. Formalities took an hour while I fretted in the freezing cold, and I was mighty relieved when the Russian border guards stamped the passport, handed it back, raised the barrier and waved me through. The Kazakh officials welcomed me into their country and gave me a paper to fill out and keep with my passport, explaining that it had to be presented within five days to the police for an official stamp of approval and advising me to check into a hotel for assistance with this procedure.

I rode 40 km from the border through a bleak treeless landscape to the first village, Taskala. Wild horses roamed, night was falling and it was cold, barely above freezing. Under the clear starry sky it was only going to get colder, so I really didn't fancy camping out, but the nearest hotel was over 80 km away in Uralsk, and as far as I knew there was no accommodation for travellers in this tiny border village. I approached the first people I saw, the money changers in their portacabin, to ask if there was a hotel in the village. As I had expected the answer was no, but would I care to join them in their warm cabin, share their dinner, and sleep on the floor in the corner? I could have kissed them both – the legendary Kazakh hospitality I'd read about was kicking in early! I spent an enjoyable evening with Marat and Marat, who generously shared the hearty meat stew and bread which their wives had prepared for them. We swapped tales about our families and home lives as best we could via Google Translate. They were fascinated by my blog and tweets – despite their remote location they were fully hooked up onto the internet. Once again I hit the sack with my head reeling – every day was bringing new and unpredictable adventures. What would the following days bring? I was rather hoping that things might settle down into some kind of steady routine, but as I drifted into sleep here at the western edge of the eighth largest country on earth, a country comprised mostly of desert, I somehow doubted it.

145 km today / 3,910 km since London

Sunday 27th April

I slept soundly in the money changers' warm portacabin through till 07:30. They recommended a nearby café for breakfast, but finding it closed I tried the local petrol station and shop where I was made most welcome by Olga and her team. Although the garage had no café, Olga sat me down in the small shop and brought me porridge and coffee, and when I'd finished she arranged a photo-shoot with other staff. Then I went back to see the two Marats to change some Russian Roubles for Kazakh Tenge, but they advised me that I'd get a better exchange rate in Uralsk – perhaps that's why they were still running their business from a portacabin.

It was still icy cold when I left the super-friendly village of Taskala in bright sunshine at 09:00, but an hour later it was warming up so I stopped to take a couple of layers off. Within minutes two drivers had stopped to check I was ok, offer bread and water, and ask about my trip. As usual, the magic letter was deployed to good effect. An entire extended family disgorged from one of the cars to have their photos taken with me, and one of them gave me a little red tulip, a lovely and moving gesture of welcome. I attached it to the bike handlebar.

The 80-odd km road to Uralsk was better than most Russian roads in that the craters were further apart and thus easily avoidable. I arrived in Uralsk at 15:00 and crossed a bridge over the River Ural. "Blimey", I tweeted, "I've cycled to Asia!"

I pootled into the city looking for a hotel – a bit of a nuisance really as it was mid-afternoon, riding conditions were good, and I'd only done 83 km. However, I needed to register with the police and the next opportunity would be in Aqtobe, 500 km further across the desert. So I stopped outside the first hotel I saw, the Pushkin. It looked rather grand and I noticed it was a four-star establishment, so I dithered about where to lock up the bike, or indeed whether I should just move on to a cheaper looking place. A man approached, introduced himself as Anvar, and asked in good English if I needed any help…did I need a room? Perhaps, I suggested, he could pop in and find out if they had a vacancy, and at what price. Oh, and ideally a room on the ground floor please, so I could take the bike in. He asked me what my budget was for the room. I had no idea of room prices here, having just arrived in the country and not yet au fait with the new currency, so hazarded a guess at 6,000 Tenge (about £20). Five minutes later he was back out and announced he'd secured me a room on the ground floor, bike welcome, and a 6,000 Tenge balance to pay. "Balance?" I queried, at the front desk. Indeed sir, the receptionist explained after Anvar had disappeared: the room price was actually 16,000 Tenge (£50) and Anvar had

paid the 10,000 (£30) difference. More legendary Kazakh hospitality! Anvar was, the hotelier told me, a frequent guest and worked for the state oil industry, so presumably wealthy enough to be generous to strangers.

It was an excellent hotel, a far cry from my recent experience in Borisoglebsk. I steered the fully laden bike into the grand marble lobby and

Anvar who paid for my four-star hotel in Uralsk

settled the remaining portion of the bill, by which time a small crowd of other guests had arrived, interested in the eccentric Englishman and his funny bike, evidently an unusual sight in these parts. A long photo session ensued as apparently all staff and available guests wanted their pictures taken with me and the bike. After a while I had to call a halt as I wanted to settle in and take full advantage of the luxurious accommodation that I had part-paid for. When I finally got into my executive-sized room I spent an hour in the bath, then washed my filthy kit and shaved, emerging quite the new man. The wifi was good so I sent out a slew of tweets to reassure family and friends that I was still on the planet, just a bit further round, then went out to the cash point for some Tenge and to shop for tomorrow's picnic. Finally I ate a splendid dinner of local fare back at the hotel and fell into the rather sumptuous bed at 22:45.

83 km today / 3,992 km since London

Monday 28th April

I treated myself to a lie-in in order to fully appreciate the opulent magnificence of the Uralsk Pushkin four-star, followed by a long sitting at a top quality all-you-can-eat buffet breakfast where I attempted, successfully, to eat a little bit of everything. There was no particular rush this morning because I had to report to the police station, which didn't open until 09:00. A helpful, youthful and frankly delightful English-speaking hotel manageress offered advice and explained how to get to the police station…I gently persuaded her to join me. It was just a few hundred yards from the hotel and I might have found it easily enough by myself, but I thought she might be a useful ally and interpreter. And indeed she was! She efficiently helped me negotiate a swift path to the main man in the big office with the rubber stamps. He looked at the paper I'd been given at the border, sucked his teeth, nodded and muttered something which Efficient Hotel Manageress (EHM) interpreted for me: I had to fill out another form. That was accomplished with some difficulty because the English version of the official form had lost something in translation and some of the questions were rather less than crystal clear. Nonetheless I had a good stab at it, crossed my fingers, and handed it back. It was scrutinised, along with my passport and visa, teeth were sucked some more, and finally a colleague was brought in to venture his opinion on the small pile of documents I had generated. They were handed back to me as I'd missed a bit; well to be frank I had left it blank as I had not the foggiest idea what the question meant. EHM helped out again, and I handed it back duly completed and waited anxiously. Eventually it was explained, through EHM, that he could only stamp my authority-to-stay paper through to 5th May because I was not planning to remain solely in his jurisdiction of West Kazakhstan. So by 5th May, EHM explained, I would have to go through the whole procedure again at another police station in a new province. A major pain in the proverbial – I'd stopped early the previous day in order to register here and was finally ready to leave at 11:00, some 20 hours later, having lost a huge chunk of time. Further time would be similarly squandered the following week…and maybe the week after that too. It was all very trying for one on a mission and a tight schedule; the 200 km/day target was starting to slip badly.

Fortunately the road south was excellent; rather less fortunately I faced another headwind – I never seemed to get both good wind and road together. Nonetheless I made good time to Zhympity where night was falling as I entered the only café in town. I was quickly surrounded by a crowd of friendly locals who wanted to pose with me and the bike for photos, which I went along with for a few minutes. But I was hungry and eager to get back out on the road as the wind had dropped and conditions were ideal to make up some time and get close to the 200 km target despite the late start. That plan however was thwarted five minutes later. As I was sitting eating my dinner, a young girl approached me and, with some difficulty, managed to convey that a room in the hotel over the road had been booked for me and paid for by Omar, the man outside with the big black car who'd choreographed the photo shoots a few minutes earlier. More traditional Kazakh hospitality, it was explained. It was a much smaller hotel than the Pushkin, but friendly, clean and comfortable. I accepted gracefully and resolved to set off early the following day.

147 km today / 4,139 km since London

Tuesday 29th April

At 06:00 my hotel benefactor Omar came to meet me at the café opposite the hotel for breakfast, but it wasn't yet open so he invited me back to his house for bread, yoghurt and coffee and showed me photo albums of his family and surprisingly extensive worldwide travels. I think he'd have liked me to stay all day but I managed to extricate myself at 07:00 and get back out on the road. He insisted on driving with me to show me the way out of town – even though there was only one road.

There followed another hard day riding into a stiff headwind at an average of just 15 km/h, so blustery it was at times hard to control the bike, and particularly dispiriting because the road surface was unusually excellent and progress would have been swift with a more favourable wind. Distances between towns and villages seemed vast and the landscape was increasingly arid – just a few weedy, scrubby trees and hardy grasses punctuated the empty, pancake flat, sandy landscape. Traffic was sparse, just a few dozen vehicles all day, from which passing travellers showed great interest in me, slowing down to take photos and videos. Several drivers pulled over ahead of me and motioned for me to stop and pose for photos with them. The novelty soon wore off and I rode past most waving a cheery greeting, reluctant to lose yet more time, especially as I had just learned that three days of national holidays were about to begin, so I had to reach Aqtobe the following day in order to register with the local police before the deadline.

It took until 16:30 to do 120 km at which point, energy levels running low, I finally found a café and ate a huge meal – the usual great joint of lamb floating in a bowl of hearty broth with loaf on the side. When I went to pay my bill I was told it had already been paid by one of the other diners. Kazakh tradition had kicked in again.

The wind dropped as usual at dusk, but once again I was thwarted: I crossed the provincial boundary from West Kazakhstan into the Aqtobe region, and the road surface, which had been good all day, promptly turned to dust. Furthermore I was in a region of small hills – nothing severe but just lumpy enough to keep me pegged back to the stately 15 km/h I'd been doing all day. I plodded along to finish and collapse, exhausted, for a roadside camp at 22:00.

179 km today / 4,319 km since London

Wednesday 30th April

Rain woke me at 05:30 and I was struggling into the wind again 30 minutes later. After four hours of laboured pedalling I'd covered just 40 km to Qobda, where I pulled in at the only café. A level of self-doubt was creeping in and for the first time I noted in my diary that this was not actually much fun; I'd not had a combination of good roads and tailwind since Germany. Why was I here if I wasn't enjoying it? I worked hard to rationalise and convince myself that things could only get better...couldn't they? Almost on cue an exotic bird perched on the handlebar to cheer me up, a beautiful creature sporting black, white and brown plumage, a fan-shaped tail and a long beak. It was gone before I could get a snapshot but I looked it up later – a black-winged stilt, perhaps?

By 16:00 I'd covered just 100 km at an average speed of 13.5 km/h. After another brief café stop where once again my standard fare of soup, meat, veg, bread and dumplings was paid for by fellow diners, I entered a region of long draggy hills and bad roads. It felt chilly despite an average temperature for the day of 15°C (and a maximum of 23), and there were sizeable snowdrifts lying on shady north-facing slopes at the roadside. I finally arrived in Aqtobe at 20:00 and stopped at the first hotel I came to. I went through the usual routine (shower, kit wash, dinner), and for the first time in Kazakhstan I actually paid for myself (didn't they know who I was, I wondered). Wifi was available – I summed up recent days in a brief tweet: "500k of not much from Uralsk to Aqtobe. Except headwinds! All better now. Beer helps."

154 km today / 4,472 km since London

Thursday 1st May

It was raining when I woke up, and the hotel breakfast wasn't till 08:00, so I went back to bed for an hour. Then I dawdled over a generous buffet breakfast, hoping to give the weather a chance to improve. It didn't, so I steeled myself and set out at 09:30 into the rain, against the wind, and, as would become clear over coming days, in the wrong direction.

There was a choice of two roads leaving Aqtobe, one going south towards Algha and Shalqar, the other east towards Qarabutaq. They both eventually converged at Aralsk, some 600 km distant, with little in between. The map showed the road east to be the more major route, and therefore possibly the better highway, but with fewer villages; whereas the Shalqar route passed through more settlements where I'd get food and water, but was shown as a secondary highway so the road surface might be inferior. Dilemma: ride faster between fewer towns and villages, or more slowly between more? The total distance to Aralsk was similar either way. I had sought advice before leaving London, and again a couple of times since arriving in Kazakhstan, but had not reached a decision. My gut feeling was to go south and no one had advised against it, so that's the way I went. It wasn't until two days later, far beyond the point of no return, that I realised it had probably been the wrong choice.

Things were fine to start with and I enjoyed a relatively easy day for a change – the rain soon cleared and the wind was moderate. Every passing driver hooted and many slowed to film me as they overtook or pulled over to stop for photos and videos. It was all very amicable, if becoming somewhat tiresome. The wind shifted to westerly in the afternoon, which would have been useful in recent days, but today I was going south for a change.

By 16:30 I'd covered the 100 km to Qandyaghash, where I stopped in the only café for soup and a delicious beef stew. Other customers bought me drinks and the café ladies sent me on my way with a parting gift of cakes. The road was smooth for another easy 40 km at good speed, then suddenly the surface disappeared and I was reduced to 10 km/h on a stony track for 13 km. I stopped to don my night gear at dusk – a few more layers and some hi-vis – and a van pulled up beside me. Three men emerged and surrounded me, taking an intense interest in the bike and firing fast questions which I didn't understand. I showed them the magic letter, which they read slowly while I anxiously pondered their intentions. After all, it was almost dark, there was no one else about, and I was in the middle of the desert. After what seemed an age they offered me water and cakes and asked if I needed a lift anywhere. Phew! I accepted the sustenance and declined the lift as graciously as possible and they drove off, leaving me to potter on a little further before chucking in the towel at 22:00 because the road was too bad to ride safely in the dark. I retired some 20m from the road to make camp in the lee of a small dune under a star-studded sky in total silence. This was a beautiful moment, it was a privilege to be here – and yes, I was enjoying myself!

164 km today / 4,636 km since London

Friday 2nd May

I was up at 05:30 and riding at 06:00 into a beautiful clear dawn. There was no wind and the road was smooth, a rare perfect combination – hurrah! It was 30 km to the small village of Embi but there was no café so I tucked into some rations from the seat bag by the side of the road, basking in the warm early morning sunshine. It was a lovely location to linger so I decided that now would be as good a time as any to do a spot of bike maintenance, specifically an oil change in the hub gear, a recommended procedure every 5,000 km. I was happily busying myself with this task when Tuligen the

Tuligen the shepherd, and flock

local shepherd approached, evidently curious. He read the magic letter then stood and watched, apparently fascinated – this was probably a rare sight on his patch. His flock grazed lazily about 50 yards away and periodically Tuligen would look round to check that none were straying – he had a pocketful of small stones for that eventuality, which he threw with great accuracy to keep them in check. Then his mobile phone rang – it was his wife summoning him home for elevenses. A surreal little episode!

Oil change completed, I got back on the road, which stayed good for another 10 km, then disappeared again. There was a choice: stay on a rough, loose and stony surface where it seemed the original road had once been, or use a smoother parallel road forged in the dust by frustrated drivers in an attempt to go faster. I tried the latter for a short while but deep sand drifts caused me to wobble and skid and eventually fall off the bike, so it seemed safer to ride on the stony road. The surface did not improve, progress was painfully slow and tiring, and at times I wondered how much more shaking

60

and rattling the bike would bear before falling to bits, like the *Blues Brothers'* car at the end of the film.

In the afternoon I passed a young woman on foot. She looked about 20 years old, pretty with long dark hair, bug-eye sunglasses and a London/New York t-shirt with crossed UK and US flags on the back. She was walking this desert road alone, far from any settlement, in sandals and swinging a handbag. As I approached I caught a whiff of this most unlikely fellow desert traveller: she smelt like a parfumerie. With the assistance of Google Translate, I tried to ask if and when the road surface would improve, but I don't think she understood, and I got the sense that she was probably a little anxious or suspicious of my intentions…especially when I began to unzip my lycra shirt to reveal the magic letter…

At 70 km I arrived in a bonus village – it wasn't on the map so I'd not been expecting anything. I stopped for supplies and was immediately surrounded by a small group of boys who all wanted autographed cards, making for a pleasant interlude.

Back on the unmade road again, I was feeling increasingly remote. There was almost no other traffic now, a passing vehicle every hour perhaps. I crossed a small range of hills up to around 500m altitude and noticed that every gradient sign stated 12%, even though most were well under that, probably more like 5%. The road continued in a terrible state for a further 30 kms then there was a small improvement but still no tarmac. The going wasn't too hard at this stage but still demanded 100% concentration to avoid the potholes, and I was anxious for the bike, so my stress levels were rising. I met a couple of guys in the late afternoon who gave me the unwelcome information that the next café was 100 km away in Shalqar, and there would be no improvement in the road surface until then. It was just as well I had stocked up with plenty of water and food in the bonus village earlier. There was no other traffic at all now, just an empty, silent, unmade desert road stretching to the horizon. Had I bitten off more than I could chew here? I realised now that I'd almost certainly not made the right choice of road from Aqtobe, but was in too deep to turn back now. I stopped at dusk on just 123 km and camped in the gully by the roadside for a troubled sleep despite the utter silence.

123 km today / 4,759 km since London

Saturday 3rd May

Up at 05:00 and soon back on the "road", in reality a dusty stony track with no sign of tarmac ever having been present. It was a gorgeous, sunny, windless morning nonetheless, and the birds were tweeting merrily from the scrubby desert grasses. I was walking some bits now, averaging only 10 km/h, and after a couple of hours I flagged down the first passing car to gather local intelligence. Yesterday's information was confirmed by the five occupants: there was no tarmac on the road to Shalqar, still some 60 km away. On a good day I'd do 60 km in a couple of hours before breakfast, but in present conditions it might take five times that long.

Sharing the road

Wild horses and camels were by now my more frequent companions of the road than cars and lorries, and an occasional train passed in the distance on a line which the map showed to be going to Shalqar and then on to Aralsk. A few kms further on the railway converged towards and then crossed the road at a manned level crossing. I stopped for a few minutes to greet the operator, Numba, who welcomed me into his hut and shared a pot of tea with me.

Mid-morning I arrived at a river where a few crumbling pillars testified to the previous existence of a bridge. Vehicle tracks were visible in the dirt down to the water's edge, indicating that drivers simply forded across, but I hadn't seen a vehicle for some hours, so waiting to hitch a lift across seemed a tad over-optimistic. The prospect of fording the river with my bike wasn't appealing – the river bed was stony and I couldn't be sure of its depth. Safest I thought would be to go for a trial paddle empty-handed in my bike sandals to the other side, pick out the best route, then come back first for the bags, then the bike. It turned out to be fairly shallow and not too fast-flowing. So that's how it was done, in three stages, and another half-hour lost.

Very shortly after that mini adventure I took another tumble, this time a bit harder. The handlebar was twisted and I scraped some skin off a kneecap – ouch! Two further falls in quick succession convinced me that I'd have to give up riding altogether, the risks of bike or body damage being unacceptably high now. So I set off on foot – teasingly there was a nice tailwind at this point. It was sunny and pretty hot by now, 30°C, and to be frank I'd just about had enough. I was facing a tough five-hour walk across the desert to get to Shalqar, and it was starting to look like I might not even make that destination by nightfall. Food and water would have to be rationed now.

I concluded that I was in a bit of a jam and that it was BIG DECISION time! I'd set out to bike round the world, not to kill myself, so I reluctantly decided I would try for a lift – which might not be easy as there were three roads now: the official stony road and two parallel tracks running about 50-100 metres each side, and hardly any traffic. The first passing car was fully occupied, and bore further bad news for me: the road was bad like this to Shalqar and beyond, indeed all the way to Aralsk, over 200 km away. So I decided that however and whenever I finally made it to Shalqar, I'd get a bus or train from there to Aralsk. Perishing in the desert would not have been a great way to finish the trip.

At 15:30 I heard a lorry approaching fast, but on the track about 100m over to the left. I waved…the driver waved back, and kept going. I yelled and started waving both arms energetically, animatedly, frantically… he slowed a little and peered out, kept going a bit…was he going to stop? Was this the ship that would miss me on the desert island? Eventually he slowed and drew up to a halt. I made my way across the scrub as sharply as I could and appealed for a lift into town, using hand gestures to convey that I was hot, exhausted, thirsty, and the road was bloody awful. He got the gist, jumped down from the cab, and opened up the back which was bare but for a few empty sacks. He helped me haul the bike in, introduced himself as

Fatima and Eraly

Eraly, and invited me to climb up into the cab where I found myself sitting next to his wife, Fatima. Pressing the pedal to the metal, Eraly crunched up through the gears, and we were soon careering at terrific speed across the bumpy desert sending up clouds of dust in our wake. Fatima fed me some small but powerful balls of dry goat cheese while I gripped onto my seat for fear of being catapulted up into the ceiling, with rising concern for my bike bouncing around like a ping-pong ball in the back. It took about 30 minutes to cover the 20 km into Shalqar, on paper not a dazzling speed, but across that rough patch of desert it was like a fast and furious fairground ride.

Thankfully he slowed down as we drove into town, negotiated a few back streets, and pulled up smartly into the courtyard of their house, where we unloaded the bike, surprisingly still intact. I asked for directions to the station but they insisted I first join the family for tea, so a moment later I found myself sitting on the matted floor around a low table with Fatima and Eraly, their young son Dinislam, and Orazhan who I think was Fatima's brother. The table was laden with all manner of homemade delicacies, both savoury and sweet, and large pots of tea. For a moment I felt quite overwhelmed – just an hour previously I had been alone and worried about surviving a desert crossing; now here I was, in the bosom of this kind family, being looked after like a returning prodigal son. It was very moving and I found myself welling up a little as I tried to thank them for their kindness. The cakes were divine and I drank gallons of hot sweet tea.

At the conclusion of the feast I mimed a steam train and made some puffing and whistling noises – for a moment they looked at me quizzically, probably wondering if I was having a bit of a turn, heatstroke perhaps. Then the penny dropped and they twigged that I intended to travel to Aralsk by rail and could they point me towards the station? Dinislam was despatched to fetch the laptop. Like small children everywhere he was soon on the page, and it transpired my timing had been fortuitous – there was a train due to leave for Aralsk in a couple of hours. So I said my goodbyes to this lovely family and tore myself away; it would have been nice to stay a while longer in that safe and cosy haven, but I needed to keep moving – the expiry date on my visa was looming large.

Dinislam showed me to the railway station, where I met my next helper in the chain, Aslan. I was obviously looking a little lost and he asked in pretty good English if he could assist. Yes please, would he help me buy my rail ticket to Aralsk? But of course, no problem! At the ticket office he engaged in earnest conversation with a lady in state rail uniform. Then he turned round to inform me that the ticket price to Aralsk was 3,000 Tenge (about £10). Did that include the bike, I asked? He turned back to the ticket lady, further parley ensued, and then she picked up the phone, spoke for a few moments and passed it to Aslan. He spoke for a minute or two and handed the phone back to ticket lady, they exchanged a few more words, then he informed me that the price for me *and* the bike would be just 2,000 Tenge – a price he'd negotiated directly by phone a moment ago with the guard on the train! Needless to say, there would be no actual ticket involved. When the train drew in at 19:00, Aslan (who by now had spent a whole hour helping me) and the guard both helped me haul the bike aboard, I paid the guard cash and was shown to a sleeper berth opposite a Kyrgyzstani lady called Sara who was travelling home to Bishkek. She soon insisted on sharing her pot noodle dinner with me as the train rattled into the darkness, and once again I was touched deeply by the kindness of complete strangers in this remote yet most hospitable corner of our world.

At 22:00 the train stopped at Sekseuil station and a local woman came through our carriage hawking various comestibles, including cold beer. Yesss!!! It was sublime nectar and all was momentarily perfect with the world on this toughest of days...until the guard passed through and told me sternly that drinking alcohol was not permitted on the train, leaving me to wonder why selling it was absolutely no problem. We pulled into Aralsk an hour later and I found a cheap hotel just outside the station.

83 km today / 4,843 km since London (including 20 km by lorry but not the 180 km by train)

Sunday 4th May

After a quick, cheap and cheerful budget hotel breakfast I enquired at the station where I might find a police station to get my card stamped, and was advised to take a taxi. It turned out to be a straightforward journey which I could have walked in ten minutes. This time I was unaccompanied, but managed with little trouble to locate the right officer who, naturally enough, gave me a form to fill out. It was the same form as the one I'd completed back in Uralsk, so I'd had recent practice and made a conscious effort to do better this time before handing it back, like late homework. I waited a few anxious moments while he scrutinised the completed form, together with my passport and the stamped paper from Uralsk police station. He began asking some questions, then the phone rang and he was diverted for five minutes on other business while I tried to stay calm, desperately hoping that he'd sign it through till 20th May, the expiry date of my visa, so I wouldn't have to repeat this bureaucratic rigmarole a third time.. After hanging up he conferred with a colleague, then signed the paper and reached for the rubber stamp. Bang! 20th May! Result!

I walked back to the hotel with a spring in my step and ate another breakfast to celebrate this good fortune, then found an internet café and sent a series of cheery tweets while my mood was upbeat. Finally, I availed myself of a quick third breakfast at the station before hitting the road at 11:30...or rather 12:30. The GPS confirmed I had unknowingly crossed into the Astana time zone.

The M32 road south from Aralsk was excellent, an indescribable joy and relief after recent days. This was the road I could and clearly should have taken from Uralsk, but it was too late now for any such regrets. A crosswind was sometimes helpful, sometimes not, and the temperature gradually rose to 32°C. I was carrying my maximum capacity of 6.5 litres of water, and camels and wild horses congregated at infrequent water holes. By 18:00 I'd covered 85 km and stopped at a spartan roadside café; in reality I think just an open house. There were no chairs so I sat on the floor and was brought a filling meal of bread, mutton, potato, and tea.

After tea I got going again and was making great progress: the road was still good and, in great contrast with recent more testing days, my spirits were high... until I was overtaken slowly by a police car and ordered to stop. Oh no! What now? I produced the magic letter and passport with the paper their colleague had stamped that very morning, and they appeared satisfied. But where was I going to sleep, they asked. Thinking that they may take a dim view of my intention to camp at the roadside, I pointed to the next town on the map – Zhangaqazaly. They waved a cordial greeting and shot off up the road at high speed.

An hour later I arrived at Zhangaqazaly...and kept going. I really didn't want to stop yet – I was still going well, the road was good, the wind and temperature had both dropped, and I had the road to myself; in short I was enjoying the perfect bike ride! Then I saw a car approaching in the rear-view mirror, oh dear...a flashing blue light on top! It was the same police car, and the same three officers flagged me down. I thought they might order me to go back to Zhangaqazaly, or perhaps even lock me up in the cells for a night? I wasn't breaking the law, was I? Using Google Translate I managed to explain that I'd changed my mind and wanted to keep riding because conditions were good, and I demonstrated that I had good bike lights both to be seen by other road users and to light up the road. I added that I'd been delayed that morning by their colleagues at the police station in Aralsk getting my papers in order, so hadn't been able to start riding till after midday. They were clearly facing a new situation. Puzzled, they discussed it among themselves for a few moments while I fretted for the second time that day as my destiny was decided by armed police with unknown powers. When they finally gestured that I was free to continue I was so relieved I shook their hands. Then I jumped back on the bike and set off before they could change their minds.

I rode on to a convenient bus shelter, pleased with the distance covered for a half-day ride. The bigger picture was looking OK too: I'd been on the road for a month, and was about 20% along my route around the world.

148 km today / 4,991 km since London

Monday 5th May

The day dawned beautiful and sunny and I was off to a good early start at 06:15, but as the sun climbed so the heat and headwind increased – as did the number of cars stopping to take photos. It was time to test a coping strategy that I'd been formulating: since I was on an old trading route – the Silk Road – perhaps I could trade photos for food and water. The great advantage to me would not be to save money – eating was cheap (and often free) – it would be to save time. Most towns and villages were some way off the highway down a rough track, so diverting off-route to stock up on a few provisions could easily take an hour. This new tactic worked a treat and the seat bag was gradually replenished by passing travellers with bread, cheese, olives, dried fruit...

Shortly before midday I rolled into a roadside café, having ridden only 68 km at a slow average of 15.7 km/h against a hot headwind. Unusually there was a choice of mains: beef or chicken stew. Ravenous as usual, I ordered both; they were served with a whole loaf of bread and a gigantic pot of hot sweet black tea. I bagged half a portion for a picnic later in the day and went back out, but it was like a furnace so I retreated into shade at the first opportunity, a remote fuel stop where I learned of another café just down the road. I pushed on and stopped there for iced tea and biscuits and a lie-down for an hour. At 15:00 it was still a ferocious 40°C, but I felt compelled to try again, being only a third of the way to the daily target distance and beginning to wonder if I'd ever achieve another 200 km day under my wheels. 5 km further on there was yet another café, making three within about 10 km following a café-free expanse of 100 km – so Kazakh cafés come in threes like London buses. I stopped again as the shade was irresistible. It was an easy job convincing myself not to stay out too long on the road in this heat – surely I'd get sunstroke.

It had cooled down a little by 17:00, the wind had gradually dropped too, and I managed to put a good spurt on for a few hours on a fine road. I pedalled past the Baikonur cosmodrome, but it was a good way off the highway so there was little to see apart from a few distant towers. I finally stopped for a roadside camp at 23:00 near Zhosaly.

166 km today / 5,157 km since London

Tuesday 6th May

Today started promisingly: I was up at 05:30 and after a quick snack and packing away the camping kit I was bowling along the wonderfully smooth M32 highway at a good lick. There was no wind and I began to daydream indulgent thoughts that today might bring a rather overdue lucky break. Morale was further boosted at 08:00 by a great café breakfast of eggs, sausages, bread and coffee. Keen to get going again as soon as possible and make the most of the favourable conditions before it got too hot, I was back out racking up a few more fast kms until at around 09:30 the fine smooth road surface came to an abrupt end and a warning sign announced 50 km of roadworks. All traffic was diverted to use parallel rough tracks and I was immediately pegged back to 10 km/h where I could ride, but often forced to dismount to walk through sand drifts. My hopes were dashed – another hot tough day was on the cards. There were occasional usable bits of resurfaced M32, but the highway was banked up out of sight above the level of the diversion track, so every few km I climbed up to check if the road menders had yet been in attendance. The good stretches were superb, wide and smooth enough to land a jumbo jet...then suddenly they ended at a sharp edge and there was no surface at all, or indeed any sign there had ever been a road there at all. It was really quite bizarre – how had the road ever evolved to this?

Trading with the road menders

The day was a partial success in that I concluded some more good trades, including with a road-mending crew, which saved me losing even more time diverting off-piste for shopping. By midday the mercury had climbed to 37°C but shelter was non-existent – no towns, villages or cafés – so I plastered on the factor 50 and soldiered on, eventually finding refuge in a culvert under the road just big enough to squeeze into with the bike. I picnicked and made the pleasant discovery of a nice hot cup of sweet black tea – an hour earlier I'd gained a bottle of iced tea in one of my trades which had since been strapped on the back of the bike in full sun.

After lunch I took a siesta till 16:00 and then set off again. Inevitably, within 10 km of my hole under the road, a café materialised at the side of the road. It was still hot and the road was still appalling so I was tempted in and surprised to see something on the menu I'd not seen recently, nor would expect to see in the middle of the desert: fish! I checked the other diners' plates and they were all eating fish. So I ordered fish, and it was delicious. Reassuringly, on checking the map, I saw that there were a number of lakes and rivers in the vicinity.

It was 19:00 by the time I'd ridden and pushed through the roadworks, so about nine hours at little above walking speed to cover 50 km. They ended as abruptly as they'd started and suddenly I was on a beautiful and obviously expensively engineered stretch of highway every bit as good as the best in Europe with motorway-style interchanges, slip roads, bridges and other paraphernalia designed for high levels of fast moving motor traffic. The only element missing was the traffic – I was mostly alone. At sunset, riding though yet another costly but empty spaghetti junction, I did spot one other road user on a distant slip road – he was riding a donkey.

Engineering for donkeys

By and by, gradual signs appeared that I was beginning to emerge from the desert: a few wiry trees and shrubs, a lake, a river, some wildfowl… By 20:00 it was mercifully cooler but the headwind didn't drop as usual so the night shift was hard work too, and when I pulled into the verge to camp just outside Qyzylorda at 22:30 I was once again utterly drained.

I'd been on the go for over 16 hours, and riding for 12 at an average speed of just 12 km/h.

148 km today / 5,305 km since London

Wednesday 7th May

It was another dawn start on the M32, which remained good all day, but once again, alas, the combination of good road and wind eluded me – a stiff north-easterly held me back at 14 km/h. Interest from passing motorists remained high, and despite some good trades it became irritating; I felt rather like an exhibit at the zoo. Some slowed right down to my speed and drove uncomfortably close to get their shots; when they got home and reviewed their photos and videos I suspect they saw some excitable hand gestures as I tried to shoo them away. Hopefully the accompanying robust English outbursts escaped their comprehension. I later came to regret such a churlish reaction; after all I really must have looked quite extraordinary out there, plodding sedately and alone across the desert. I hadn't seen another cyclist since Russia, let alone someone riding what was effectively a wheeled-deckchair – I might as well have dropped in from Mars. It occurred to me that if the tables were turned and one of them was riding his camel around the world and came down, say, the Broadway in Wimbledon, we'd be pointing our cameras at him, equally curious. But would we be equally hospitable, paying for his lunches and hotels?

By 13:30 I'd ridden only 70 km but it was too hot to go on so I retired under the road into another useful culvert for lunch and a siesta. Emerging from my hole at 16:00, the wind had stiffened, so progress remained slow through to 110 km by 18:30, at which point I repaired into a café for eggs, meat pasties, cakes and provisions to refill the seat bag. Following a fifth mug of tea I went back out for the final shift of the day, which thankfully became less breezy as night fell. I managed another 50 km before striking camp at 23:00 in an open field some 100 metres off the highway.

163 km today / 5,468 km since London

Thursday 8th May

At 02:00 I was woken by a dazzlingly bright light. I unzipped the bivi bag a few inches to investigate: car headlights were shining directly at me – highly unnerving. I waited, motionless and transfixed, improbably hoping they hadn't seen me, my heart beating faster than it had all day. Silence reigned for a long minute. It was like a stand-off – who would move first? I watched and waited, feeling exposed and defenceless. Slowly the driver reversed back onto the road, then sped off into the distance. I'd obviously not hidden myself well enough, and lay wide awake wondering whether to find a more secluded spot. I didn't wonder for long before another passing car also slowed down to take a gander. That was enough; I broke camp in record time and moved on about 2 km, where I found a well-hidden culvert under the road and slept through till a glorious sunrise at 05:30.

At 06:00 I was back on the move and back in the groove: the MP3 was pumping, the road was good and there was no wind – let the good times roll! A series of long gentle hills made for a fine early morning work-out before it started warming up again.

During elevenses at a roadside café a well-dressed driver pulled up in a large and expensive-looking new car, took an interest in the bike, read the magic letter and promptly proffered 5,000 Tenge (£16). I was flummoxed. Kazakh tradition again? How to react? He was pretty insistent but I felt uneasy, how could I possibly accept a cash donation? I was proudly self-funding my trip which, all said and done, amounted to a self-indulgent extended holiday, so I declined the offer. He seemed surprised by this as he put the notes back in his wallet; on reflection he was probably mildly offended that I had not accepted his well-intentioned gift. Clearly what I should have done, I concluded moments after he'd left – and resolved to do should the situation arise again – was to accept the donation graciously on behalf of RoadPeace.

At lunch a few hours later, while I was tucking into my eggs, sausages, bread, jam, tea, and a large and tasty rice dish not dissimilar to paella, two young boys playing out near my bike were scolded by their mother before I could intervene to say it was fine, they were welcome to look at the bike, just don't touch please! The mother and women running the café then joined me at my table and, as we shared a pot of tea, three men arrived and crowded around the bike, and suddenly one of them was astride it posing for photos – the cheek of it! Their intentions were good and friendly but I had to echo the young mother's words of a few moments earlier – look but don't touch.

I rode on for a further hour then stopped for a siesta till 16:00 in another culvert – fortunately there were plenty on this road as shade was otherwise still scarce. When I emerged the wind was up again, and once again in my face. The heat was still fierce, 40°C, so I stopped at the first café for cold drinks, another rice dish and a deliciously spiced-up carrot salad. I was beginning to worry now about how I'd cope with the heat in Southeast Asia. Here it was dry; I imagined it would be steamy and even harder to deal with in Vietnam, Thailand and Malaysia.

On the approach to Turkistan a small van drew up alongside and the driver leaned out smiling and giving a thumbs-up gesture. I smiled back and noticed a cycling logo on the side of the van so I motioned him to pull over for a quick chat. He turned out to be the Kazakh youth cycling coach, and proudly showed me a silver cup they had won in a recent competition. He read my magic letter, took some photos, and gave me 2,500 Tenge. I put my earlier resolution into practice and accepted with good grace, explaining it would be for RoadPeace.

I arrived in Turkistan at 19:30, a large town where I'd planned to find a hotel – it had been five days since my last hotel stay in Aralsk, five days of hot dusty desert riding without washing more than my hands and face in café toilets. I don't think I'd ever been filthier in my life, so the hotel would be a justified necessity rather than a frivolous luxury. To meet my simple undemanding standards, I'd developed a three point hotel checklist: friendly reception, safe cycle parking (ideally in the room), and wifi. The first I passed had no wifi but the second ticked all three boxes and furthermore sported a combination of opulent splendour and reasonable price tag. I checked in, and the bike was stored in a locked luggage room.

Large and luxurious, the room did not disappoint, so I made full and extended use of all facilities, emerging quite the new man after an hour of washing, scrubbing and shaving. Bike kit was hung out to dry all around the room, then I settled down to tweet reassurances to the world that all was fine – I hadn't sent news in four days and didn't want anyone worrying. Blast! The wifi wasn't working. I asked at reception and was told it would be fixed in the morning. Then into dinner, where all was good except that there was no beer – double blast! I was gasping for this beer, but the hotel wasn't licensed. There was no English menu nor did the staff speak any English, so I got myself invited into the kitchen to choose my dinner from a number of bubbling pots and went for soup, salad and beef…washed down with fruit juice.

134 km today / 5,603 km since London

Friday 9th May

I awoke fully refreshed from my night of luxury and went down at 07:30 to see if an early breakfast might be possible – yesterday I'd been told different times by two staff members: 08:00 and 09:00, both of which struck me as rather late, certainly for a busy man like me! Today's receptionist split the difference, informing me that breakfast would be served from 08:30. I'd just had time to settle down to wait in the lobby and discover that the wifi was still not working when I noticed people dressed remarkably like kitchen staff slipping into the dining room, so I followed them in discreetly and they obligingly served me breakfast at 07:45.

After breakfast the wifi was still not fixed so I went out in search of the nearest internet café. It took a little while to track down and as I was

Bloody camels, think they own the road, pay no road tax

wandering down the wide main street a boy rode past on a camel. Turning the tables for once, I asked him to stop so I could get a photo. Shortly after that I found the internet café, only to discover it didn't open till 10:00. In all likelihood there would be no more wifi till Bishkek in three or four days' time, so I decided to wait, highly frustrating though this was, as it was a sunny, cool and windless start to the day – perfect conditions for making good progress on the bike.

I passed the time doing a general sort and tidy through my bags and washing more kit, then packed up and left the hotel to make my way back to the internet café, fervently hoping their punctuality was better than the hotel's. It was still closed at 10:00 so I knocked, then again more forcefully. A sleepy-looking youth emerged and I explained I needed wifi; he nodded and switched on some computers and a router then gave me a login code. It didn't work. He got on the phone to technical assistance who guided him through some electronic fiddling and tweaking while I sat with crossed fingers watching the minutes tick by. At 10:15 he coaxed the IT into a co-operative mode and I sent out a slew of previously drafted emails and tweets, including one with the photo of the boy on his camel I'd taken that morning. In response to that I received a cracking reply from Yeti Pilot @TransAlpUK: "That's the problem with bloody camels, think they own the road, pay no road tax..."

I finally left Turkistan at 11:00, by which time, as usual, the wind and heat were both up and against me. Once out of town I was straining to cruise at 12 km/h, buffeted all over the road by a hot, strong, north-easterly cross-wind which was forecast to continue over the coming days all the way through to Almaty, the end of the Kazakh road for me, about 800 km away. After just 20 km it was literally too windy to ride, so I retreated into another culvert under the road – it was siesta time anyway. More lost time of course as I was neither hungry nor tired. Exasperating. I had another eleven days on the Kazakh visa. Normally 800 km would be easy going in that timeframe, but against this wind it would be slow and challenging. Again I lamented my lack of luck with the wind – I'd been riding against it now for the best part of 5,000 km.

Back out on the road at 15:00, I was banked over against the side-wind. When lorries passed, the wind was momentarily cut resulting in some alarming wobbles. A hard slow ride ensued, reaching a roadside shop at 18:00 with only 58 km under the wheels and most of the day gone. But they had cold beer – probably the best sports drink in the world – so I didn't care. A terrific café stop followed just 12 km later where I put away a large bowl of soup, a loaf of bread, four kebabs, three yoghurts and three mugs of tea.

Morale substantially boosted, and the wind down a notch, I made better progress through the evening to 100 km, at which point the road bore round to the right in a more southerly direction and the wind was finally behind me – boy that felt good! I changed up through several gears and settled into an unfamiliar new cruising speed approaching 30 km/h...for exactly 13 km...at which point the road once again did its all too familiar disappearing trick. I walked across dust and stones for a couple of kms after which a road of sorts reappeared. It comprised chiefly old cratered tarmac, so the going remained laboriously slow as I passed through a dimly lit, dusty and edgy-feeling township where I encountered no problems but felt acutely uneasy, the centre of unwanted attention. Crowds of people milled about aimlessly, it was nearly midnight, many were drunk, and I felt their eyes on me – especially when I had to stop for what seemed an eternity at the town centre crossroads.

Emerging unscathed back into quiet open country I decided to call it a day, pulled in well off the road, laid the bike down, and got myself tucked into my bivi bag shortly after midnight.

124 km today / 5,727 km since London

Saturday 10th May

I was woken at 03:00 by more unwanted attention: three inquisitive types gawping at my prostrate form. And again at 04:30 – I was obviously not well enough hidden. Once again it was most unnerving. After that I couldn't sleep so I got up to try and discover why I was so visible in the dark. I walked about 50 metres away from the bike and turned a torch onto it, whereupon it lit up like a Christmas tree. Reflective bits all over the bike, designed to be visible on the highway after dark, were doing their job effectively. I felt rather foolish, and was surprised it was only the second night I'd been spotted – or of course possibly not; I might have been observed and ignored on other occasions. I resolved to be more careful in future.

Hurdles training for pedestrians

So it was an early start, back on the road at 05:00. An hour later I arrived at a junction not on my map – a brand new highway had been built bearing east and bypassing Shymkent. It was the ideal direction for me, so I turned onto it. Somewhat less ideal, once again, was the wind – I had turned into the teeth of a ferocious headwind and was down in the lowest of my 14 gears at something under 10 km/h, wobbling around in the gusts. Fortunately there was virtually no traffic. It was less than 700 km now to Almaty, the end of the first leg of the world tour, but I was increasingly doubtful I'd make it under such conditions before my visa expired.

Three hours and some 30 km of hard grind later the new highway deposited me back on the old narrow M39 road to Taraz, thick with heavy lorry traffic. The wind was now blowing up a dust storm and visibility was down to a few metres. Attempting to ride felt suicidal under these conditions; it was pretty tricky even to walk with the bike. At 11:30 I stopped at a roadside shop for supplies, having covered barely 45 km in over six hours. I'd moved into hilly terrain now and snow-capped peaks dotted the southern horizon, giving pause for reflection: it was hard to reconcile my present snail-like progress with the fact that I'd ridden in just a few weeks from London to the foothills of the Himalayan chain.

Back out from the shop I'd ridden scarcely a few metres when a terrific gust blew me right out into the middle of the road, momentarily and fortunately unoccupied by other traffic. A minute later I was buffeted violently the other way, right off the road into the verge. I walked a few metres further then stopped for breath – this was utterly exhausting. These were the windiest conditions I'd ever tried to ride in – I could barely move. I laid the bike down and flopped to the ground beside it. Traffic rumbled by while I sat with my head in my hands, feeling defeated.

After five minutes I pulled myself together and began pushing the bike along the rough verge when a driver pulled up in a large empty car and offered a lift. I didn't hesitate. He dropped me at a café some 15 km later – very conveniently, for it was lunchtime. I parked the bike and sat at a table on the terrace under a wildly flapping roof of plastic sheeting. A fine meal of broth, salad, rice, kebabs and tea appeared before me within moments and I settled in for the long haul – the wind was now up to gale force strength so I clearly wasn't going anywhere soon.

Before long I'd attracted benevolent attention and was invited to join other customers who plied me with beer and more kebabs. The local police pulled up in a gigantic 4x4 and sat down with the owner and I was invited to join the party. We drank more beer and exchanged niceties. I spotted that the police car had bald tyres but decided it might be wise to keep that observation to myself.

At 16:00 I shook hands with my new friends, went back out onto the road and tried to ride. It proved impossible, and I imagine it looked quite comical to any onlookers who might indeed have wondered if I'd ever ridden a bike before. I fell off three times in rapid succession then gave up and tried hitching a lift for 15 minutes with no success. I was warmly welcomed back at the café.

A steady trickle of new customers came and went as afternoon slipped into evening. Many of them read the magic letter and there was a further donation of 2,000 Tenge to RoadPeace. My third kebab and beer dinner was paid for by other diners, who confirmed that the exceptionally high winds should abate by the following day. The café owner invited me to stay and doss down for the night, so I made myself comfortable, fired up the Kindle app on my smartphone, and settled down to read a rather apposite

Sherlock Holmes short story: *The Adventure of the Solitary Cyclist*. This was the first opportunity I'd found time to read a book since London.

My worries gradually dissipated as I quaffed beer, scoffed kebabs and lost myself in one short story after another. The café remained busy throughout the evening, but the clientele changed: earlier it had been travellers – this being a busy trading route from Tashkent to Bishkek and Almaty – and now it was full of locals. The barbecue was working overtime; in the kitchen several generations of the owner's family toiled to produce dinners and drinks; all was calmly overseen by the patriarchal figure of my generous host. I was invited to meet, eat and drink with many clients and made sterling efforts to limit the beer intake just in case the wind dropped and I could make my escape. I was also keen to stay as sober and alert as possible in case of any less well-intentioned interest in me and my kit, though as the evening wore on I felt more and more relaxed – these people were looking after me like family.

Reading Sherlock Holmes under the madly flapping awning next to my bike and a nonstop barbeque in the middle of Kazakhstan suddenly felt quite surreal. The wind didn't abate and by 20:00 I'd decided to accept the accommodation offer. One of the locals insisted on giving me a lighter, despite my protestations that I'd given up smoking in 1989. Pascale rang at around 21:00 and we had a nice long chat. Then I ordered more soup, bread and beer.

My bed was made up for me outside on a picnic table under the fluttering canopy and I began to wonder when I'd be able to retire into it – the café was still thronged at 22:00 and most guests were outside on the terrace, some of them hitting the bottle enthusiastically now, effectively in my bedroom. But it was hardly my place to ask them to leave. Then suddenly, with rather excellent timing, all the lights went out – a power cut, hurrah! The music died and so did the party. Within fifteen minutes the place was deserted and I was free to go to bed in peace, if not quiet – it was still windy and the feverishly flapping plastic roof kept me awake and worrying what I'd do in the morning if conditions didn't improve. There were just ten days now to visa expiry, and still 600 km to Almaty. Today I'd covered just 63 km, 15 of which by car. My GPS was recording 10 km "laps"; today I'd ridden and walked five laps at 13, 11, 8, 5 and 4 km/h respectively. Setting out to ride the world, I had not expected an easy ride...but how much harder could it get?

It stayed windy all night.

63 km today / 5,790 km since London (including 15 km by car)

Sunday 11th May

By dawn the wind had dropped to stiff but rideable, and I finally got away from my refuge of some 17 hours at 06:00. The scenery was much more varied and interesting now I was out of the desert, featuring hills, grass, trees and rivers. It was a gorgeous sunny morning, rather slow going in the hills, but towards midday the wind had picked up again to blowing-me-off-the-road speed and I was once again forced to stop, frustrated, by the side of the road. In six hours I'd ridden just 45 km. While I sat on the crash barrier picking at some lunch from the seat bag and increasing anxious about the slow progress, a lorry driver stopped to offer a lift. This was becoming a rather bad habit, but I accepted on account of the looming visa deadline – I needed to keep moving.

As we stowed the bike, the driver made it clear that he wasn't offering a free lift, so we quickly agreed on a fee that he scrawled by fingertip on the dusty back door of his lorry. I climbed up into the cab, we exchanged a few pleasantries as best we could across the language divide, then I settled down to enjoy the ride. A fine ride on the bike it would have been too, in better conditions – the road was good and smooth and I dozed off in the sunny sanctuary of the cab. A couple of hours and 85 km later he dropped me in Taraz. There was a tense moment relating to a significant misunderstanding of the agreed fee – 500 or 5,000 Tenge? We settled amicably on 2,000. This, as it turned out, was to be the last of 300 diesel assisted kilometres of the whole trip (two lorries, one train and one car).

In town I found a new source of free wifi: a mobile phone shop. Of course! They need wifi to demonstrate the phones. Why hadn't I thought of that before? The owner was happy for me to connect and I spent a happy 30 minutes tweeting updates and replying to emails.

I set out from Taraz – on the bike – at 16:00, conditions still breezy but rideable. On the outskirts of town a rather excellent little café served soup so delicious I managed double portions, fuelling a sustained effort without further ado through to 23:00 and within 200 km of Bishkek and 400 km of Almaty. What a difference a day had made – this thing now looked doable; the end of the Kazakh road was looming into view.

Making camp at the roadside, I took greater trouble to hide the bike and cover all its reflective bits from nosey neighbours.

123 km today (not including 85 km by lorry) / 5,914 km since London

Monday 12th May

Another lovely sunny day dawned, and just a gentle breeze blew. It was a headwind of course, but I couldn't have everything, could I? On my right, to the south, ran a long chain of lofty snow-capped peaks; on the other side a flat empty wilderness. I was gradually climbing a long, steady, gentle gradient on a fine quality four-lane highway, and traffic was still sparse. It was much cooler and easier going now I was out of the desert – a huge relief. Dozens of honey vendors lined the roadside for a number of miles so I stopped and bought some rather delicious local honeycomb.

Shortly after midday I reached Merke where the road forked: decision junction; should I take the main highway direct to Almaty, or a smaller road via Bishkek? The map showed the reverse: the main road going via Bishkek and the minor more northerly route direct to Almaty. I dithered a while, recalling the recent bad choice I'd made in Aqtobe. Apart from road quality, another potential downside was that going via Bishkek, the capital of Kyrgyzstan, would necessitate exiting and re-entering Kazakhstan and possible red-tape hassles at one or both borders. On the other hand, my papers were in order as far as I knew, and I had bought a double-entry Kazakh visa in anticipation of using this route, so in theory there shouldn't be a problem. I also had a warmshowers host arranged in Bishkek and was rather looking forward to that, my last one having been in Russia almost three weeks previously. The pros outweighed the cons so I plumped for the Bishkek route and took the right fork towards Kara-Balta, the first town in Kyrgyzstan.

After emerging from the thronged and bustling town of Merke, the road turned out to be a wonderful refreshing change from the highway – a pretty tree-lined avenue, light traffic, and low wind. The road surface was perfectly adequate and I arrived at the border in the late afternoon. Sidling to the front of the long queue of stationary traffic, I was accorded priority attention

Fellow riders on the highway to Kara-Balta

and processed efficiently through the formalities and into Kyrgyzstan in a matter of minutes. After changing some money and scoffing a quick ice-cream, it was a slow but fun-packed 25 km into Kara-Balta, dodging between large herds of cattle and goats being rounded up and driven, presumably homewards, by mounted cowboys.

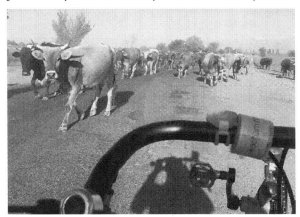

In town I checked into a solid, Soviet-looking, concrete monolith of a hotel, a bargain at just 250 Som (£3) but a real dive of a place – I'd been in more luxurious bus shelters. The shower wasn't working so I made do with a quick sponge down, rinsed some kit under a cold dripping tap then went out in search of dinner. Twenty minutes later I'd retreated back into the relative safety of my dingy bedroom with a quickly procured picnic because all the streetlights were out and the town felt distinctly edgy and unwelcoming. Luckily I had managed to procure beer too, so everything turned out fine in the end. I'd finally enjoyed an easy day, and another was in prospect for the morrow – it was a mere 60 kms to Bishkek.

You looking at me mate?

144 km today / 6,057 km since London

Tuesday 13th May

A day of luxury began with an indulgent lie-in listening to Mozart violin concertos followed by a spot of bike-fettling (adjusting the brakes and checking all nuts and bolts were still tight after bumping across the desert for three weeks). I checked out of the hotel at 09:00 and found a lovely looking place for breakfast where I could sit outside on the terrace in the bright early sunshine. But the ubiquitous meat dumplings were cold and tasteless and there was broken glass on the table and even in the sugar bowl! I was rapidly tiring of pretty much identical menus at every café since Russia, and starting to look forward to both the complete change and wider variety that Southeast Asia would surely bring.

Conditions were ideal for riding today: cool, sunny, a good road, and no wind…in short just perfect for a 200+ km ride. On a day when I only had 60 km to go this was a little irksome. Along the way I stopped for iced tea and yoghurt at a roadside place being run by Jehovah Witnesses Nadia and Bermet. I had my tea and yoghurt and resisted conversion.

At midday I arrived in Bishkek, the capital and the largest city of Kyrgyzstan with a population of just under a million, and followed directions, provided by my warmshowers host Nathan a few days earlier, through noisy crowded streets to a city centre café where he'd meet me and take me back to the flat. After five minutes, just as I realised that I was probably waiting at the wrong café, a voice called "Are you Richard?" Alex from Brighton introduced himself – another warmshowers guest staying with Nathan who'd perchance spotted my bike, there being not many heavily-laden, wheeled deckchairs on the streets of Bishkek. He was cycling from Australia back to the UK (as one does, in warmshowers circles) and had been languishing here for two weeks waiting for an Uzbek visa. He led me back to Nathan's flat, I took a quick shower and changed, then we headed out for lunch. The Sierra Café was a modern, stylish establishment serving European food, great coffee and fabulous monster-sized English breakfasts. There was working wifi and the staff spoke English – this was heaven! Alex and I gassed non-stop for about two hours – this was the first proper conversation I'd had in over a month since parting with Dave in Warsaw.

Back at the flat we cracked open some beers and continued chewing the fat. Nathan arrived home from work and joined the party – it was so good to relax in English speaking company. We were finally joined by Nathan's girlfriend, Angie, and went out to a nearby Turkish restaurant for dinner – no soup and dumplings tonight! Sharing the table with others and not having to eat quickly and get back out on the bike was an indulgent, luxurious moment to savour; I was surprised at how much I'd missed it.

The flat was compact and cosy, and rather crowded for four adults with bikes. Furthermore, after dinner Angie had to pack her bags to fly off to a three-day conference in Athens and would be leaving the flat at 02:00, and when she returned on Sunday she and Nathan would be moving into a new house on the other side of the city. I was amazed that they were still receiving warmshowers guests under such circumstances, completely relaxed and unfazed.

62 km today / 6,119 km since London

Wednesday 14ᵗʰ May

I paid a return visit with Alex to the Sierra Café for another of their excellent breakfasts before pedalling out of Bishkek towards the border, where I arrived at around 10:00. Formalities were once again swift and I was processed back into Kazakhstan without incident, but for a minor episode with one of the guards who thought it would be hilarious to sit on my bike. It made me anxious but was also a great photo opportunity. I'd just started framing the shot when a second guard appeared and made it clear photos weren't permitted in the border zone…and simultaneously the first guard fell off the bike. The photo that got away – damn!

Towards the end of the Kazakh road

Fortunately the bike was undamaged and I set off in fine weather but fighting against a stiff headwind into the biggest range of hills I'd encountered since the trip began. I fuelled up with a big plate of noodles and kebabs for lunch and got friendly with a busload of Uzbek women who were touring on a religious vacation. One of them, Louise, spontaneously donated 5,000 Tenge (£16) for RoadPeace.

After lunch there was a monster climb of some 1,100 metres in such high winds that once again I was reduced to walking up almost half of it, but I resisted the temptation to thumb for a lift. Towards the end of the afternoon I reached a mountain pass and descended onto the plains in the lee of the wind to a roadside café, apparently in the middle of nowhere. I ordered the house special: an enormous shank of tough mutton floating with potatoes and cabbage in a giant bowl of broth, and a half-loaf of bread on the side. Suitably fortified I ploughed on until 22:00 to my final Kazakh roadside camp, now within 100 km of Almaty – the end of my Kazakh road.

141 km today / 6,260 km since London

Thursday 15th May

My final day in Kazakhstan dawned gorgeously sunny. I breakfasted at 05:30 and was on the road at six. Feeling peckish an hour later I snacked on bread, cheese, nuts and honeycomb. 20 km further on I got an excellent café breakfast of eggs, sausage, bread, jam and tea in Samsy. Such feasting made me dozy so I took a mid-morning kip for an hour under a tree; the pressure was off and it was great to finally have some time to relax. After all the worry of a few days ago I was now arriving in Almaty five days ahead of the visa expiry date. At 14:00 I plunged into the motorised mayhem of Almaty and followed up on two arrangements I'd made before leaving London: a possible warmshowers host called Tasman; and a bike shop called Extremal with a big cardboard box for me to pack the bike into for onward transit. I rang Tasman but there was no answer, so I rode to the bike shop where Alexander and Tatiana were expecting me with a choice of boxes at the ready. The bike was clearly not going to fit into a standard bike box so they taped two together to build a super-sized custom model while I dismantled the bike, removing both wheels, the rack, seat, mudguards and pedals, and folding down the handlebars before I could squeeze it all in. It was hot thirsty work, but fortunately a restaurant next door served ice cold beer.

Next I had to decide where to fly. I'd been mulling over this question for some weeks. The Chinese border was less than 300 km to the east, a no-go zone since I didn't have the visa. Applying for the visa in Almaty could take up to a week and, I'd been advised, would be unlikely to succeed. My original route plan across China had been to ride east, veering gradually south via Urumqi, Lanzhou and Chonqing, crossing the border into Vietnam, and on to Hanoi, Bangkok and Singapore. So the obvious place to fly to now would be the first city on my route the other side of China: Hanoi. But there was no direct flight – I'd have to change planes at…Bangkok. So the decision was: Hanoi or Bangkok?

I chose Bangkok. There were a number of reasons for this quite apart from the direct, easier, faster and cheaper flight. First and foremost I needed a break. Russia and Kazakhstan had been far tougher than I'd expected – 6,000 km against the wind on those terrible desert roads had taken its toll, and I really fancied a few shorter, easier days on the bike, something more of a relaxed cycle-touring holiday as opposed to a daily 18-hour assault course. Hanoi to Singapore was about 4,000 km; from Bangkok that distance would be halved. I'd also decided it would be rather fun to arrive at my brother Jonathan's place in Perth, Western Australia, in time for his birthday on June 13th. So I now had four weeks to ride either 500 km a week from Bangkok or 1,000 km a week from Hanoi. Both in theory should be achievable – after all the original schedules had called for 1,400 km a week. But my self-confidence had taken a dent over recent weeks and I wasn't at all sure how well I'd cope with the high temperatures and sweltering humidity of the monsoon season across Vietnam and Laos. I'd read great accounts of cycle touring in these countries and I'd be missing both, but the attraction of riding relaxed sub-100 km days and indulging in a little sightseeing along the way proved irresistible.

Once the bike was boxed up I got online to try and buy an air ticket to Bangkok. Bingo! My luck was in – there was one daily direct Air Astana flight departing at 01:00. Trying to make the booking on the smartphone was a fiddly job, which ultimately failed – once all the little boxes had been filled, clicked, checked and ticked, the payment was not accepted. The bike shop manager invited me into the office to try on his computer, but that too failed at the same stage – cyber security was preventing my payment from going through.

By now it was early evening and too late to go and find a travel agent, so I decided to chance my luck at the airport – rock up, buy a ticket and fly. Alex the mechanic drove me in the shop's van to the airport for a small fee, and after a few anxious moments with a hesitant credit card machine at the Air Astana counter I had a one-way ticket to Bangkok for that night's flight – I could hardly believe it. The last few hours had been something of a whirlwind and I wouldn't even be staying a single night in Almaty, whereas, had my intended warmshowers host answered the phone, I might have been there for two or three nights.

At 21:00 I checked in and put my outsize, overweight luggage on the conveyor belt: one large bike box and a huge laundry bag containing a pannier, sleeping kit, bike seat and seat bag. I kept one heavy pannier as hand luggage to minimise the excess baggage fees. Almaty airport was tiny and peaceful; there were hardly any other travellers or flights. I spent a pleasant few hours catching up on emails and writing glowing online feedback on my four wonderful warmshowers hosts in Warsaw, Kursk, Engels and Bishkek. And I sent a message to a few potential hosts in Bangkok.

100 km today / 6,360 km since London

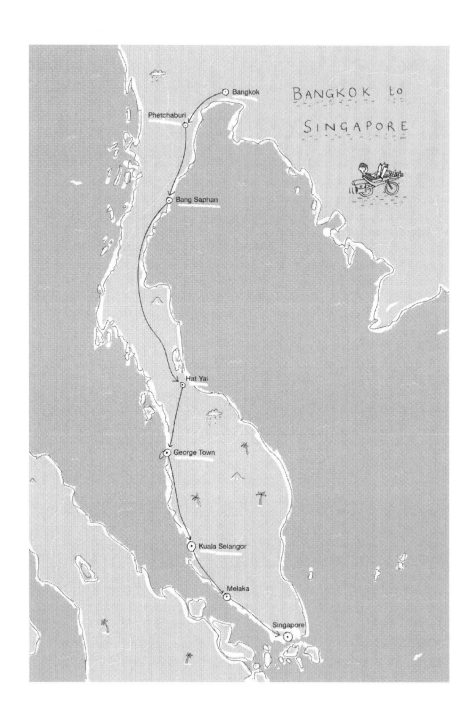

BANGKOK TO SINGAPORE

Friday 16th May

My flight left on time at 01:00 and the plane was half empty, so after an airline tray of warm veggie pastie and a beer I managed to stretch out over three seats for a pretty good sleep. A half-decent omelette was served for breakfast and the onscreen map showed we'd flown around the west of the Himalayas via Bishkek and Delhi. We landed in Bangkok at 08:00 local time, one hour ahead of Almaty, and the big laundry bag and bike box emerged quickly and unscathed. I reassembled the bike in the baggage hall, much to the bemusement of the handlers, contacted my warmshowers host to give an ETA, and bought a Thai curry for lunch, a refreshing change for the palate after so many weeks of stodge.

It was 14:00 when I finally left the air-conditioned sanctuary of the airport and pushed the bike through the automatic sliding doors out into the sweltering Bangkok afternoon: 37°C and almost 100% humidity – I was drenched in sweat within minutes. The heat in Kazakhstan had been bone dry, so I'd need to take things easy while I acclimatized. Any lingering doubts about my decision to fly here rather than to Hanoi were now dispelled – riding three weeks of 200 km days in these conditions would have been a daunting prospect.

I pedalled westwards away from the airport towards the city centre on roads choked with traffic, but most drivers were reasonably patient. Around half the vehicles on the road were small motorbikes, many ferrying entire families, some with pets squeezed in between first and second pillion. The intermingling noises and smells were intense: roadside mechanics bashing metal interspersed every few yards with street vendors wielding woks – there wasn't much chance I'd go hungry here! I stopped at a food market for a large iced kiwi and strawberry smoothie, made on the spot. It was so good I immediately had another, apple and yoghurt this time.

Back on the bike, inching westwards through the manic traffic, a cycle lane appeared and a few metres later it was blocked by a parked 4x4 – I felt right at home. The bike was attracting plenty of attention, but it was less intrusive here: people smiled and waved but fewer cameras were poked up my nose. It took almost four hours to cover under 40 kms across the congested city, but thank goodness once again for the GPS, which led me directly and unfalteringly to my warmshowers host, a Headteacher. I was met by the caretaker who installed me in a huge, airy, ensuite room in a wooden building near the school, and gave me a set of keys, some bottles of water and a bucket of ice. I flaked out on the bed for an hour then set about some ablutions before going out to dinner. I didn't need to walk far: there were street vendors every few yards. I chose a delicious chicken stir-fry which cost 50 baht (about £1), then found a 7-11 mini-market selling Leo and Chang Thai beers which I took back to the room and settled down for a nice bedtime read – I was on holiday now.

There was a set of bathroom scales in the flat. I was alarmed to see that despite eating probably three times as much as normal since leaving London I had lost seven kilos in seven weeks. With 19 weeks to go I hoped this weight loss would stabilise soon!

38 km today / 6,398 km since London

Saturday 17th May

The holiday began with a lie-in till 08:00, followed by a wifi session to find out what advice my tweeps (twitter followers) might offer on how best to spend a day seeing the sights of Bangkok. This would be my first whole day off the bike since leaving London, and the first time I'd spend a second night in the same place, and I wanted to make the most of it.

Inevitably I suppose, the answer came: Bangkok (like all cities in my experience) is best visited...by bike! CoVanKessel, a Dutch bicycle tour operator, was highly recommended, so I called to make a booking. They would supply an upright commuter style bike, more practical for city riding than my chaise longue. I set off on foot towards the city centre, found good coffee along the way, and arrived with 30 minutes to spare at the bike tour office for their five-hour afternoon tour. The other seven clients on this tour were all Dutch, about half my age, and six of them women. We set off with two guides at 13:00 out into the narrow alleyways and small side streets of Bangkok visiting temples and mosques, the frenetic market environment of Chinatown, then down to the waterside where our bikes were loaded onto a classic longtail boat. We boarded and set off at a terrific pace along the extensive canal network which, our guides informed us, constituted "the Venice of the East". The tour included a sumptuous all-you-can-eat Thai buffet lunch on a floating restaurant, and a further boat trip out of town into the rural hinterland for a final bike ride through the luscious green belt and forgotten plantations. For a tour of one of the world's mega cities it was all surprising tranquil, and the most remarkable city tour I've done anywhere by any means.

I took a ferry back across the river and a tuk-tuk (three-wheeled motorised rickshaw) back to the school-house, got a quick haircut for 70baht (£1.40) then briefly met my warmshowers host, a busy lady of 68 who had started cycling just the previous year and now hosts dozens of cycle tourists. We chatted for 15 minutes then she had to dash off to another appointment, inviting me to get in the car so she could drop me at her favourite street market for dinner. Once fed and back at the school-house, I spent the evening lounging around in bed reading and taking frequent cold showers to cool down – the heat and humidity were so intense that just sitting or lying in bed was a sweaty business.

The day had been a brilliant start to my sojourn in Southeast Asia.

0 km today / 6,398 km since London

Sunday 18th May

An early start: I loaded the bike, had some breakfast and left at 06:20 before the city streets got too busy. After seven weeks of heading east, mostly into the wind, I was headed west today... unbelievably still into a headwind. It was a mere breeze however, and Highway 35 was fast rolling, so averaging an almost dizzying 24 km/h I made 80 kms in four hours including breakfast and coffee stops. Then I turned off the main highway onto a quieter and more scenic route, still on good tarmac and making decent

progress – my mojo had quickly returned following the rigours of Russia and Kazakhstan.

I'd done around 100 kms by just past noon when quite suddenly I became acutely aware of the extreme heat and humidity and the need to stop as soon as possible to avoid dehydration and heatstroke. I pulled in at the first

Roadside kitchen and cyclist pampering station near Phetchaburi

opportunity, finding myself in a small family-run roadside kitchen and obviously looking somewhat the worse for wear. I was immediately taken into care like a long-lost prodigal son, properly pampered with a cold water sponge down, electric fan, smelling salts and iced water, and made to lie down on a camp bed while my brow was mopped and my pulse taken – it was racing. After 15 minutes and a litre of cold water I'd recovered sufficiently to scoff three bowls of vegetable soup with noodles, pork and tofu: delicious.

Two hours later, fully rested, fed and watered, I was pronounced fit and well by my lovely adoptive family, bade them goodbye and headed south. At Phetchaburi I found a café just in time to escape a drenching monsoonal downpour which cleared the air while I ate another lunch and tweeted a video of the spectacular weather. Within an hour the rain stopped as abruptly as it had started and I moved on through an area of salt farms, spotting reptilian life thrashing about energetically in roadside pools, just a couple of feet long but looking fierce and powerful, like small crocodiles.

Being in the tropics dusk came earlier, at around 18:00, by which time I'd done well over the average daily distance I'd need to reach Singapore in three weeks, so I stopped at an excellent holiday camp in Cha-am. For 700 baht (£14) I was comfortably installed in a self-contained small villa and, following a quick wash and brush-up, invited to share a specially prepared duck and rice dinner with owners Picky and Joy on their patio. A couple of beers rounded off another easy day and the perfect evening. Later I tweeted a photo while watching TV in my room with my feet up: "Thais are good at luxury. At £14 a night it'd be rude to camp out. Foot art c/o Shimano sandals". My sandals had produced the most extraordinary suntan patterns on the tops of my feet.

160 km today / 6,558 km since London

Monday 19th May

Despite the lower daily distances, I decided early starts would be a good plan so I could get most of the riding done before the tropical heat became overwhelming at around noon every day. So I was up at 05:15 and on the road by 06:00, with a quick stop for roadside doughnuts at 06:30, 40 winks in a bus shelter at 09:00, and a duck/rice snack with added wifi at 11:00.

The going here was so much easier than in Russia and Kazakhstan in pretty much all respects: better roads, food, wifi, wind, and many locals had a basic command of English. Interest in the bike and me was less intrusive – rather than honking and barking orders at me to stop for photos, people simply smiled and waved.

The delightfully quiet and scenic detour route ended shortly after Hua Hin, where I joined Highway 4 heading south. This was not as pleasant but there was a good rideable shoulder, though this was used in both directions by motorbikes and even by some cars, which came as a shock at first but I soon adapted to the rather anarchic lane discipline. Driving standards were generally not too bad, most other road users being patient and calm…but

there wasn't much use of mirrors when moving off, and there appeared to be no minimum age or basic competence required for riding motorbikes. This may be related to the high Thai road death toll of some 12,000 per year.

At noon it was hotting up, prompting a quick stop for iced coffee.

Is there a lower age limit?

It was a really good homemade one so I had their iced cocoa to follow, then a quick snooze before setting off again at 13:30. This turned out to be far too early – the heat was still oppressive – so I stopped again in a roadside kitchen 5 kms further on for pork and rice, glad once again not to be on a 200 km/day schedule. A small party of customers arrived soon after me and ordered the speciality of the house: a homemade ice cream produced on the spot from ice shavings off a huge block, syrup, condensed milk, bread bits and an unidentifiable sweet gelatinous gloop on top, all of which combined to produce a most attractive and refreshing looking dessert. Sensing my interest, they ordered the same for me too. It was divine.

Then the monsoon started so I sat that out reading another Sherlock Holmes short story before moving on a few kms to check in at the Golden Beach Hotel in Prachuap Khirikhan, where a luxury room with a view set me back the princely sum of 800 baht (£16). It was just across the road from the beach, which was indeed golden, so I popped over to take a quick dip in the tepid Bight of Bangkok, my first sight of the sea since Holland.

A route-planning session followed: I unfolded my map of the Malaysian peninsula and marked up where I needed to ride to each day in order to arrive in Singapore on 8th June, a pleasant exercise serving to emphasize that the nature of my tour had utterly changed now and I was effectively on a gentleman's paced cycle-touring holiday for the next few weeks – hurrah!

The hotelier advised on a good local restaurant, just a few hundred metres down the road, where I chose a fish curry described by the waitress as "medium spicy" – it almost blew my balls off…

123 km today / 6,681 km since London

Tuesday 20th May

I woke at 06:30 well rested. Prachuap Khirikhan is a pretty beach resort, but early in the season it was almost deserted. I found a decent breakfast and coffee then headed back out onto a good, tree lined, shady Highway 4. A chain of air-conditioned coffee shops called Amazon had outlets at frequent intervals on all the main highways doing a fine range of iced coffees and cakes, so I became a regular visitor. They were good for wifi too – a great way to while away the time now the pressure was off.

By noon it was 37°C and time to stop for lunch with barely 60 kms on the clock, but on my relaxed three-week schedule to Singapore that was enough – this was easy street. I hardly needed to carry bonk rations as there were roadside kitchens every few kms along the highway. English or illustrated menus were often available; otherwise I could point at another diner's meal to communicate my order. After lunch today I was offered a camp bed in a shady nook of the café for a siesta – how marvellously civilised! I slept solidly for two hours then ate another stir-fry.

Soon after setting off again I turned off the main highway towards the coast and spent a couple of hours riding through paradise: a series of exquisite quiet lanes through palm plantations and small villages to Bang Saphan where I had a warmshowers host booked. There was just one interruption to this tranquil episode, which I happened to catch on video: a dog attack! But no serious attempt on me was made, just a lot of excited yapping which didn't even warrant the withdrawal of my formidable dog stick.

James, my warmshowers host, was a retired policeman from Mexico. After a couple of cold beers we set out on his motorbike-sidecar combination for a fresh fish dinner at a local beach restaurant and he told tales of his former professional life – he'd been on the front line against the drugs barons. With such a colourful past he was a marked man and had been on the run around the planet for a number of years, and had converted to Buddhism somewhere along the way. Warmshowers members do comprise an interesting cross-section of humanity.

92 km today / 6,772 km since London

Wednesday 21st May

James cooked me a splendid early breakfast of eggs and potato on his efficient home-made beer can stove and I was away by 06:30 on a quiet,

Pak Khlong Saphli

rolling, pretty coastal route. By noon I had arrived at Pak Khlong Saphli, a luxury seaside resort full of deserted holiday villas, and I went into a restaurant/bar to escape from the heat. I waited a few minutes, then had a mosey around looking for some sign of life, but all was ghostly quiet. Behind the bar I found a wifi code, so I settled down under a straw-thatched dining area to update friends and family on recent progress. After 20 minutes or so an old lady appeared, looking rather sleepy, obviously roused from recent slumber, and after exchanging pleasantries she cooked me a large plate of delicious fried rice. After a cold shower and siesta I set off again at 15:30 on another quiet scenic road down to Chumphon, where I rejoined the busy main highway. By 21:30 I was ready to stop but there were no obvious accommodation options, so I decided to camp out for the night, and bedded down in the forest just off the highway. This turned out to be a mistake.

153 km today / 6,925 km since London

Thursday 22nd May

Overnight I discovered that Thailand in May is far too hot for camping, especially as I had to zip the bivi bag right up to keep the mozzies out. As I lay awake sweating and swearing profusely I resolved not to sleep out again till Australia.

Another easy day followed on the busy but bland Highway 41, punctuated by regular stops for drinks, snacks, siesta and reading another Sherlock Holmes short story in a bus shelter during the monsoon. Shortly after leaving that refuge it started raining again and I was drenched within minutes, but the downpour was warm and refreshing so I carried on regardless for another 40 kms to Surat Thani, where I found another excellent value hotel. Spotlessly clean with ensuite facilities and air conditioning for around a tenner, why would anyone camp out here?

I bought a take-away dinner from the street market and a couple of beers from the 7-11 store to have in my room while I caught up with world news: there'd been a military coup in Bangkok the day after I'd left the city, and the country was generally on high alert with terrorist activity looking likely, especially a little further down the coast on my planned route around Hat Yai. I set about planning an alternative route.

129 km today / 7,054 km since London

Friday 23rd May

Highway 41 got a little samey today, but the tedium was relieved by frequent roadside stops for stir-fries and at service stations for Amazon iced coffees and wifi.

It was hot and sultry as usual, but nonetheless I'd made steady progress at around 22 km/h since Bangkok, covering well over the 100 km/day minimum I needed to get to Singapore by 8th June, so I was ahead of schedule and starting to look forward to a day or two off the bike for sightseeing perhaps in Penang and Melaka. Such easy going got me wondering about whether I'd be able to step up the pace again when the time came and get back on the 200 km/day schedule I'd planned for my mid winter crossing of Australia.

At midday I stopped for a read and a snooze, then rode through another monsoonal afternoon to an early stop for fried rice and checked into a hotel chalet for 450baht (£9). After showering, shaving and washing my kit it was still raining; fortunately dinner was being served just next door. I pointed at a couple of pots and was served a fragrant vegetable soup followed by a ball-blowing green curry. Luckily there was beer.

114 km today / 7,168 km since London

Saturday 24th May

It was another early start at 06:30 in an attempt to get as far down the road as possible before it got too hot. Regular stops at Amazon cafés for reliably good tea, coffee and cakes were helping to deal with my weight (loss) problem. At Thung Song, following Foreign Office advice to avoid the troubled area around Hat Yai, I turned right onto Highway 403, heading south towards the western coastline of the Malay/Thai peninsula. It was scorching hot by 11:00, forcing an early and prolonged stop right through to 15:00 – time put to good use eating, sleeping and reading. At Trang I found chalet accommodation, ideal with easy ground floor access to get the bike in. After settling in and getting my daily chores done, I went out in search of dinner, and as usual did not have to travel far before finding excellent street food with beer. There was plenty of time left in the day for a long phone call home and a relaxed evening's reading, just as planned from Kazakhstan. This world cycling tour thing was, for the time being at least, a walk in the park – I had never dared imagine that riding round the world would be this easy.

97 km today / 7,265 km since London

Sunday 25th May

The chilly fog that enveloped me as I set off at 06:00 southbound on Highway 404 was soon burnt off by a fierce morning sun to reveal a jogger, some cyclists and a couple playing badminton – the highest level of physical activity I'd seen anywhere since leaving Europe. Was this the sports capital of Thailand, I wondered?

Amazon provided more iced coffees and cakes on the road down into the far south of Thailand, where I was beginning to feel just a tad uneasy, having read recent news that the army had dissolved the senate and was tightening its grip on power, arresting and locking up journalists, and had decreed a nightly curfew from dawn to dusk. At 10:00 I hit a queue of traffic: a military roadblock and checkpoint. But was it manned by official military or rebels? And who should I be more afraid of? I advanced slowly towards the machine-gun toting guards, who were chewing gum nonchalantly and exuding an air of lazy menace. I presented my passport together with the magic letter. They took a great interest in the letter and the bike, and after a couple of easy questions waved me through. Phew!

I was now approaching the Malaysian border on a scenic road twisting gradually upwards into the rainforest. After an exquisite picnic and siesta stop by the lake at Thung Wa I rode a further 25 kms to Langu and took refuge in a bar just ahead of the opening of the heavens for the day's monsoonal downpour. The bar was bang opposite some chalets I'd selected for the night's accommodation, so I drank my beer slowly, willing the rain to ease off just enough to allow me to cross the road. It didn't, even after a second beer, so I made a dash for it but got drenched in the ten seconds it took to cross the road. I've never known rain so powerful.

After hanging my sodden kit around the room to dry I popped out for a street kitchen stir-fry, then some shopping for breakfast and another lazy evening under a lethargic whirring ceiling fan catching up on twitter, world news, and Sherlock Holmes.

108 km today / 7,373 km since London

Monday 26th May

I was back on the highway at 06:00 for a couple of hours before turning west onto a small twisty lane up into the hills and thick jungle rainforest where troupes of monkeys were calling to each other across the valley. Turning onto a side road into the Thaleban National Park, I immediately spotted a small monkey in a tree by the roadside and managed to get a few seconds of video, not quite up to David Attenborough's standards but hugely satisfying. The road continued to climb gently up to the Malaysian border, where I arrived at 11:00. It was a relaxed affair involving photos with the guards, one of whom noticed that my big right toe was bleeding – I'd picked up a stowaway leech in the jungle. He helped me remove it with care, and then sold me some Malaysian Ringgit in exchange for my remaining Thai Baht. Camp kitchens and souvenir vendors lined the roadside, proudly offering western food – I couldn't resist a burger and chips.

And so I set off with full belly into country number ten of the tour on a small road coiling inexorably upwards through a series of hairpin bends, the steepest climb since London, in full midday sun, wondering why the clouds so often dissipated by noon just when I was most in need of shade. I also wondered if the Brits were responsible for building this road straight up the mountain – it had been a much gentler climb on the Thai side of the border.

A sign at the roadside graphically warned of the dangers of this mountain road, depicting a steering wheel and skull and bearing the warning *kawasan kemalangan*, which google translate helpfully rendered as "accident area". Sure enough, just around the next bend a yawning gap in the crash barrier revealed an upturned bus about 20 feet below. I stopped to catch my breath as the climb had been so brutal and was immediately pestered by wasps, so I pressed onwards and upwards towards the summit – thankfully it was only a few more kms of sweat and tears and no more blood. A fast, exhilarating, swooping descent led to flatter roads threading between paddy fields, then a heavy downpour at 15:00 brought proceedings to a temporary halt in a handy bus shelter – picnic time.

After a couple more hours I arrived in Alor Setar, a large town where I had a warmshowers arranged in a bike shop. My host, Zul, met me in the town centre and showed me to the shop, which he runs with his dad. I parked the bike and changed, we locked up the shop and went out for a street-food dinner, followed by a trip to the off-licence. He sent me in to buy the beers, explaining that it was both illegal and impossible for him to do so – he'd have to show his ID card which identifies him as a Muslim. Back at the shop we cracked open the cans and he asked me not to tell his dad in the morning – perhaps, I speculated, this was his chief motivation for being a warmshowers host…but it would of course have been most ungracious to ask.

We polished off the beers and chatted easily about bikes and cycle touring while he inflated an airbed for me and explained that he too would sleep on the floor in the shop. As I started to settle down for the night he said he had to go out for a hospital appointment. At midnight, I queried – yes, he needed a scan and the hospital was very busy. I asked if he was pregnant but the joke fell flat: he had bone cancer. I felt pretty awful after that; he looked about half my age. It was a hot night and I slept rather fitfully despite the three fans.

152 km today / 7,525 km since London

Tuesday 27th May

Zul took me to a tandoori place near the shop for a tasty local breakfast of bread and eggs with dahl, then I was off down Highway 1 sharing the road with some pretty careless drivers generally going too fast and indulging in some hairy overtaking manoeuvres. Many pestered me for photos and videos, slowing alongside to get action shots. Sometimes it was the driver taking the photos, just as in Kazakhstan, except that the roads were empty back there. Here a tailback formed behind me leading to resentment and further risky overtaking. When I was swarmed by some 20 small motorbikes buzzing around me like crazy bees, I finally lost my trademark laid-back cool, stopped and unleashed a tirade of robust Anglo-Saxon. They seemed to get the gist and moved on a little sheepishly.

At Bandar Amanjaya I found a European style café: Italian pasta for lunch – hurrah! Eastern street food was good but so was the change. Dessert followed an hour later at a roadside place where two sisters, Yati and Beti, were hawking fresh coconuts, expertly hacking the tops off with a few well-aimed strokes of the machete, inserting a straw for the punter to suck out the milk, and finally delivering the death blow, splitting the nut clean in two so that the thin layer of soft white flesh could be scooped out with a spoon – delicious! A large car pulled up and a large new client oozed out. The coconut sisters set about their hacking routine while the newcomer took an interest in my bike, then me, and started asking questions. I referred him to the magic letter, but he wasn't interested and just barked the questions a bit more loudly. I tried to protest that I did not understand a

word of Malay; he responded by upping the volume another notch. I started to feel uneasy, even threatened, and wondered how to cope with this apparent lunatic. An edgy silence reigned momentarily as I deliberated. The thing to do, I decided, was to meet fire with fire. So I raised my voice to match his decibels, jabbed my finger at the magic letter, and

Yati and Beti, the Coconut Sisters

invited him once again in reinforced terms to read its contents. It was the second time that day that I had descended to the use of coarse language, and once again it proved jolly effective: he quietened down, paid his bill, then paid my bill, shook my hand, and drove off! The coconut sisters were open-mouthed, and Yati, eyelashes batting, asked for my phone number, declaring an undying love – my winning manful display of strength had evidently made an impression. I decided it was high time to move on, pointed to my wedding ring and said I was cycling back to London. She said she would walk to London and marry me…I'm still vaguely expecting a knock at the door.

Driving standards continued to shock: there was no apparent use of mirrors, and lane discipline was so lacking that some drivers did not even drive on the left side of the road. Somehow I muddled through the mayhem and arrived intact at Butterworth ferry terminal by 16:00, took the ten-minute ferry crossing to Penang, disembarked and made my way into central Georgetown. Here I had an address: Derrick Tan, now working in a small family-run engineering business on Chulia Street, had ten years previously been working in Bournemouth at my grandmother's care home. Expecting me, he downed tools and took me to a nearby food court for beer and a bowl of the delicious local hokkien prawn mee noodle soup. We then returned to the shop, a veritable Aladdin's cave of engineering parts stacked floor to ceiling and stretching back a hundred feet or more, and

Derrick and his brothers began closing up for the day, along with their sister who was doing the accounts in a small back office.

Once the dozens of display items were safely off the pavement and piled up precariously just inside the front of the shop, the shutters were brought down and padlocked, and Derrick kick-started his little step-through Honda C50 motorbike, ubiquitous throughout Malaysia, into life. He set off slowly into the evening traffic and I followed for half an hour to his home in the residential suburbs where I was introduced to his wife, Lee Mee, sister Doris, son Yi Jun, and a family friend – round-the-world Kiwi yachtsman John Ivey. We exchanged travellers' tales over a fine Chinese dinner then went out on the town for a local speciality dessert: *ais kacang* – a great medley of ice cream, gelatinous sweetcorn, red beans, shaved ice, syrup, condensed milk and mixed fruit, topped by a pile of jelly which looked rather like frog spawn. Divine!

109 km today / 7,634 km since London

Wednesday 28th May

Today was my first non-cycling day since leaving London 53 days ago – I went motorcycling instead! After a walk with Derrick around the stunning botanical gardens and a good breakfast in the food court, he went off to work leaving me the Honda to do an island tour.

The island of Penang is a similar size to the Isle of Arran in Scotland, a special place for me which I have visited many times since my childhood, being the home of my wonderful Great Auntie Sheila and her daughter Laura. I remember joyful outdoorsy family holidays there with five Scottish cousins who seemed to speak a different language, and great long distance walks up into the hills and across the island with my dad, who showed me how to read a map and use a compass. And how to survive on bread, cheese and apples. Pretty much like audaxing but without the bike. There are other Penang-Arran similarities too: both are a short ferry ride off the mainland west coast, both enjoy damp climates, both have a hillier north than south, and both sport first-class beaches. There are of course notable differences: Penang is a tad warmer, produces no malt whisky, and is home to 1.4 million people. Fewer than 5,000 live on Arran.

So with a circumference of about 100 km I could quite comfortably have cycled round the island in a day, but that would have left little time to see the sights, which included the fabulously ornate Kek Lok Si Temple and pagoda, where I spent most of the morning enjoying panoramic views high above Georgetown. After a quick duck-rice combo for lunch I completed the tour on hilly scenic roads. Petrol-powered assistance felt a bit like cheating, but I did rather enjoy my first day on a motorbike in over 20 years, stopping for a swim at one of the many idyllic beaches and visiting the snake temple on the way back into town.

0 km today / 7,634 km since London

Thursday 29th May

I devoured a scrumptious early breakfast in the local food court with Derrick and Lee Mee, ordering two Penang specialties: curry mee – thin noodles in a spicy curry soup with dried tofu – and char koay kak – fried rice cakes. Both were outstanding and set me up well for the rigours of the day ahead – except it didn't need to be a rigorous day at all. I just needed to stick to the 100 km/day schedule to reach Singapore by 8th June.

I crossed back over to the mainland on the 13.5 km motorway bridge to Prai, then decamped over to Highway 1 where I jockeyed for position among thick traffic all day, stopping frequently for snacks, drinks, a tepid car wash hosepipe shower, a bus shelter at monsoon time, and finally for the night at the modestly named *Wonderful Motel* in Taiping – a veritable bargain at just 55 Ringgit (£11) for my first paid accommodation in Malaysia.

97 km today / 7,731 km since London

Friday 30th May

Another easy day started with a late food court breakfast and an 08:30 departure on a variety of roads ranging from a four-lane arterial highway to a sinewy lane through the jungle, but mostly on quiet single carriageways – a big improvement on the previous day. The only hilly bit inevitably came at high noon. I took in all the usual stops for drinks, food and rain, terminating for the day in Bota for chalet accommodation. The 60 Ringgit price struck me as a little high compared to the previous day, especially as there were no ensuite facilities, air-conditioning, TV or wifi. But Bota was a tiny village and there may not have been anything else available – I certainly couldn't be bothered to look – and for goodness sake it was still only £12.

I took a shower and was about to walk into the village to eat when Zahuri, the owner, offered me a lift...then paid for my meal and beer! Over dinner he told me about his family and his expansion plans for the chalets he'd recently bought, and then listened attentively to some tales from my travels. Once back at the chalets he would only take 50 Ringgit for the room – perhaps he'd expected me to haggle?

91 km today / 7,822 km since London

Saturday 31st May

I hit the road at 07:00, stopped five minutes later for roadside noodles, and when I went to pay, the bill had already been settled by another diner. The next pause came mid-morning after 50 kms for ice cream and drinks at a garage. By noon (80 kms) it was too hot to go on but luckily there was an *ais kacang* vendor to hand – just the job! He was also selling stir fries and curries, so I had a squizz round to see what others were eating and pointed to a dish on the neighbouring table, whose owner warned me it was hot and would I like to try his first. I ate a tentative forkful and waited a moment expecting to explode, but Malaysian food is generally less spicy than Thai, and in any case my palate had by now had time to acclimatise. So I ordered a plateful for myself, and the man on the next table whose dinner I'd tasted paid my bill. Hat-trick! Three meals bought for me in a row!

After a siesta stop I rolled on till 17:00 and found a cheap hotel in Sekinchan – just 35 Ringgit (£7) but perfectly adequate. I headed out for dinner and managed to find beer – increasingly rare in these parts as many restaurants and shops are run by Muslims, so I'd been teetotal for a while and barely drunk at all since leaving the UK with one or two notable exceptions (Warsaw and Brest were fond but distant memories). So just one beer now was enough to get me feeling pleasantly light-headed and ready for bed, if not quite under the table.

123 km today / 7,946 km since London

Sunday 1st June

Over a leisurely breakfast I unfolded the map to assess recent progress, and came to the conclusion that I needed to slow down – with a week and just 500 kms to go I was getting down towards Singapore too early. The obvious choice for a multi-night stopover was Melaka, a city port steeped in colonial history just under 300 km away. So I set off at 09:30, considerably later than normal, stopped for more breaks than usual, took a scenic detour, rode through the hard, driving but refreshing warm rain of the monsoon, and found a hotel in Klang at 15:30 after just 76 lazy kms.

After showering and a siesta I ambled into town for dinner and found a wildly popular restaurant with tables spilling out onto the street and dozens queuing. This was obviously the place to be, so I joined the queue, caught the waitress's eye, and within five minutes had a small corner table – as a single diner I was probably easier to place than larger groups. There was no menu; everyone was eating steamed clams and fried noodles, so I followed suit and they were excellent, washed down with two beers which had the effect of five – marvellous!

I passed through the 8,000 km milestone today, so I'd averaged 1,000 km/week, but the second 4,000 had taken five of the eight weeks since London: slower in Kazakhstan due to wind and roads; slower in Southeast Asia by design. The current easy-life pace wouldn't be sustainable after Singapore; would I be able to step back up to the 200 km/day across Australasia and America?

76 km today / 8,021 km since London

Monday 2nd June

A new approach today: leave early, do 70 kms by noon, and book into a hotel in time for afternoon siesta. All was going well with this plan until I caught up with Ellis and Willem Janssen. They'd been cycling for a year since leaving their home in the Netherlands, riding sturdy-looking, flat-bar touring bikes, fully laden with four panniers each plus camping stuff. We swapped tales of the road for ten minutes and agreed to meet up in Melaka. I noticed that like me they were using Schwalbe Marathon Plus touring tyres, the choice it would seem of most inter-continental cycle tourists, and we all agreed how fantastic they were – I'd not yet punctured in over 8,000 km since London despite those terrible Russian and Kazakh roads.

Needless to say, I'd tempted fate and summoned the puncture fairy – a few kms further down the road my back tyre exploded with a loud BANG! Luckily I'd just passed a handy roadside café, so I retreated into the shade of the verandah, ordered a drink and some lunch, and set about fixing the flat tyre. It was worse than a simple puncture – the sidewall had split. I tried a quick fix with a tyre boot and a patch on the tube. It held up for just long enough for me to get the wheel back in the bike and the bags loaded back on and all ready to set off...then pshhhhhhhhhh...bugger! The tyre was abandoned and the emergency folding spare deployed along with a new inner tube.

Once all was reassembled I got going again and found my way down to the seaside playground of Bagan Lalang near Kuala Lumpur airport, a rather swish resort with hotel prices to match. Rooms at the first four I called in at were around 200 Ringgit, over triple the high end of my usual price range. The magic letter produced a couple of meagre 10% discount offers – not enough to tempt me in. The fifth place however, a little further along the beach, had chalets for 100 Ringgit and offered a generous 30% discount, perfect! It was a stunning location, right by the beach, and busy: Malays were on school holidays, and this was clearly their resort – there were no westerners to be seen.

After a full service – shower, shave and kit wash – I settled down at the bar to try and book my flight for the following week on the Skyscanner app. Being a relative newcomer to the smartphone, and something of a Luddite, this was not a task I welcomed with great relish; however it proved quicker and easier than I'd anticipated and after only 15 minutes I had a booking from Singapore to Perth on 10th June for just £120. Cause for celebration! A barbecue fish dinner at an idyllic beach café, with sunset view and beer, proved just the ticket.

87 km today / 8,108 km since London

Tuesday 3rd June

I took a glorious dawn dip in the tepid sea opposite my chalet before departing the resort, sharing the quiet early morning roads with monkeys scampering about scavenging rich pickings from the detritus of the night before – much like the foxes of Raynes Park and other London suburbs. I stopped for an Indian breakfast of bread, curry and coconut at the side of the road, and at 10:30 rolled into Port Dickson for coffee, cake and wifi. Still with time to kill, and comfortably installed in the coffee shop, I started drafting a blog update – it had been left sadly neglected since London.

Just as I was setting off to ride out of town, I spotted a small café doing western breakfasts – sausages, eggs, toast, beans...the attraction was irresistible, and another hour was whiled away. I left around noon and rode on for a couple more hours before checking into a budget hotel in Taman Bayu at 14:00, with just 57 kms on the clock. After a short siesta I went for a walk along the local beach, crowded with Malays on school holidays. Back at the hotel I continued drafting the blog update and booked a hostel in Melaka for the next two nights. From there I planned a three-day, 220 km ride to Singapore. What could possibly go wrong?

I ate at a Chinese restaurant next to the hotel, and then discovered a 9% Skol beer in the local 7-11 shop which put me under the table.

57 km today / 8,166 km since London

Wednesday 4ᵗʰ June

It was an uneventful but pretty morning's ride featuring a couple of stops for breakfast and ice cream before I arrived in Melaka at noon and checked into the utterly delightful Rooftop Guest House. A safe berth was found for my bike in a garage down the road and I was served an iced lychee juice as I filled in the hotel register. My room on the second floor adjoined the spectacular rooftop terrace, which was planted out like a jungle, and the only sound was the Muslim call to prayers. What a wonderful place to kick back for a couple of nights.

Mine's a pint!

The city centre is a UNESCO World Heritage Site, so after a light lunch of omelette and spring rolls and a pint of fresh watermelon juice it was time to start taking in the sights. I started with a 45-minute river cruise, then visited a maritime museum set in the *Flor de la Mar*, a replica Portuguese Nau – a warship and trading vessel – where I learned about Melaka's colourful colonial history: a Sultanate until 1511, Portuguese till 1641, Dutch to 1795, British to 1941, Japanese to 1945, British again till 1957, then finally independent. There was so much to look at and read I only had time to see half of it before closing time and was glad to have the following day to finish the job.

I walked around town sampling various exotic juices and ice creams followed by dinner at a riverside restaurant serving the apparently famous Melakan chicken rice balls.

70 km today / 8,236 km since London

Thursday 5th June

My third day off cycling since London started with a forensic search of the bijou city centre for a decent English breakfast, something I'd been craving since…well since leaving England really. Happily I found a good one close to the marine museum, to which I returned once I'd eaten to complete my visit. Then I was hungry again – there was no diminution of appetite just because I wasn't riding. An unctuous slow-cooked Chinese pork belly and rice hit the spot and fuelled me up for the rest of this lazy day, which I spent seeing a few more sights before taking a siesta with half an ear cocked to the afternoon play on BBC Radio 4 – I was pleased with myself for managing to tune into that on the smartphone.

Tonight I had a dinner date! Dutch couple Ellis and Willem, whom I'd met a few days earlier, had arrived in town so we met up and went out for Indian street food and they told me of their year on the road: they'd covered 17,000 kms, about twice as far as I had so far, and were planning another year to get to Melbourne, with plenty of non-riding days in the schedule. They'd both been made redundant, were without dependants and seemed to be having the time of their lives. The evening was rounded off with a few fine beers on the roof terrace of their guest-house. Roof terrace living is the way to go in Melaka.

0 km today / 8,236 km since London

Friday 6th June

After a leisurely but mildly disappointing breakfast (too small) I was away at 09:00 and looking forward to better breakfasts in Australia in a few days with my brother, Jonathan. It was overcast and cooler than usual but still 33°C by noon. Entering the Johor province of southern Malaysia, I passed a couple of pieces of rickshaw inspired architecture: a bus shelter in the shape of a rickshaw where I took a quick snooze, and a giant sized rickshaw model against which I leaned my bike to take a photo – it came only about a third of the way up the back wheel. In Batu Pahat I found a cheap budget hotel with adequate rooms for just 50 Ringgit (£10) and had duck and rice for dinner.

95 km today / 8,331 km since London

Saturday 7th June

I was rudely woken at an unearthly hour by high-spirited conversation in the corridor outside my room, and opened the door to express my displeasure – a large family gathering dispersed sheepishly. After that I couldn't get back to sleep so made an early getaway at 07:00 and rode 113 uneventful kms against a moderate headwind down to Skudai, near Johor Bahru, a stone's throw from Singapore, where I found a 40 Ringgit room (£8) room and had an Indian dinner.

113 km today / 8,445 km since London

Sunday 8th June

After a delicious Indian breakfast I was out at 08:00 and straight onto 10 kms of unavoidable, busy and noisy multi-lane highway before striking off on a small scenic alternative route up into a secluded area of low hills and expensive real estate near Danga Bay. Blissfully there was almost no traffic, but for one large car which settled behind me to film for an extended period before picking the most dangerous moment to overtake as we approached a blind bend. During this moronic manoeuvre he slowed to get more footage, giving me plenty of time to offer caustic comment on camera in respect of his imbecilic driving. Sadly this was all too commonplace – bad driving in Malaysia tended to be thoughtless and idiotic rather than fast and aggressive, with little use of either mirrors or common sense.

At 10:00 I crossed the bridge onto Singapore island and into the customs shed where a giant sign informed travellers that the maximum penalty for drug-smuggling was death. As I queued and dug out my passport it occurred to me that I had left my bike and three of my four bags unattended in hotel reception areas over the previous two nights where anyone might have exchanged some of my kit for a bag of smack... Now I'd either be arrested and hanged by the state or gunned down by gangsters reclaiming their goody bags. How the imagination can work overtime at stressful moments… I duly arrived at the front of the queue and passed through without incident.

Woodlands Road is a quiet, pleasant alternative to the main highway for the 20 km run down into Singapore City, and once there I headed for the home of the brother of a fellow Kingston Wheelers member who'd issued an invitation well before I'd left London. It was around lunchtime and, thinking it wouldn't be good form to arrive hungry and expectant, I wolfed down a quick bowl of duck and rice before phoning my host Ivan, who met me at the bottom of his 50-floor high-rise residence in the central business district. He was smartly dressed and had been at work for the morning. I enquired what work that might be – he's a minister. Working on a Sunday? Oh right, a church minister! I followed him into the lift and up to the 19th floor, where I was introduced to his wife, Renata, and their two lovely children, Ethan (7) and Talia (5). Despite my best efforts I had clearly mistimed my arrival as the family were just sitting down to a late lunch of sushi and invited me to join them… After brief mild protestation that I'd already eaten, I gave up any pretence of resistance and managed a second sitting very nicely.

I spent the afternoon thoroughly washing the bike before dismantling and packing it into a giant screen TV box that Ivan had thoughtfully procured. Australian customs officers are very particular that no foreign dirt should enter their pristine territory, and after two months of all weathers and terrains my bike was stubbornly filthy. After toiling for three hours it looked pretty clean but not spotless, so I'd just have to hope it was good enough. I removed the chain and the one remaining original tyre to leave behind as I'd had spares sent out to my brother in Perth – the chain was binned but amazingly there was still plenty of tread on the tyre, so Ivan stored it away as a spare for his own bike.

We all went out together to a local Japanese place for the kids' favourite dinner, Tonkotsu Ramen, a tasty Japanese pork noodle soup, followed by an amazing green tea ice-cream. Back home we took the fast lift up to visit the 50th floor for the most stupendous cityscape views. There are seven blocks each with 50 floors, all connected by wide bridges at levels 26 and 50. Ethan and Talia took me on a guided tour: this was luxury high rise, beautifully landscaped and planted out with grass, small trees, children's playgrounds, deckchairs and lounge areas. On level 26 a 1 km running track links all the blocks. The flats, Ivan proudly explained, had won a design award, and all 2,000 had been sold at affordable prices with low interest, government-backed mortgages to low-income families earning less than $4,000 pa chosen by ballot – astonishing. In London, I mused, such flats would have sold for millions to the highest bidding oligarchs and oil barons.

49 km today / 8,493 km since London

Monday 9th June

Ivan did eggs and coffee for breakfast and is obviously a passionate amateur barista with a great flair for intricate artwork in the froth on a cappuccino. Today was another planned day off the bike to visit the city…and what better way than by bike? The Bacchetta wouldn't have been ideal for pootling around the city and in any case was now in bits in a box, so Ivan lent me his British-made Brompton folding bicycle and I set off through Chinatown and down to the Singapore River, where I found more good eggs and coffee in a quiet riverside café. That was followed by a leisurely spin around the spectacular Marina Bay before a quick lunch and retreat from the heat back into the flat for a cold shower and siesta. I then made one more visit up to the 26th and 50th floors to admire the views again and get some photos of the fantastic facilities these lucky residents enjoy.

When Ivan got in from work we took Ethan and Talia out for a bike ride around Marina Bay, where we watched a gorgeous sunset, picked up some street market Satay for dinner, and caught the daily sound/light show on the bay, where a fine spray of water is used as a projector screen. A pint of Old Speckled Hen in an English pub rounded off a perfect lazy day.

Marina Bay, Singapore, with my new biking buddy Ethan

0 km today / 8,493 km since London

Tuesday 10th June

After a final fabulous coffee with Ivan, he went off to work and I spent the morning washing out my bivi bag and airing the sleeping bag, both frankly rank having been packed away damp and neglected since that hot sweaty night almost three weeks previously. I then packed my bags for the flight to Perth, helped Ethan with his piano practice, and went out for a final lunch with Renata and the kids at the local food court where we had wonton soup, chicken, rice, noodles, a bean curd dessert and some healthy yet delicious ABC juice: apple, beetroot and carrot.

A half-hour taxi ride took me to the airport where I was in for two substantial shocks to the system: a $240 excess baggage fee was rather higher than expected, indeed double the price of the flight itself. But worse was to follow. In the duty free shop I chose a bottle of Lagavulin malt whisky for Jonathan, his favourite, only to be told at the check-out that I was too late – for some bizarre reason such a purchase must be made at least 90 minutes before a flight to Australia.

The flight departed on time at 15:50, and there were limited whisky choices on board; I selected a rather bland blend hoping that Jonathan would accept it with humour and good grace. We landed in Perth a little ahead of schedule at about 21:00 and my luck changed – there was a duty free shop in the arrivals hall stocking some reasonable malt whiskies; I picked a Macallan.

My bike box and bags emerged promptly onto the baggage belt and I stared at them in some horror – the two panniers were filthy – I'd cleaned the bike as thoroughly as possible but overlooked the luggage. I shoved them both under the hot tap in the gents and scrubbed them as best as I could with liquid soap from the dispenser and my fingernails, then held them under the dryer for a few minutes. After all that I sailed unimpeded through customs with scarcely a glance or a question from any of the officers on duty, and strolled out into the arrivals hall where Jonathan greeted me with a traditional fraternal back-slapping routine before driving me some 15 minutes back to his home in East Victoria Park.

The house exterior was festooned with bunting, balloons and posters bearing the legend: *Laid Back Around the World Welcome Down Under!* Very touching. Sister-in-law Jenny served a fabulous prawn pasta dinner and we cracked open a couple of cold tinnies and sat around chewing the fat till the small hours. It was great to be back with family!

0 km today / 8,493 km since London

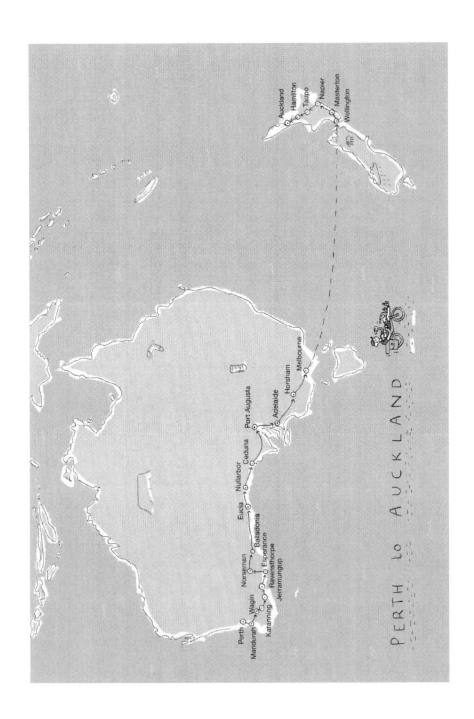

Auckland
Hamilton
Taupo
Napier
Masterton
Wellington

Melbourne
Horsham
Adelaide
Port Augusta
Ceduna
Nullarbor
Eucla
Balladonia
Norseman
Esperance
Ravensthorpe
Jerramungup
Katanning
Wagin
Mandurah
Perth

PERTH to AUCKLAND

PERTH TO AUCKLAND

Wednesday 11th June

A lazy day of domesticity started with coffee, eggs and snags (Aussie sausages) followed by the school run, or dawdle rather, with my nieces Lana (7) and Kayla (5). Hurrah, they walk to school! The half-mile journey took us about 15 minutes and, just as when I walked my own kids a similar distance to school back in the 1990s, we walked past houses from which children were being loaded into cars to be driven to the same school by lazy parents, cooped up and denied the opportunity to stretch their legs with their friends. A sad worldwide scourge, contributing to filthy air quality, climate change, road danger, traffic congestion, obesity, heart disease and early death (to name but a few). It occurred to me as I thought these thoughts that perhaps I was beginning to miss the day job.

Back at Jonathan's place I got on the computer to download the Perth-Albany-Perth 1,200 km Australian audax route and load it onto the GPS – this would be a good way to get across the south-west corner of the continent and on a heading out towards the Nullarbor Desert and Melbourne, some 3,700 km distant. After that I rebuilt and serviced the bike, fitting new tyres, brake pads and a chain spliced together from 2½ normal chains to achieve the requisite length of 3.5 metres. Then it was time for lunch at a nearby Vietnamese restaurant and a pint in the local with Jenny before strolling back to school to collect the girls.

A long and slow-cooked beef shoulder ragout was produced for dinner, rather splendidly married up with a fabulous 2002 Pomerol. Cheese and malt whiskies followed. There had been some hard days on this world cruise, but this wasn't one of them!

0 km today / 8,493 km since London

Thursday 12th June

I finished and published my first new blog entry since London, then took the girls to school again and with avuncular pride watched Lana sing in assembly. I then went for a swim with Jonathan, who has gone native and become something of an expert swimmer, sailor and surfer. He watched and commented helpfully on my freestyle; apparently I resembled a drowning squirrel.

After that, we cycled into the city centre for lunch and on to the best Italian butchers in town to pick up a whole 11kg suckling pig to slam on the birthday boy's barbie, as they do out here. After relaxing with a leisurely beer by the Swan river we pedalled back home for a great Thai duck curry dinner, and Alan the neighbour popped in with some of his fabulous homebrew beer – a bitter golden ale which reminded me fondly of Hopback's delectable Summer Lightning.

0 km today / 8,493 km since London

Friday 13th June

Jonathan's birthday! After toast and coffee we were off to the beach to watch Jonathan demonstrate his new surfing skills – he could do it standing up and looked pretty impressive, but the waves were tiny! Coffee and muffins in a beach shack were followed back in the city by Dim Sum for lunch, then back to the pool for a second swimming lesson – my crawl technique was so terrible it was leaving me breathless after just a couple of lengths. Something to work on then just in case I ever decided to enter a long distance triathlon – I'd need a new challenge after this adventure after all.

Half a dozen neighbours piled in for the birthday feast – the suckling pig in a home built wood fired oven, washed down with more than a few bottles of Alan's finest beers. This was the life – would I ever have the willpower to get back on my bike and leave this nirvana?

0 km today / 8,493 km since London

Saturday 14th June

Perth parkrun day! The third of the trip including Wimbledon at the start and Warsaw a week later. The 5 km course runs along the banks of the serene Swan River at Claisebrook Cove, conveniently just a 20-minute bike ride from Jonathan's house. I'd emailed in advance so they were ready with some running shoes to lend me, and I was given a special mention and warm welcome by the race director in his briefing to the gathered multitudes. It was a simple out and back route, so no chance of getting lost, with a humorous Aussie twist at the end – after running on pancake-flat paths by the riverside for 4.97 kms, there is a completely gratuitous steep climb for the last 30 metres or so up "Heartbreak Hill" to the finish line – brutal! I finished in 21:46, 38th out of 225 runners, over five minutes behind the winner...but, and I checked, he'd not ridden there from London.

Riding back home after the run on the super-smooth shared-use path by the river – Perth pedallers are provided for wonderfully well – I was paying rather too much attention to the picturesque views and not quite enough to the edge of the path, against which I managed to catch the front wheel and catapult myself sprawling across the tarmac. Fortunately no-one else was about, either to crash into or snigger at my misfortune. I picked myself and the bike up gingerly and inspected the damage: the bike was ok, that's the main thing! I suffered a few scrapes and bruises in the usual places but nothing serious, a ripped glove and base layer.

The afternoon was spent doing a big sort through my kit, discarding as much as possible to be posted back to UK and lighten the load, then re-packing the panniers. This was mighty thirsty work, so I paid a courtesy visit to Alan next door to admire his home brewery and taste some samples.

A visit to the local park to play with Lana and Kayla for an hour, skype calls home to siblings and Pascale, a pork risotto dinner and a dram of fine Arran malt whisky all combined to ensure a sound night's sleep before I set off on the ride across Australia. My third continental crossing was about to begin.

0 km today / 8,493 km since London

Sunday 15th June

After eggs, bacon and beans – breakfast of long distance champions! – three of us hit the road at 08:00: Jonathan, Alan the neighbourly brewer and myself. It was a cold start at just 3°C but a beautifully crisp, clear, sunny winter's day as we rode southwards out of Perth towards Mandurah on Highway 2, a busy six-lane highway but designed considerately for cyclists with a high quality, smooth and fast-rolling segregated bike route alongside. Alan managed about 30 kms then took the train home to get back to more important things, probably involving yeast, hops and barley. By lunchtime it had warmed up to a pleasant peak of 19°C and we stopped for fish and chips in Mandurah, a wealthy looking pleasure port for the playboys of Perth.

Jonathan and me wearing our compulsory plastic hats

I was reluctantly wearing a new item of headgear. There are a few (fortunately very few) misguided countries in this world which no doubt think they are making a contribution to cycling safety and public health by forcing their cycling citizens to wear plastic hats. Australia is one of them. Cycle helmets can provoke fierce debate among cyclists but most would agree that to wear one or not should remain a matter of personal choice. Compulsion results in fewer people cycling which is bad for public health – the risks around sedentary lifestyles are vastly greater than the risks of cycling. However, I digress. This is not the place for an essay on cycle helmets. www.cyclehelmets.org is a brilliant place to go to see the evidence.

Jonathan was to be with me for four days and we'd planned them to include plenty of down-time. Our first night was spent in a bungalow in Pinjarra caravan park, where we arrived mid-afternoon. After ablutions we rode into the one-horse town to shoot some pool and drink beer at the only pub, then eat at a rather threadbare Chinese restaurant where we were the only clients. Only 100 kms from Perth, it already felt like the back of beyond.

106 km today / 8,599 km since London

Monday 16th June

We downed a bowl of muesli in the bungalow, then some coffee in town followed by haircuts – Jonathan tweeted a photo of me in the barber's chair, commenting "only 2 km into day two of Perth-Albany and vanity kicks in for @laid_back_rich".

By 09:30 we were on the quiet Pinjarra-Williams road, rolling steadily across a lush, scenic and gently undulating landscape in bright but cool winter sunshine.

A billboard poster caught my eye: *WATCH OUT FOR KILLER ROOS, BELT UP!* More back-to-front "road safety" – let's blame wildlife for the carnage and put a seatbelt on in case those naughty kangaroos hop out and we've no time to stop. There was no suggestion of drivers slowing down (perish the thought!) to a safe speed to enable them to stop within the distance they could see to be clear.

We stopped mid-morning for a high quality large breakfast of bacon, eggs, hash browns, mushrooms, tomatoes, toast and coffee served by the lovely Shelley Sturgeon at the Blue Wren café in Dwellingup – absolutely fabulous! Then on to Ye Olde English Inne at Quindanning by 16:30, an old characterful pub with basic but comfortable rooms and a good range of fine bottled beers. We spent a fine relaxing evening there playing pool, with good steaks for dinner.

101 km today / 8,700 km since London

Tuesday 17th June

An excellent full cooked breakfast was served at the Quindanning Inne, during which our hotelier learned of my world tour and fundraising efforts for RoadPeace, resulting in a full refund of the $100 room fee...astonishing generosity! We hit the road at 08:00 and got our heads down for a fast non-stop ride over 96 kms of rolling hills to stay one step ahead of a huge storm system which had lashed Perth and the coast overnight and was now chasing us inland. We just made it, arriving at our small town destination of Wagin ten minutes ahead of torrential rain and gale-force winds.

After checking into our motel we went out in search of lunch but nothing was open except the local supermarket, so we bought bread, cheese and paté and ate it in our room while reading and watching the storm. There was a handy pub open later for dinner and a game of pool.

96 km today / 8,796 km since London

Wednesday 18th June

The storm passed through overnight, the morning dawned sunny, and we were back on the road at 08:00, using the unexpectedly quiet Great Southern Highway down through Katanning (meat pies) and Broomehill (coffee and cakes), where we turned east and picked up a terrific tailwind for a fast final 40 kms to our B&B in Gnowangerup.

Here I faced a minor dilemma. The original intention had been to ride down to Albany with Jonathan, stay a night there with friends of his, then ride on towards Jerramungup, Esperance and the Nullarbor. But from Gnowangerup, Albany would be a significant detour. Cutting it out would save at least a day, and Australia seemed big enough. The downside would be one less day riding with Jonathan, or rather Jenny, who had joined us in Gnowangerup with the girls at 17:00 and was planning to ride the following day with me, with Jonathan assuming parental duties. We discussed it over dinner and beer in the local pub and concluded that Jenny would ride east with me directly towards Jerramungup for the morning, then we'd all meet up and they'd head south for Albany, leaving me alone to get on with the main job and with a day gained.

116 km today / 8,912 km since London

Thursday 19th June

Breakfast at the B&B was excellent and copious, and the plan we'd hatched worked out well – Jenny rode some 80 kms with me, Jonathan and the girls caught us in the car, we all had a quick roadside picnic, said our goodbyes, and I was finally alone again.

It had been a fantastic and relaxing ten-day mini-break with family, but now it was time to buckle down, speed up and beetle over to Melbourne by around 7th July. 18 days to do 3,000 kms should be doable...but it had been almost two months since I'd last ridden a 200 km day, so I was certainly not feeling over-confident. Plus there was the minor matter of the Nullarbor Desert to traverse, which sounded scary. But all Nullarbor means is that there are no trees. Furthermore, I'd recently survived a Kazakhstan crossing – surely it couldn't be that hard, could it? I crossed my fingers for good roads and good winds, and rode a solid 210 kms to Ravensthorpe by 20:30 with barely a stop – there was little to stop for on these roads. Feeling pleased with this early progress I celebrated with curried snags, mash and beer in a busy pub. Rain threatened as I was leaving so I found an excellent sheltered camp spot on a quiet, dark shop verandah.

210 km today / 9,122 km since London

Friday 20ᵗʰ June

I was woken early by the sound of vacuum cleaners being pushed around the shop, and after a quick bowl of muesli got going just before 07:00 on a rolling road under clear sunny skies for 100 kms in six hours to a roadhouse lunch in Munglinup; thence on to Dalyup crossroads, where I turned off Highway 1 onto a gravel road for some 20 kms to cut a big corner, miss the town of Esperance, and save probably another half a day.

Traffic was thin all day and roadhouses were far apart. The sense of vast open space was overwhelming, yet enticing and exciting. Carrying all I needed to survive alone across these huge distances gave a rewarding feeling of self-sufficiency and independence from the world. I felt at one with the bike, it was now part of me, and we were both rolling reliably well. Ticking off the miles in these conditions was enormously satisfying, liberating, therapeutic...

But I came down to earth with a bump. Of the few drivers sharing the road with me today, most passed with care, with one notable exception. I was buzzed at very close range by a speeding swerving car full of probably drunk youths – an unnerving experience anywhere of course but here in the utterly silent middle of nowhere it was quite surreal.

At Gibson I rejoined Highway 1 heading north towards Norseman, and found the Gibson Soak, a homely country pub serving fine burgers, chips and beer. These winter days were short and it was pitch dark and cold under a clear starry sky for the final push on to Scadden, where I dossed down on the verandah of the town's primary school.

204 km today / 9,326 km since London

Saturday 21ˢᵗ June

Midwinter's day! It was a chilly night outside the school at 6°C, but a bright sunny day followed and the mercury climbed steadily to 20°C. There were only ten hours of daylight, from 07:00 to 17:00, so I was riding a few hours in the dark every day to hit the 200 km target. Today's ride north to Norseman was against a stiff headwind, so my average speed nosedived to 15.4 km/h and it took till noon to cover the 55 kms to Salmon Gums, where I munched on toasties in the solitary roadhouse. The wind was a worry – would I be facing this across another entire continent? At

Norseman I'd be turning east and hopefully winds would be more favourable, otherwise Melbourne by 7th July might be impossible, with knock-on effects to my planned schedules for New Zealand and North America.

Just over to the right of the road there was a railway, barely used – just two trains rumbled slowly by all day, the longest goods trains I'd ever seen, hauled by two engines in front and two in the middle. I was puzzled why more freight was not travelling by rail across such vast distances – for every railway train I saw, scores of roadtrains passed me (huge, powerful, American-style trucks pulling up to three long trailers), each of them hauling probably a mere 1% or so of the capacity of their rail-borne competitors.

The wind eased off around 15:00, my speed crept up to something approaching reasonable, yet it was well past dark when I finally reached Norseman at 20:00, the last town before the Nullarbor. It felt very much like the last town too, a frontier town at the edge of civilisation; an eerily quiet, dusty, edgy, rundown place with minimal street lighting and barely a soul to be seen. I had a list of things to do before setting out across the desert: re-stock the seat bag; fill up the four water bottles and the hydrobag; eat some dinner; and find some wifi – I'd already been out of touch for four days and after this it could be a week or more, so I wanted to reassure folk back home that all was fine and to prepare them for radio silence. The trouble with daily updates was that people came to expect them, and some might worry if things went quiet.

I turned a corner and there they all were: a large proportion of the local population was rammed into a lively and noisy pub, so I locked up the bike and joined them for dinner, sharing a table with a family who'd driven up from Esperance, a round trip of some 400 km, just for dinner. It was good but not exceptional...perhaps dinners in Esperance were particularly bad.

The barman told me that the BP Roadhouse at the Eyre Highway junction was the only place in town with working wifi, so I pedalled up there where BP woman informed me that the wifi wasn't working – damn! I went round the shop stocking up on the essentials for a desert crossing, finding milk in a chiller cabinet labelled Moo Juice. Then I tried connecting to the wifi and, to my amazement, it worked. I quickly tweeted that all was well, there'd probably be no more wifi for 2,000 km, and normal service would be resumed ASAP.

Then, feeling not a little daunted, I stepped outside and loaded my shopping onto the bike. It was nearly 22:30 and I wondered if it might be more sensible to find digs in town and set off in the morning. But that would set me back another half day and it was a fine if chilly night, the wind had dropped to negligible, and the road had a certain mesmeric appeal. As I was dithering a truck pulled in, the driver jumped down from his lofty cab and eyed me up, smiling: "You're not riding tonight are you, you crazy bastard?" he queried, apparently incredulous. I said I was minded to do just that, prompting further colourful opinions on barmy poms before he headed into the warm roadhouse for his dinner, leaving me alone outside in

a deathly silence to further ponder the sanity of my project. The garish green and white neon lights were in stark contrast with the inky blackness of the road heading east. The next roadhouse was 189 kms down that highway, with nothing in between. To go or not go? I referred myself back to the yardstick, Kazakhstan – it was never

Into the night...scary distances on the signposts!

going to be that hard was it? With that thought in mind I set off into the night and into the great Oz interior, soon passing a foreboding distance sign: Adelaide 1,986 kms.

Once out of town my eyes adjusted and it was not actually pitch dark at all; a clear night sky revealed possibly the most magnificent wall-to-wall starscape I'd ever witnessed and I spent one of my happiest and most rewarding hours ever on a bicycle revelling in that perfect exquisite silence before stopping at midnight to camp at the roadside and fall asleep looking up at the magic show in the heavens above. Cycle touring doesn't get better than this!

180 km today / 9,505 km since London

Sunday 22nd June

It rained overnight and a cold wind was up as I emerged from the bivi bag in the forest (the Nullarbor proper was a few days away yet) but, happy days, it was blowing my way! I rode 75 kms by 11:30 and pulled off the road a kilometre or so into the Fraser Range "oasis in the outback" sheep station and caravan site, not marked on my map but I had heard of it a few days previously from another traveller. It's in an isolated and stunning location set in a range of granite hills covered by dense eucalyptus forest. Facilities include a small shop and use of a kitchen with a roaring fire which was being stoked by local tourists playing cards and sheltering from the bitter winter weather. I bought and cooked up half a dozen eggs, a pot noodle and a tin of soup and shovelled it all down the cake-hole with a loaf of bread and a pot of tea.

It was something of an effort to tear myself away from that safe warm haven and back out onto the cold, desolate and arrow-straight Eyre Highway (named after explorer Edward John Eyre, first to cross the Nullarbor in 1840–1841[19]). The road rolled gently across low hills through light rain for around five hours to the roadhouse at Balladonia, where I arrived at 18:00 and decided to stop for the night – another cold wet one was forecast and camping held no allure whatever. "Cheap" backpacker accommodation was available at $50 for a small, spartan, windowless room with bunk beds in a converted shipping container, but it was clean and substantially more appealing than stopping outside. After ablutions I found myself in the bar tucking into a tasty plateful of snags and mash and a pint of Coopers Best served by a rather lovely German girl running the bar. I was joined at my table by a fellow traveller, who told me about the dramatic crash landing nearby of the Skylab space station in 1979 – apparently the local council presented NASA with a littering fine, and President Jimmy Carter rang the roadhouse personally to apologise!

167 km today / 9,672 km since London

Monday 23rd June

Bullet holes in the bin – Aussies presumably get bored driving the Eyre Highway

A giant high quality cooked roadhouse breakfast at 06:30 fuelled me up for the day, and I was back out on the long straight highway at 07:20. After 35 kms I entered the famous 90 mile straight – 146 kms right through to Caiguna without a turn, and pancake-flat too. Today was pretty much a perfect

---

[19] https://en.wikipedia.org/wiki/Eyre_Highway

winter's day awheel. The trees were thinning out and giving way to scrubby bushes, there was a helpful gentle tailwind, the sun shone and I saw kangaroos, a camel, pink and green parrots, and two giant emus dashing across the road and into the distance. It made a change to see so much living wildlife; road kill was usually more prolific.

I arrived at the Caiguna roadhouse at 18:00 where they served a delicious homemade pumpkin soup followed by burger, chips and beer. It was a fine evening, so I set off again for a final 70 kms in the dark to Cocklebiddy, where I arrived by 21:30 and discovered the local time was actually +45 minutes, so 22:15. With the owner's permission, and a promise that I'd be in for an early breakfast, I camped on a covered picnic table opposite the roadhouse.

247 km today / 9,920 km since London

Tuesday 24th June

A big blackboard sign outside the roadhouse welcomed travellers to Cocklebiddy and imparted the following useful local statistics:

- Population: 8
- Budgies: 25
- Quails: 7
- Dogs: 1
- Kangaroos: 1,234,567

The breakfast was pricey at $30 but once again it was of premium quality, 100 km portion-sized and included coffee. I guess they could charge a lot more if they wanted to, given that the nearest competition is 100 kms down the road, and they probably pay a premium too for their supplies and their staff since they are out in the middle of the desert. All things considered, pretty good value after all.

I was away by 07:30 and traffic was very light, just a handful of vehicles passing by every hour, many of them roadtrains carrying explosives for mining. It was a grey, cloudy, chilly and windy day, but once again the wind was from the west, and there was never any sign of the road turning to dust like it had so often in Kazakhstan. A quick lunch stop for pie and chips at Madura, then an uneventful ride – other than passing through the 10,000 km milestone – on to 20:00 where, a stone's throw from Mundrabilla roadhouse, I found an ideal sheltered camping spot with picnic tables under a roofed water station. As I looked around in the pitch dark with the aid of my head-torch for the best spot to doss down, I saw that I wasn't alone – a motorcyclist I'd met at Madura was tucked up inside his tent and my arrival probably freaked him out a little. He called out to ask who was there and was hopefully reassured by my cheery reply, "Just the harmless crazy pom on the laid-back bike you met at lunchtime – sleep tight, happy dreams!" It was a cloudy night, and mild at 12°C. I unrolled the bivi bag on a picnic table, had a quick snack, wrote up the daily diary, and climbed into bed.

205 km today / 10,125 km since London

Wednesday 25th June

I broke camp at 06:00 and rode 4 kms to the Mundrabilla roadhouse for yet another high quality big breakfast, and spotted that they had wifi. Bizarrely and frustratingly however, this turned out to be not for public use. They'd make good money selling it to travellers keen to send news home and find out what's happening in the world outside the desert.

Mid-morning a wedge-tailed eagle alighted majestically on a branch at the roadside so I stopped to observe quietly from just a few feet away; he didn't appear to be in the least bothered by my intrusion. After a few moments he took lazily to the wing, slowly and nonchalantly flapping away out of view.

It's a long, long road

At Eucla the road tilted upwards for some 100 metres onto an escarpment where a roadhouse afforded terrific views over the vast Southern Ocean. Here I ate lunch and met Shayne, a miner driving to Esperance. He was doing some basic vehicle checks and obligingly paused to take a great photo of me against the ocean backdrop. I took a photo of him too which I saved to tweet at the next opportunity: "so I ride half way round the world for a spot of peace and quiet and here's Shayne using a noisy electric pump to check his tyre pressures..."

A signpost showed I still had some way to go to reach the half-way point across this vast continent: Perth 1,435; Melbourne 1,989. 12 kms later

I crossed into South Australia at Border Village, which consisted of a single roadhouse. Internet was available! But at a dollar a minute I had to be quick so fired off a couple of quick tweets, checked emails and headlines then ate another lunch. Refuelled to the brim, I rode on through the rest of the afternoon and four hours into the night under a cold, clear, star-spangled sky. Other vehicles, mostly roadtrains, were few, and their headlights were visible either ahead or in the rear-view mirror for five minutes or more before actually passing me; if approaching from both directions it was impossible to judge the moment they'd pass so I moved well off the road to wait in safety as these giant behemoths of the road thundered by. I called it a day at 22:15, pitching camp at a cliff edge viewpoint under a freezing starry sky.

195 km today / 10,320 km since London

Thursday 26th June

It was a bone-chilling 2°C at dawn, but the ocean view from my cliff edge perch offered spectacular compensation. I'd moved into another time zone and was now 90 minutes ahead of Perth, so I started riding a little later at 07:45, slowly against an unhelpful cross-wind. I shared a long stretch of road with thousands of migrating caterpillars all attempting to cross from left to right, a bizarre sight. The cannier among them had worked out that it was faster to go broadside and roll with the wind; green stains on the road marked the squishy end of those that had failed to complete the treacherous crossing.

At 14:00 I stopped for a burger at the Nullarbor roadhouse where, annoyingly once again, the wifi was for staff use only. There was a roadtrain at the fuel pumps so I took a closer look, and counted the wheels: 34! Shortly after hitting the road again, a sign indicated I had finally arrived at the Nullarbor plain itself: a flat and treeless stretch of sparse grasses and bush, but only about 20 kms across. I rode until 23:00 but didn't quite hit the 200 km target due to the unfavourable wind and some long rolling hills for half the day, pulling in to camp in a rest area under another clear starlit sky, mercifully not as perishingly cold as the previous night.

192 km today / 10,512 km since London

Friday 27th June

After a quick bowl of muesli at a picnic table, I rode 27 kms into Nundroo and saw green fields: farmland – I had survived the Nullarbor crossing! It had been one of the most daunting prospects of the whole tour, but on the ground it had been just another long bike ride presenting no serious challenges, and far, far easier than the yardstick that was Kazakhstan. I pulled into the roadhouse for the full works breakfast, with mixed feelings about emerging from the desert – it had been a week of sublime peace and quiet (apart from the occasional roadtrain and Shane's noisy tyre pump). The lack of wifi had definitely had its advantages too.

I left Nundroo at 10:00 in bright sunshine and with a good tailwind. Within 30 minutes it was all change: a fast-moving cold front swept in bringing a series of brief but vicious icy showers. Luckily they pushed me 70 kms down the road to Penong in time for lunch – a delicious homemade chicken and vegetable soup, burger and chips and iced coffee. Following that it was a stormy cold afternoon's ride to Ceduna featuring hail, thunder and lightning, but fortunately the wind was still behind me; I think riding west that day would have been nigh-on impossible. I arrived in Ceduna at 18:00, planning to have dinner and push on to Wirrulla by 22:00 to take further advantage of the gale-force tailwind.

However, darkness was falling and the cold stormy weather showed no sign of abating. I ate a full roast dinner in the roadhouse then went back outside to re-assess the weather – it had further deteriorated to vile. There was no question of riding now, so I checked into the motel next door then paid a quick visit to the bar for a beer. With hindsight it would have been wise to shower and spruce myself up a little beforehand. Propped at the bar was a couple engaged in earnest conversation which stopped abruptly at the moment of my entrance. The woman studied my face intently for a moment and pronounced (it clearly wasn't a question) that I had just crossed the Nullarbor desert. How did she know, I wondered. "Just do", she said, "you've got that look". She was being sensitive, of course – the clues were plentiful. Perhaps it was the facial grime or the stubble, the bloodshot eyes or the stench...probably all of the above. I downed the beer and returned to my room for a thorough scrub and shave under a hot shower before returning to the roadhouse a new man to enjoy a second roast dinner. Freezing rain lashed against the windows and staff and fellow diners were in agreement that such a huge storm system was unusual in these parts. I quietly congratulated myself on my wise decision to hole up here.

After dinner I lazed in bed watching the TV weather channel, full of repeated severe warnings about the storms which were forecast to continue over the weekend, further vindicating my decision to stop early for decent accommodation; anyone riding or camping out in that would have to be a notch or two further round the crazy scale than me! I enjoyed a long wifi session sending emails and tweets from my luxurious warm dry bed, imagining where I might be and what trouble I'd be in had I continued earlier – it sent a shiver down my spine just to think of it. As I turned out the light, the wind howled, the rain pelted against the window – the noise was phenomenal. But I had no trouble getting to sleep: the bracing bike ride, two roast dinners and a large beer proved more effective than any sleeping draught.

178 km today / 10,690 km since London

Saturday 28th June

Another big roadhouse breakfast set me up nicely for the morning and I was riding by 07:40. The expected strong crosswinds were less helpful than the previous day's tailwind, and the bike wobbled in the lee of occasional roadtrains. Weather conditions alternated every ten or fifteen minutes between warm sunny intervals and icy cold showers all morning, during which I managed 93 kms to Wirrulla, where the general store sold a mean steak sandwich.

I devoted some thought to the time of my arrival in Melbourne. Since Perth I'd had around 7th July in mind, which looked achievable and fitted nicely with the New Zealand schedule. The 7th would be a Monday. Hmmm…could I possibly get there three days earlier in time for the Albert Park parkrun on Saturday 5th? This crazy idea gradually took hold. I'd need a fair wind and I'd need to ramp up the daily distances, but it looked distinctly possible, in theory at least. Furthermore, it would give me an extra couple of days in hand to pay a visit to my Arran cousin Craig and his young family in Tasmania – such opportunities don't arise that often – *carpe diem!* It wasn't long before I was determined and fixated on the new schedule: Melbourne by Friday 4th July.

The wind that afternoon did not immediately co-operate with the new plan – I struggled into a stiff headwind until 16:00, but then it dropped abruptly and I rode a couple of easier hours in light winds under blue skies until nightfall at 18:00 when it started raining again and traffic rose to levels I hadn't seen since leaving Perth. The last 40 kms to the small town of Wudinna were thoroughly unpleasant and miserable on the dark, wet, busy highway with vehicles passing close and fast and leaving clouds of icy spray in their wake. But a $40 budget hotel room, good dinner, beer and wifi were sufficient recompense, and I was pleased with the distance covered – a decent result in adverse conditions.

It was about 1,300 kms from here to Melbourne, and there were six days to do it in – the race was on!

212 km today / 10,902 km since London

Sunday 29th June

Amazingly the $40 room price included a generous buffet continental breakfast, and the total bill including dinner and two beers was $73 – life was substantially more affordable now I was out of the desert. I was back on the bike at 07:20 riding once again through rapidly changing weather conditions: warm sunshine one minute, icy cold showers the next. My rain jacket was on and off repeatedly and I needed to get the timing right for my mid-morning picnic – a sardine sandwich between showers. The spray from oncoming roadtrains was like riding through a cold carwash at 100 km/h.

Nullarbor Plastic bottle recycling initiative

I stopped for a pastie in Kimba (100 kms) after which conditions improved for the afternoon with a dry tailwind, but the litter-strewn verges were a depressing sight in such remote country. In an Aussie variation, many trees were decorated with plastic bottles. Litter had been a feature in most countries, with the notable and honourable exceptions of pristine Holland and Germany right at the start. Plastic water bottles and aluminium drinks cans girdle our globe with filth.

Once again there was a railway running parallel to the road, but the only trains to be seen were roadtrains, many of them marked "Oversize", and hauling vast bits of plant and equipment around the country. Extraordinary loads that we'd rarely see in UK seemed to be commonplace in Australia. Why don't they use their railways?

At 18:30 just after dark I arrived in Iron Knob, which made me smile – how childish! A former mining town and birthplace of Australia's steel industry, it's now a small isolated backwater between Kimba and Port Augusta. It was an unsettled and wind-chilled 6°C and looking like further rain so the prospect of camping out was unappealing. On the map the town looked bigger than recent towns I'd stayed in, and the town sign I'd just ridden past had boasted a hotel. On the ground however there were a few houses dotted about, but no town centre, no shops…and no hotel.

I knocked at a door to ask for directions to the hotel and three elderly ladies informed me it had gone out of business two years previously. However, they thought a new couple who'd recently moved in just up the road might be letting rooms. The kindly ladies attempted to provide directions but it was rather confusing, especially when they contradicted one another. They came outside to point up the road and reinforce their instructions, to no avail. Finally they took pity (or perhaps decided I was a hopeless case) and got in their car to lead me to an unwelcoming, dark back street full of howling dogs – I'd never have found it alone. The ladies added to the cacophony by blaring their horn repeatedly for attention until Stapie, a youthful South African girl, emerged to confirm that this was the old hotel, she and her partner were the new custodians, rooms were $50, and they'd be delighted to welcome me as their first guest. She showed me into a room as big as a school classroom with two double beds, a pair of bunk beds, a sofa, fridge, TV, bathroom and enough floor space to turn it into a dormitory for 12. She confirmed my suspicions that there was no restaurant in town; this was disappointing news – a hot dinner and a beer would have gone down extremely well – but not a serious problem as I had plenty of survival supplies.

However, before I'd had time to start delving into the seat bag, there was an unexpected and welcome knock at the door: Stapie reappeared bearing a hot, tasty cheese toastie and the remains of their recent barbecue – a large steak and pork chop.

1,112 kms to Melbourne, five days to go.
193 km today / 11,095 km since London

Monday 30th June

I pedalled out of Iron Knob at dawn into bright sunny settled weather, chilly at just 4°C but warming up gradually during a brisk 70 kms to Port Augusta, the first sizeable town since Mandurah near Perth, over two weeks behind me now. I stocked up on essentials at the supermarket, got a steak sandwich for breakfast and found wifi to catch up on twitter and emails which included a tempting offer from cousin Craig in Tasmania to book return flights for me. I dithered for a few minutes – it would be a solid financial commitment to the new schedule. Emailing back "yes please" turned out to be the easy bit.

Back on the road again, I was bearing south now on the highway to Adelaide, much busier than anything since leaving Perth but happily for the time being with a good, smooth, fast-rolling tarmac shoulder. Feeling the pressure to get a wriggle on, I rode non-stop to dusk at 18:00, refuelled at the pie shop in Crystal Brook, then pressed for four hours in the dark, finally stopping for the night at 23:00 on a shop terrace under an awning – a useful find as it had been drizzling for the final hour.

865 kms to Melbourne, four days to go – it still looked doable so long as the weather co-operated.
247 km today / 11,342 km since London

Tuesday 1st July

It was a foggy start at 06:40 just before dawn, but that soon cleared and I made good time over the 130 kms into the suburbs of Adelaide by 15:00. After a fortnight in the outback, city riding was a jolt to the system and tediously slow in thick stop-start traffic through a series of busy junctions. I ate at an Australian fast food place then found the road out of town towards Murray Bridge, a road with something of a reputation for a fearsome climb up into the Mount Lofty Ranges. It didn't disappoint, rising steeply through a series of switchbacks up to 700m, affording spectacular views back over the city at sunset.

That was followed by some tricky and stressful navigation in heavy evening traffic on a rolling, pitch-dark, narrow twisting road between a chain of satellite towns: Crafters, Stirling, Aldgate, Bridgewater... I eventually emerged onto the old Princes Highway, escaped the gravitational pull of the big city and its suburbs and had the road to myself again; normal service was resumed, exquisite silence at last. The road continued to roll up hill and down dale through to Murray Bridge, no doubt highly picturesque in daylight. This was the second hilliest day since London with over 1,400m of climbing according to the GPS; it had been a good workout. But, I reflected as I finally rolled into Murray Bridge at 23:00, it had been a walk in the park compared to the 1,500m hilliest day on those dreadful Russian roads on 20th April.

The awning of a warehouse in the northern industrial suburbs provided a useful sheltered camp spot, well placed to roll a couple of kms into town for breakfast.

657 kms to Melbourne, three days to go.
208 km today / 11,550 km since London

Wednesday 2nd July

Out of my pit at 06:00, bowl of muesli, then into town for a fast food second breakfast, wifi and ablutions. Today was a generally easier day than yesterday – much less lumpy, no big towns or cities to slow me down, and light traffic...until just after dark when suddenly all the truckers came out bearing gigantic, oversize loads including fully built houses and, most bizarrely, a roadtrain hauling three trailers of rail wagons...on the Western Highway, beside which there is a railway. Bonkers!

Around 21:00 I crossed the state border into Victoria and the clock jumped forward 30 minutes to Melbourne time, and the end of the Aussie road suddenly looked a lot closer. Conditions were favourable and I was feeling good so I rode on to Kaniva by 23:00, where I found a covered spot to camp in a back yard behind the village bank, vaguely hoping as I bedded down that no armed gang had planned a break-in for that night.

412 kms to Melbourne. Two days to go. Game on!
245 km today / 11,796 km since London

Thursday 3rd July

I was up and out on the road again at 07:00, once again running on muesli power for the early shift. It was freezing cold for the first 30 kms to Nhill, where I procured a large and much needed cooked roadhouse breakfast and slowly thawed out. 40 kms further down the road free teas and coffees were being served at the roadside, with homemade cakes on sale for a local charity. The stall was manned by the editor of the *Dimboola Banner*, who interviewed me and took some photos for the following issue. Truck driver Chris overheard proceedings, professed admiration for my exploits and contributed a slice of his girlfriend's delicious carrot cake. I was asked what sponsors were funding my trip and was met with incredulity that it was all self-funded, it surely must be costing a small fortune, they thought. Well not as much as you might think, I started to explain, and in any case how could I expect anyone else to pay for my extended holiday? I was thoroughly enjoying this chatty break from the road but suddenly noticed a whole hour had ticked by. I had to move on – Time is Miles.[20]

The finance query, which had come up a number of times, prompted me once again to reconsider the relatively small costs of the trip, the highest by far being the forgoing of six months' salary. That could easily be

---

[20] Overused audax proverb

recovered, Pascale had helpfully suggested, by continuing to work six months past my retirement age. Other costs were pretty small beer: cycling is cheap, I would be eating anyway (perhaps not as much), accommodation was mostly free in the bivi bag and with warmshowers hosts, and there were only five long-haul flights to pay for. The whole enterprise had in fact been funded several times over, I mused, by my having given up two expensive habits a quarter of a century ago, namely smoking and car ownership, producing combined savings in the region of £100,000 I calculated happily as I pedalled onwards towards Stawell and Ararat.

I passed through a succession of small towns and called in at four or five fast food places mainly to try for wifi to contact my Melbourne hosts and give them an approximate ETA for the following day, but it wasn't working in any of them – Australia seemed to be a bigger wifi desert than Kazakhstan! I pushed on long into the night across a rollercoaster series of big hills for the last 90 kms to finish at 01:00 and cut the distance I would need to cover on the final day in order to arrive at a respectable hour…with luck, in time for beer and dinner!

I unrolled the bivi bag for a final time in Oz on a garage forecourt at Beaufort.

160 kms to Melbourne, one day, looks easy, all but in the bag!
251 km today / 12,047 km since London

Friday 4th July

It was a short, cold, night with noisy roadtrains pulling in at all hours for rest and refuelling just a few feet from where I was trying to get a spot of shut-eye – most inconsiderate! The roadhouse opened up at 06:00 and I was straight in for the big breakfast. There I met Travis the trucker, who proudly drives his own rig up and down the highway several times a week – today he was hauling steel cladding. He smiled as he warned of the hills ahead and provided an explanation for something I'd been puzzling over for days, namely why were there so many more trucks on the road at night? Most customers, he said, want overnight deliveries.

It was a chilly and overcast 3°C for the 50 km ride to Ballarat, where I finally found working wifi in a well-known international purveyor of fast fattening food. But why was the waitress holding back the giggles as I ordered my coffee? I got her to take a photo of me, and my suspicions were confirmed – in full winter gear sporting facial grime, substantial scruffy beard growth and head torch, my appearance was rather outlandish, something between intrepid polar explorer and wizened coal miner.

What's so funny then?

I emailed my hosts with an ETA between 5-7pm. The weather brightened up for the afternoon but stayed cold, and Travis had been right about the undulating terrain. However, I managed to escape from the main highway onto a lovely quiet scenic route over the Pentland Hills and directly into the north Melbourne suburb of Carlton at 18:30. I felt pleased with myself for hitting a target arrival date I'd set six days previously with some 1,300 km to go. At times I hadn't been sure I'd make it, but reasonable conditions, single-minded persistence and a lot of night riding had produced the required result – I was in time for parkrun!

Bill and Rosemary were generous, talkative and warm hosts. Parents of a work colleague in London, they rose in stupendous fashion to the occasion, fussing over me like a long lost son. What did I need first? Beer, shower, dinner, sleep? That was an easy question! I was given a glass of what had come to be a favourite, *Little Creatures* – oh sweet nectar after such efforts. Ablutions and a sumptuous dinner followed in quick order and I was made to feel right at home and truly welcome in their comfortable and recently modernised town house. Getting into a warm, soft, cosy bed was an indulgent luxury after the previous four cold nights outside.

It was exactly three months since I'd left the UK and I was pretty much exactly half way round the world – these were strangely and satisfyingly symmetrical statistics.

161 km today / 12,207 km since London

Saturday 5th July

Sadly there was no chance of a lie-in...parkruns in Australia start at 08:00, an hour earlier than in Britain, because for much of the year it would be too hot by 09:00. So after a hurried bowl of muesli I rode seven kms across the city centre and over the river into Albert Park where 202 other runners made me welcome. A loaned pair of running shoes fitted perfectly and I jogged rather gingerly around the five km course – one lap of the lake –

finishing in 61st place on 23:19, not wanting to take any chances with rather stiff calf muscles. Obviously I'd not been doing enough running recently.

Back at the house an hour later I had a distinguished guest. Pete Matthews, President of Audax Australia no less, had arrived with a bike box for me for the flight to New Zealand. I'd met him in July 2013 when he'd been over in the UK to ride London-Edinburgh-London. He stayed for an hour drinking coffee and chewing the fat, and I spent the following hour dismantling, cleaning and packing the bike in the box he'd provided.

The next job was to get online for flights to New Zealand and onward to the USA – New Zealand border control officers won't let you in unless you can show them your ticket out. These dreary desk jockey tasks always take longer than they should and by the time I had the air tickets in the bag the whole day had slipped by and it was time for dinner. My shout tonight, the three of us walked about ten minutes down to the Kent Hotel, a great local gastro pub, where I indulged myself with pork belly twice cooked with sauerkraut, crispy prosciutto, pomme frites and apple cider glaze, washed down with some fine craft beers.

This rather perfect day continued back at the house – Rosemary is a big cycle sport fan, and Stage one of the Tour de France was just being waved off from its Yorkshire Grand Départ. The ten-hour time difference meant we could watch the action live, so we settled back on the sofa with a couple of bottles of *Little Creatures*…and I promptly fell asleep.

0 km today / 12,207 km since London

Sunday 6th July

Two emails came in overnight: one to confirm my USA flight; the other to say I'd been bumped onto a later flight to Hobart – some three hours later, giving time to visit the magnificent 820 hectare Woodlands Historic Park adjacent to Melbourne airport, full of kangaroos and providing "a fascinating glimpse of the landscapes and wildlife seen by European settlers in the 1840s...a 150-year old homestead, indigenous canoe trees, native woodland and grassland".[21]

Bill then dropped me off at the airport (without the bike – this was a holiday!) for the 13:40 flight to Hobart, Tasmania, where cousin Craig and his kids Finlay and Evie picked me up and took me back to their place, just 15 minutes from the airport. It's probably the coolest address I've ever stayed at: Surf Road, Seven Mile Beach. Craig's wife Liz was at home and we spent the afternoon playing footy, hide and seek and reading with the

---

[21] http://tinyurl.com/hgnq23s

kids. Liz did homemade pizzas and a Tasmanian wine tasting for dinner and we were chatting, quaffing and reminiscing till midnight.

0 km today / 12,207 km since London

Monday 7th July

After a late breakfast we all piled into the family car to drive up the east coast to Nine Mile Beach, where Craig and Liz have a "shack" (beach chalet) and we had a spot of lunch. Then we moved a little further up the coast to Wineglass Bay for a trail walk out to spectacular coastal locations at one of Tasmania's most popular tourist attractions. Despite the grey overcast and drizzly weather conditions the stunning views lived up to their reputation.

We stopped for dinner in the pub at Coles Bay on the return journey, and back home caught up with live coverage of Tour de France stage three from Cambridge to London on roads I know well, exchanging emails with my brother Antony who was watching the action at Blackfriars Bridge.

0 km today / 12,207 km since London

Tuesday 8th July

I took the dog and kids for a beach walk while Liz cooked a fabulous Eggs Benedict for breakfast. Then we all drove into Hobart and up to the cold wind-swept summit of Mount Wellington for stupendous views over the city. After ice creams Evie and Fin were deposited with a babysitter, releasing Craig, Liz and me to go out on the town for dinner and some rather excellent local beers and ciders.

Back at the ranch by 23:00 it was time for whisky tastings. We all agreed that Scotch Glenlivet was vastly superior to the Tasmanian single malt whisky which Craig had recently been given, presumably by someone who doesn't like him much, and which was pronounced undrinkable and poured unceremoniously down the sink.

Then it was time to settle down for Tour de France stage four which came down to an exciting bunch sprint for the line and another win for Marcel Kittel, his third win out of the four stages so far, putting top British sprinter Mark Cavendish firmly in the shade.

0 km today / 12,207 km since London

Wednesday 9ᵗʰ July

An in-betweeny day consisting of a morning flight back to Melbourne, an afternoon back at Bill and Rosemary's place packing my bags, and an evening eating lamb cutlets for dinner followed by stage five of the Tour on the wet cobbles of Flanders during which the 2013 Yellow Jersey winner Chris Froome fell off his bike twice and threw in the towel.

0 km today / 12,207 km since London

Thursday 10ᵗʰ July

Another day, another flight. I have never been a frequent flyer; this was surely using up my lifetime carbon allowance! Bill dropped me back at the now familiar Melbourne airport at 06:30, over three hours early for the New Zealand flight to beat the morning rush hour...inevitably the flight was then delayed.

After almost four hours airborne plus two hours further round the planet, I landed in Wellington NZ at about 16:00. The bike and bags came through with minimal delay and I took a shared airport shuttle bus up to the lofty suburb of Ngaio and knocked on the door at Rob's house, where I was booked in for a couple of nights. Rob and my youngest brother Philip, who arrived to complete the party an hour or so later, have been best friends since their primary school days. Bangers, mash and beer were served for dinner, and we spent the rest of the evening reminiscing indulgently, mainly about bike rides – Rob and Philip regaled me with tales from their 1997 diagonal crossing of North America from Vancouver to Virginia Beach.

0 km today / 12,207 km since London

Friday 11ᵗʰ July

A final day off the bike – it had been a week and I was getting edgy! I unpacked the bike from its box and rebuilt it by 09:30; this routine was getting a bit quicker each time. After a bit of bike fettling, kit sorting and bag re-packing I took a bus into Wellington city centre for a restful day with Philip involving coffees, pizzas, beers, a walk along the waterfront and a Kiwi spoof vampire film at the cinema.

Despite Wellington's reputation as one of the windiest cities on earth, it was a mild and still day and I couldn't help thinking it would have been a great day for cycling, especially as the outlook was much more unsettled. But of course we couldn't have set off today, on a Friday of all days, towards Auckland – I had a rendezvous with a pair of loaned shoes at the Wellington parkrun tomorrow!

0 km today / 12,207 km since London

Saturday 12th July

After an early breakfast Philip and I were on our bikes before dawn to cover the 16 kms to Lower Hutt for the parkrun at 08:00. As usual a warm welcome and running shoes awaited. 117 runners assembled for the traditional briefing, and then we were off on an out-and-back flat course beside the Hutt River. Conscious of the need to conserve energy for the rigours of the day to follow, I jogged gently and crossed the finish line in 23:28 in 33rd place. An enjoyable leisurely second breakfast of eggs, bacon and banter followed with a bunch of parkrunners in the local café before posing for a few photos. Then we set off up the Hutt River path bearing north-east towards Upper Hutt and Featherston.

Not the easiest terrain to ride on a 40kg recumbent

It was, as I later tweeted, "good to be back on the road again. Well, off-road that is. @PhilEvans10 is our navigator today". I had delegated all New Zealand route planning to Philip, with minimal guidance. In fact the only guidance had been to say that the bike and I both had a strong preference for tarmac, a hard learned lesson from the vast road-free expanses of Kazakhstan. Philip knew better though, and after the Hutt River trail we took an all-to-brief bit of hard-top to climb steeply to around 300 metres and then onto an unsurfaced disused rail route across the Rimutaka Mountain Range. In fairness the surface was mostly rideable and the scenery was outstanding; furthermore, explained Philip, we were bypassing Highway 1, which, busy and without any sort of shoulder, would have been "suicidal". The trail climbed gradually and reasonably smoothly for ten kms up to a 400m summit, but the descent was trickier on bigger stones, through pitch-dark tunnels and at one point crossing a V-shaped gorge where evidence strongly hinted at the previous existence of a bridge. Shouldering a 40kg laden recumbent bicycle to first descend then climb a steep scree slope turned this section into something of a vigorous full body workout.

We eventually popped out of this rugged wilderness onto a good smooth minor road leading us into Featherston, where we found excellent home-made pies and beer at the Royal Hotel. From there it was an easy flat 35 kms to Masterton by 18:30, where Philip had booked us into a cheap backpacker room for $50 and we had an excellent lamb shank dinner at the pub.

111 km today / 12,318 km since London

Sunday 13th July

Muesli in our bedroom at 06:00 was quickly followed by quiche and coffee in the local bakery before we hit the road at 07:30. It was mild and cloudy with added headwind, but it stayed dry as we followed a stunningly scenic route using minor roads all day. My knees objected to some of the more challenging climbs, hurting from the excesses of yesterday's parkrun and off-roading adventures, forcing me to drop down to the 24-inch gear (two feet, i.e. walk!) to get up the steepest. Lunch was a huge plate of sticky ribs and chips at the Pongaroa Hotel and the sun made a sustained appearance for the afternoon. The final 20 kms were the hilliest yet, finishing at the Wimbledon Tavern, a simple inn with chalet-style rooms, where we recovered with steaks and beer.

135 km today / 12,453 km since London

Monday 14th July – Day 100!

After muesli and eggs in our chalet we were on the road at 07:15 and an hour later passed through Taumata, a shortened name for the longest place name in the world meaning "the hill on which Tamatea, the chief of great physical stature and renown, played a lament on his flute to the memory of his brother"[22]. It was a brutally hilly morning through spectacular scenery

---

[22] Taumatawhakatangihangakoauauotamateaturipukakapikimaungahoronukupokaiwhenuakitanatahu

134

under foreboding grey skies, but the rain held off and we found great homemade pies for lunch in the rather excellent Antkor Wat Bakery and Coffee Shop in Waipukurau. The afternoon ride to Hastings was easier going.

We arrived at 16:00 and headed to our hosts, Vince and Clare, parents of a good work colleague, Matt (I'd stayed with his partner Zoe's parents in Melbourne the previous week). Kiwi hospitality turned out to be every bit as excellent, a symphony delivered in three distinct and efficient movements: for starters, about a gallon of tea with piles of biscuits; next up, after a quick wash and brush-up, we moved seamlessly on to beers and nibbles; finally, a mountain of pasta was washed down with an excellent local Hawke's Bay wine.

Today marked a hundred days since I'd left London. Just 80 days remaining now to get back home. I still had most of New Zealand to go, and then another continent and a half. Yet the end of the road was now clearly on the radar.

117 km today / 12,570 km since London

Tuesday 15th July

Following an early full cooked breakfast – thanks Clare! – we were on the road just before 07:00, and after a short, easy, flat 20 km coastal cruise to Napier we turned left onto Highway 5, the hilliest highway in New Zealand and the most climbing in a day since leaving London – over 2,200 metres of altitude gain squeezed into 80 kms – and being a cold, miserable, wet, foggy, wintry day, it was without the scenic views we might have hoped for. Night had long fallen and the road was icing up when I finally rolled into Taupo, exhausted, some three hours after Philip, who was waiting for me in the hot springs of the DeBretts Spa Resort, the perfect place to ease our tired muscles.

Meeting us in the hot pools was world runner Kevin Carr. He'd set off from Dartmoor in July 2013 and was running ultramarathon distances most days in a bid to break the world record for 'fastest runner around the world'[23]. I'd been following his twitter feed and knew our paths were converging,

---

[23] www.hardwayround.com (I considered renaming my blog easywayround)

but it was an amazing coincidence to arrive in Taupo on the same night, especially as our routes were completely different and just happened to be crossing here. After a long chat, a soothing soak and some photos by our respective vehicles – he was pushing all his kit in a pram – we bade Kevin goodbye and bon voyage and made our way a little further round Lake Taupo to Acacia Bay, where warmshowers hosts Julie and Jim were patiently waiting for us with dinners ready: steak, mash and sticky fig pudding with ice cream – just brilliant!

167 km today / 12,737 km since London

Wednesday 16th July

It was a freezing morning and the roads were icy so we were in no hurry to finish the rather excellent porridge, toast and coffee provided by Jim and Julie whilst admiring the splendid views over Acacia Bay from their panoramic living room window. But the bright sunshine quickly worked its magic and by shortly after 08:00 the road was glistening with rivulets of meltwater and we could tarry no longer. As we set off, Philip explained usefully that today's route to Hamilton would be flat…apart from the hilly bits. By now I'd come to understand that was code for hilly again, but perhaps a bit less so than the previous day: just under 1,800m of climbing as it turned out – there are no flat roads in New Zealand.

We enjoyed a lovely sunny day and some great views in the hills, and a road safety poster caught my eye: a photo of a female cyclist wearing a t-shirt with MUM emblazoned across the chest and the caption *See the person, Share the road*. What a civilised idea – treat other road users like family. Rather spoilt however by the fact that that too many Kiwis ignore the message and drive like lunatics.

My average speed rose from a lamentably slow 14.5 km/h yesterday to a marginally brisker 16.5 today, and Philip enjoyed the novel experience of waiting at hilltops, delighted to be going faster than his older brother for once!

We arrived in Hamilton at 20:00 to yet another fabulous warmshowers reception involving a bubbling cauldron of spaghetti bolognaise and kegs of homebrew beer. Heartfelt thanks to Andy and Cia, two more members of this remarkable worldwide network of benevolent bikey beery people.

168 km today / 12,904 km since London

Thursday 17th July

After a generous breakfast with our hosts we pedalled out of Hamilton into a crisp sunny dawn and soon found ourselves waylaid by a second superb breakfast at the Bellyful Cafe in Ngaruawahia. That was followed a couple of hours later by really good fish and chips at the George in Tuakau.

Today was the easiest going in New Zealand with fewer big climbs, but I was admonished by a road worker for stopping on a quiet bridge to take a photo. The works had entirely closed one lane so traffic alternated on the open lane while I occupied the other and enjoyed probably one of the safest photo stops I'd made since London, until being asked rather curtly to move on for "health and safety reasons".

There were further imaginative road safety posters, in particular a stark simple monochrome message: "People aren't built for speed – slow down!" And a little further up the road: "Intersections, it's your call" bearing an image of half a roulette wheel sliced into 12 segments each repeating one of four possible outcomes: NEAR MISS, MINOR CRASH, MAJOR CRASH, DEATH – apparently road users must expect that getting through a junction in the Waikato District will always be traumatic to some degree. Certainly in my admittedly limited experience, driving standards in New Zealand were generally lamentable, bringing flashbacks of the scariest moments on lawless Polish and Russian roads.

Philip and family: welcome to Auckland!

It was a tedious final 30 kms on a busy multi-lane highway past the international airport and into the Auckland suburb of Sandringham, where we rode up the chalked driveway to cross a ticker tape finish line at Philip's house at 19:00 and something of a hero's welcome from my lovely Kiwi nieces Olive (7) and Lucille (5), and sister-in-law, Jane. The girls were super-excited, having plotted my position daily since April on a giant world map on the wall. A festive family evening ensued, featuring roast chicken and yams, local beers, a homemade parsnip cake iced with the Laid Back logo, and malt whiskies to finish.

147 km today / 13,051 km since London

Friday 18th July

The day started with a car trip 30 kms out of town with Jane to buy milk. Philip, Jane and quite a number of their neighbours are rather partial to unpasteurised milk, but nanny state NZ has banned it. So they've formed a small co-operative and take turns every week to do the milk run out to a dairy farm where they buy buckets of raw milk for each other. Or rather for their pets, the farmer having helpfully posted up the following advice in the milk shed:

- *YOGHURT: This is raw yoghurt. Especially helpful for digestive problems with calves, cats and dogs.*
- *MILK: Our MILK is raw, neither pasteurised nor homogenised. There are no additives. Our cows are fed 100% on grass. Truly natural – as nature intended it to be. Your pets will never want to drink supermarket milk again. In fact they will probably turn their noses up at it!*

I spent the early part of the afternoon servicing, washing and partly dismantling the bike ready for the flight to the USA, then popped into central Auckland on Philip's folding bike to buy a much needed new sleeping bag.

0 km today / 13,051 km since London

Saturday 19th July

Saturday – parkrun for the third week running! I cycled over to Cornwall Park where yet another great welcome and pair of loan shoes awaited, and I trotted round gingerly in 23:32 for 38th place out of 120. My sporty sister-in-law Jane, in training for a marathon, ran to the start, ran the event, then ran home again, clocking up some 30 kms. Coffee and cakes in the local café with a few parkrunners followed, then I rode home where a full cooked breakfast awaited.

A relaxed afternoon ensued playing with the girls on the beach, watching a gannet colony through binoculars from a spectacular cliff top walk, soaking in hot thermal pools, and wine tasting. The evening was spent dismantling and boxing up the bike, eating a Chinese dinner, and sampling a variety of locally brewed sports recovery drinks prepared from malted barley.

0 km today / 13,051 km since London

Sunday 20th July

A final indulgent day included a morning visit to an out of town mountain bike park, where I managed to fall off no fewer than three times on slippery wet tree roots (all at low speed with no more damage than a few scrapes and a bruised ego); goat curry and a selection of fine beers at Galbraith's Ale House ("beer crafted onsite by master brewers"); and homemade pizzas for dinner topped with mozzarella made by Philip from raw milk fit only for animal consumption. Malt whiskies rounded off a perfect Sunday.

0 km today / 13,051 km since London

Monday 21st July

I took Olive to school then went for a haircut, posted some excess baggage back to the UK, bought some luggage straps for the bike box and finished packing my bags. Philip and I had green-lipped mussels and beer for lunch in a great replica Belgian brasserie, then he drove me to out to the airport...sniff!

There were stressful moments at check-in as I was passed from one desk to another due to a problem with issuing my boarding pass that staff were initially unable to explain – it was eventually established that this was because I was not in possession of an onward ticket from the USA. Since I was planning to cycle out of the USA into Canada I had not foreseen that this could be a problem. I would however be flying out of the USA after my ride across Canada, and having arrived at the airport with three hours to spare, I had plenty of time to pop into the travel agents and buy a flight from New York to Lisbon for 15th September. Once this had been procured, and the $200 excess baggage fee paid, I was rewarded with a boarding pass and went through security directly to the bar to unwind with a pie and a glass of beer. Departure was on schedule at 19:15.

0 km today / 13,051 km since London

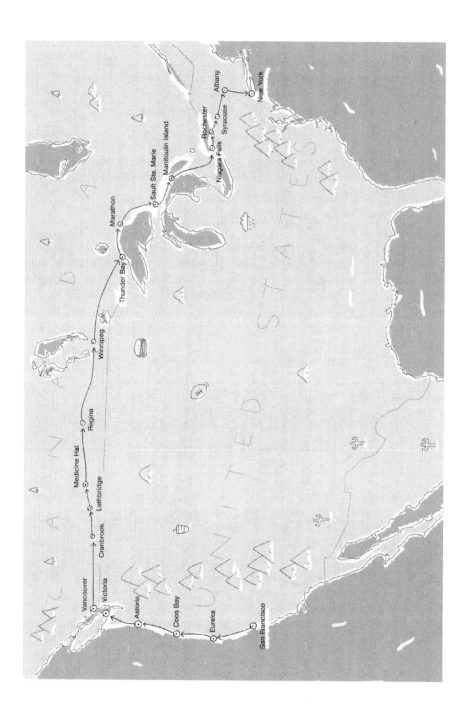

SAN FRANCISCO TO NEW YORK CITY

Monday 21st July (still!)

It was a long but uneventful flight through the night, across the Pacific and the International Date Line to San Francisco, where I landed at 12:30. After over 12 hours in the air I was in the USA, for the first time in my life, about seven hours before I'd left New Zealand!

My bags and bike took a while to appear on the carousel but getting through customs was a breeze. I'd been warned, mainly by Jonathan in Perth and Philip in Auckland, that even passengers in transit through the USA can experience long delays while probing questions are asked about the true purpose of their visit and past connections with the communist party. With the colourful variety of recent visas in my passport I was braced for an especially lengthy grilling. In the event there was no kit inspection and just one question: "Where are you headed sir?" Up the coast to Vancouver then across to Winnipeg, Niagara and New York, I replied. "Well you have yourself a real nice day sir, welcome to America!" And that was it, I was in. Ironically entry into the USA had been much simpler and speedier than into either Oz or NZ.

I rebuilt the bike in a quiet corner of the airport, then rode the 25 kms up into the city centre through warm sunshine mostly on a reasonable cycle route and found my warmshowers hosts Kevin and Kat on Geary Boulevard with no trouble thanks to the ever trusty GPS. Minor confusion arose on arrival stemming from misuse of the Queen's English – their second floor flat turned out to be on the first floor, because when they say first floor they actually mean what Brits call the ground floor. Two peoples divided by a common language, as Churchill, Wilde and Shaw are all reputed to have observed.

After a quick shower a great veggie dinner was served: home-grown salad leaves with dahl and rice followed by apple cake, all washed down with some rather excellent local beers – a truly pleasant surprise as I'd steeled myself for cold, bland, fizzy, factory pop. Talk was all cycle related; Kev and Kat had toured extensively and were also involved in the local cycling campaign, so there was much common ground to pick over as we worked our way through the tasting selection of ales that they'd thoughtfully provided.

As I went to bed I realised that my 21st July had lasted 43 hours and, though pleasantly tired, I didn't feel out of sorts at all. Perhaps the jet lag would hit me in the morning.

25 km today / 13,076 km since London

Tuesday 22nd July

I slept like a log and woke at 06:30 – no jet-lag. Kevin did me porridge and coffee for breakfast then led me across the centre of 'Frisco on his bike commute to work, thoughtfully skirting around the steepest roads that so characterise this iconic city, and leaving me by the bay at the south-east corner of the city. From there I picked my way northwards up the shoreline listening to Eric Clapton strumming San Francisco Bay Blues – what a wonderful soundtrack for setting off across another continent on a bicycle. I passed under the mighty Oakland Bay Bridge, through Chinatown and headed west to the Golden Gate Bridge for a quick photo-shoot with other tourists before crossing over into Marin County and out of the city on Highway 1 north-west towards the coast. Once I'd escaped the city's outer environs, traffic was light as most was using the faster parallel alternatives (Highway 101 and Interstate 5). Drivers were patient and courteous, the road surface was excellent, it was a fine, hot, sunny afternoon, and I was back in summer enjoying longer daylight hours again after my six-week antipodean winter sojourn. In brief, it was a rare perfect moment; all was good with the world. Even the sun was going the right way across the sky!

Highway 1 gradually morphed into a truly lovely, quiet coastal route offering great ocean views at every turn. I stopped for snacks and supplies in sleepy Tomales, then rode on through some brief, warm evening drizzle till around 21:00 still daylight! when I chanced upon a derelict and condemned residence perched precariously between road and cliff edge, marked up with posters bearing the warning: DANGER DO NOT ENTER. Bingo! A five-star international class audax hotel! Surely it would stand for at least one more night before crumbling into the sea some fifty metres below? I decided to put it to the test and unrolled the bivi bag and fell asleep to the rhythmic and soothing sound of gentle waves, hoping they'd not erode the cliff too much further that night.

143 km today / 13,219 km since London

Wednesday 23rd July

After my standard issue bowl of muesli I was back on Highway 1, the Shoreline Highway, a stupendously rugged and scenic coast-hugging corniche. Today's ride included 2,200m of undulation in variable weather conditions – scorching when the sun was out but distinctly nippy when it wasn't. At Sea Ranch I pulled into a luxury hotel for a breakfast burrito, pleasantly surprised that neither staff nor immaculately turned-out diners

 raised any objection to my scruffy and probably smelly presence in their midst.

At nightfall I reached Fort Bragg, where I found a small shack doing a brilliant brisket with chilli beans and a local beer from the North Coast Brewing Company: *Old Rasputin Russian Imperial Stout.*

According to one enthusiast: "That first sip is pure stout heaven. It's just a flavor explosion... This beer is big. This beer is bold. This beer is what all beer should aspire to be..." And at 9% ABV it proved to be a useful sleeping draught once I'd found the perfect spot to doss down under the awning of the local vet's.

166 km today / 13,385 km since London

Thursday 24th July

A beaut of a ride today after another early start at 06:15; up hill and down dale in remote country with astonishing clifftop and coastal views aplenty throughout the morning shift to Rockport, where I stopped for provisions. The village store was bountifully stocked with ripe and attractive fresh fruit and I came out with quite an armful…but where to store it? It would likely get squashed into a squishy mess in the seat bag or a pannier. I ate a peach and pondered the problem, and the solution leapt out at me – there was in fact hanging off my bike an item of equipment, redundant since NZ, which would make the perfect fruit bowl – Jonathan's bike helmet!

After Rockport the highway turned inland and sharply upwards for some 25 kms through thick redwood forest to Leggett at the end of the Shoreline Highway, where I arrived at 13:00 having covered just 70 kms. Here the locals have combined the great American passion for automobiles with an almost patriotic pride of their giant sequoias to create a drive-thru tree. Drivers flock from miles around to this remote spot in the forest to join a queue which gradually inches towards this famous attraction. They drive through it in a variety of vast vehicles, some bearing greater resemblance to small tanks than family cars, each stopping to pose for photos as they emerge back into daylight. I joined the queue and the fun and pedalled slowly through the tree to a great round of applause from

others standing around celebrating their safe passage with burgers, chips, cokes and beers.

I then set off on the celebrated Route 101, the Redwood Highway, which soon became a multi-lane freeway. Traffic levels were a little higher than on the quiet coastal route but still tolerable, and although it remained hilly the gradients were gentler – a welcome relief as the sun was fierce and the wind against me. I plodded along at an energy-conserving pace, stopping frequently to eat, drink and rest in the shade of the giant redwoods, eventually making my 150 km target by 21:00 just as it was getting dark. A bridge over the highway offered an irresistible secluded and sheltered camping spot just at the right time. Once again, the day's climbing had exceeded 2,000m, and I was pooped.

150 km today / 13,535 km since London

Friday 25th July

Today's climbs were gentler, and the day was spent mostly on Freeway 101 with occasional scenic detours. At my second breakfast stop in Rio Dell I met an English couple, Badge and Claire, cycling from Alaska to Argentina[24] – roughly the same distance I was riding around the world. Very sensibly they'd put a year aside for their trip and limited their daily distances to around 100 km. We were crossing paths as I headed north and

[24] https://bearsbanditsandbugs.wordpress.com/

they south, so I took the opportunity to find out a little about cycling in Canada. So far they'd experienced bears, moose, grumpy grouse and an earthquake, so I had plenty of excitement to look forward to!

I kept a food diary today – this was fairly typical:

- 05:30 two bowls of muesli with a pint of milk, banana and peach at roadside campsite under freeway bridge;
- 08:30 *huevos rancheros* and coffee in café at Rio Dell with Badge and Claire;
- 12:00 bread, cheese, ham, tomatoes, couscous salad, banana, outside supermarket in Eureka;
- 14:00 banana bread and coffee in Arcata at a fast food place (reliable for clean toilets and free wifi);
- 19:00 mug of chilli con carne and half loaf wholemeal with pint chocolate milk at general store in Orica;
- Snacks on the go: nuts and raisins, dry and fresh fruit, chocolate and muesli bars, 1kg of bananas…

I'm not sure how many calories this all added up to but my trousers were still loose!

At nightfall I found a lovely, dead quiet camp spot in the giant redwood forest just off the final scenic detour from the main highway.

163 km today / 13,697 km since London

Saturday 26th July

Today's ride started early and cold with a fast 10 km downhill blast which chilled me to the bone, so when I arrived in the small town of Klamath at 07:00 I was keen to find a warm refuge and breakfast. Result! Just off the highway was the Log Cabin Diner. But as I drew up outside my hopes were dashed – it wasn't due to open until 08:00. I peered in at the window and was rewarded with the encouraging sight of a chef chopping mushrooms. He spotted me and came to the door. Could I possibly come into the warm and wait an hour till the official opening time, I tentatively asked. "I can do better than that fella" he replied cheerily, handing me the menu. "Come in, siddown, read that and tell me what you want. I'm not exactly busy yet am I?" I went for the big breakfast option – and what a breakfast! Quality and quantity combined in the form of three eggs, bacon, sausages and potatoes for the main course, followed by three pancakes with maple syrup, and a jug of coffee. By the time I'd ploughed through that lot the cabin was officially open, my belly was full to bursting, and the sun had risen to a point high enough in its daily trajectory to feel its warming rays. How quickly my fortunes could turn.

Back on the road again, I was sharing space with a variety of mainly holiday traffic, and more specifically, Harleys and RVs. The Harley-Davidson is an all-American motorbike roughly the size of a small European car, commonly piloted by a similarly proportioned, middle-aged, balding, leather-and-denim clad rider sporting earrings and tattoos. These beasts are gregarious by nature and tend to cruise the highways at moderate speeds in pods of up to six brethren. Their pirate-like appearance may frighten the uninitiated, but I soon realised that they are in fact soft and cuddly like teddy bears – at least those I met were. Meanwhile, RV is the shorthand for Recreational Vehicle – in Britain we call them motor-homes. At roughly the size of a small European hotel, they are also known as Land Yachts. Despite the enormity of these pantechnicons, they were also being driven placidly, waiting for safe places to overtake and giving me a generously wide berth and often a cheery wave as they did so. Today I decided I'd like to meet some of these fellow travellers on the highway.

And so, as I rolled into Crescent City, I stopped beside an RV parked on the shoulder, and introduced myself to its super-friendly owners, Charles and Marie Fairbanks on vacation from Santa Barbara, who professed to being absolutely delighted to meet me. Theirs was not so much motor home as motor palace. They welcomed me inside and conducted a guided tour through the kitchen area, the lounge/diner, the bathroom and the double bedroom with fitted wardrobes at the back. As long as a luxury coach, Charles explained an obvious downside: once parked up at the campsite, it was rather cumbersome for nipping into town to do the daily shopping; hence the family-sized 4x4 in tow. I had spotted other RVs similarly trailing 4x4s behind them and wondered why – now I knew. Some towed trailers almost as long as the RVs themselves, reminiscent of Australian road trains. Marie explained that these were likely to be full of "holiday toys" such as motorbikes, jet-skis, speedboats, dune-buggies, micro-light aircraft...

At midday I crossed the state border from California into Oregon, and a little further up the highway I met Jim, Cindy, Margaret and Richard who were parked up and resting briefly at the side of the road with their two Harleys. They were on a day ride from their hometown of Coos Bay down to Brookings and back, a two hundred-mile round trip. They proudly led me on a guided tour of their magnificent monster-bikes, gleaming with acres of polished chrome and sporting intricate artwork on the petrol tanks. They demonstrated how rider and pillion perch regally astride these marvellous machines not on mere saddles, oh no – they are practically enthroned. With their feet either on running-boards or way out front on shiny footpegs, these are veritable laid-back Kings of the Road – just like me! When they found out I'd be riding through Coos Bay the following day I was instantly invited to join them for lunch, so we swapped phone numbers, arranged a rendezvous and went our separate ways.

Also on the road, but in rather fewer numbers, were some fellow cyclists. Without exception all were travelling south – I was alone riding north. Clearly they'd done their homework – the prevailing and lively breeze is a northerly and they probably thought I was bonkers trying to ride against it. I was fervently hoping that once I got up to Vancouver and turned east there'd be a better chance of tail winds across Canada…

At Gold Beach I ordered the biggest pizza on the menu, 16-inches across, with local Pistol River Pale Ale to wash it down. Both were excellent but the pizza proved too vast to eat at one sitting so they boxed up half of it for me to take away. Pedalling out of town I found a handy supermarket to re-stock breakfast supplies of milk, fruit and muesli. After a final ten kms I found a splendid wild camping spot in the woods just a few yards from the roadside, with the added bonus of a luxuriously soft mossy floor.

143 km today / 13,840 km since London

Sunday 27th July

It was another day of hills and headwind on Highway 101, though nothing too extreme. The road meandered inland a little into the forest from time to time providing welcome respite from the breeze. At Port Orford I scored a fabulous breakfast at Tasty Kate's Bakery and Café – scrambled eggs with lots of fresh colourful veggies, sautéed potatoes and a muffin, then toast and coffee. American portion sizes are perfect for people with active lifestyles, but judging by the ample girths of fellow diners I was in the minority on that score.

A little further up the highway I passed a sign: "DON'T LITTER. MAX FINE $6,250" Wow, they are seriously keen on keeping their highway clean! And indeed the verge was spotless. A few kms later though, another sign read: "HAND-HELD CELLPHONE USE PROHIBITED WHILE DRIVING. MAX. FINE $500". Not quite so exercised about road safety then. As if to emphasize the imbalance, I soon passed an elaborate shrine on the verge, and a poignant road sign: "PLEASE DON'T DRINK AND DRIVE. IN MEMORY OF CAROL NORMAN".

I ate my left over cold pizza for lunch in Brandon, which sounds rather sad but in fact made a lovely roadside picnic in glorious sunshine, and pressed on to my 16:00 rendezvous with my new motorbike pals Jim and Cindy in their home town of Coos Bay, where they took me out for dinner…to a pizzeria! We spent a happy hour supping beer and munching on pizzas and pasta while I regaled them with selected highlights of my trip and they described their all-American lives: they both work at the state penitentiary where he teaches electrics in the rehabilitation programme and she is a nurse with responsibility for HIV and hepatitis educational work. They have a large crop of grandchildren and own a nine-acre ranch where they shoot elk and deer, which they load onto their pick-up truck to skin and butcher at home and fill up the freezers. In their spare time they go for a spin down 101 on the Harley – just the one for the time being though ultimately Cindy would like one of her own. They seemed like good, wholesome Gun-totin' God-fearin' Republican-votin' patriots of the land of the free and the home of the brave, so I carefully avoided any mention of religion and politics and we got along just fine.

At 18:00 I hit the road again for the final stint to finish at 20:30 and camp just off the roadside. I was getting a little ahead of my schedule to hit Vancouver on 1st August so decided I'd do a shorter day tomorrow and stop earlier in a motel to get my first shower and kit change since leaving San Francisco a week ago. That would be a well-earned treat to look forward to!

152 km today / 13,992 km since London

Monday 28th July

More headwind and hills and, today, patchy fog. Scenery continued to nudge the outstanding end of the scale – this is one helluva picturesque highway, prompting frequent stops for photos. Warm sunny intervals alternated with cold fog all day, necessitating frequent adjustments to apparel. In Yachats I had a bowl of clam chowder, a delicious local speciality, then moved on to Newport and pulled in at the Money Saver Motel at 17:00 for a 1,000 km service. That was the distance I'd covered since San Francisco, justifying to my mind a shower, shave and kit wash.

I emerged a couple of hours later a new man and walked down to the main street on the harbour for an American-sized dinner of beef ribs with a couple of excellent beers from the local Rogue Brewery.

124 km today / 14,117 km since London

Tuesday 29th July

There was a microwave in the motel room so I heated the final remains of that monster pizza for breakfast and crossed the road to get a coffee from a small drive-thru booth. Back on the road at 06:45, there was more of yesterday's alternating sun and fog, but fewer stunning views to stop for, so I made faster progress towards Canada.

Riding out of Lincoln City after a magnificent second breakfast of Eggs Benedict with sautéed mushrooms at MacaDangDangs Café, a wobbly rear end signified a flat tyre. Over half way round the world now, this was just the second puncture since London. I stopped to fix it outside a church after asking permission from some elderly ladies inside who appeared to be running a happy-clappy holiday event for local children. Knowing America's reputation for religious fervour, I was mildly disappointed that they did not appear outside to bless my bicycle.

Shortly after a picnic lunch in Cloverdale I encountered some relatively mild road rage, my first experience of this in the USA. It was mild in the sense that it was merely verbal, not physical. I'd been taking the lane through a narrow bit of highway and had delayed following traffic (three cars) by perhaps up to ten seconds. A passenger leaned out of one of the cars as it sped past impatiently: "Get off the road asshole!" With long-practised restraint I replied with a cheery wave as the driver floored the accelerator and shot up the road with tyres smoking and screeching. I find it much more satisfying if I can keep my cool in these situations and react without rising to the bait or stooping to the level of the aggressor. Such aggressive displays of driving were however very much the exception to the rule; generally drivers were much better than back at home – more patient, careful and courteous and apparently in no desperate hurry to get to their destination. Many of them were obviously on holiday – perhaps driving Highway 101 *was* their holiday.

And yet the USA's per capita road death toll in recent years has been around three times worse than ours with over 30,000 slaughtered by motor every year, an appalling record but one which varies enormously from state to state. Over on the west coast, I was fortunate to be riding in some of the relatively safer states of California, Oregon and Washington, and it occurred to me that they tend to vote Democrat here. Could there be a pattern? Could it be that Democrats are safer drivers? I made a note to look into it when I got home, and it turns out there is an almost perfect correlation:

State	Deaths per 100 million vehicle miles travelled, 2014 [25]	US presidential election 2012 [26]
Massachusetts	0.57	Democrat
Vermont	0.62	Democrat
Minnesota	0.63	Democrat
District of Columbia	0.65	Democrat
Rhode Island	0.68	Democrat
New Hampshire	0.73	Democrat
New Jersey	0.74	Democrat
Maryland	0.78	Democrat
New York	0.80	Democrat
Washington	0.80	Democrat
Connecticut	0.80	Democrat
Wisconsin	0.84	Democrat
Virginia	0.87	Democrat
Illinois	0.88	Democrat
Ohio	0.89	Democrat
California	0.92	Democrat
Maine	0.92	Democrat
Hawaii	0.93	Democrat
Utah	0.93	Republican
Michigan	0.93	Democrat
Indiana	0.94	Republican
Colorado	1.00	Democrat
Iowa	1.02	Democrat
Oregon	1.03	Democrat
Georgia	1.04	Republican
Missouri	1.08	Republican
Nevada	1.15	Democrat
Idaho	1.15	Republican
Nebraska	1.15	Republican
North Carolina	1.19	Republican
Pennsylvania	1.20	Democrat
Arizona	1.23	Republican
Florida	1.24	Democrat

---

[25] http://tinyurl.com/os3h87j
[26] http://tinyurl.com/dl9s5g

Kansas	1.25	Republican
Alabama	1.25	Republican
Delaware	1.26	Democrat
North Dakota	1.28	Republican
Tennessee	1.33	Republican
Arkansas	1.37	Republican
Kentucky	1.40	Republican
Oklahoma	1.40	Republican
West Virginia	1.42	Republican
Texas	1.46	Republican
South Dakota	1.47	Republican
Alaska	1.50	Republican
New Mexico	1.51	Democrat
Louisiana	1.53	Republican
Mississippi	1.54	Republican
Montana	1.58	Republican
Wyoming	1.59	Republican
South Carolina	1.65	Republican

A little further up the coast I rolled into Bay City, which didn't really live up to its grand name: it's just a small village, population 1,293 (2013). Nonetheless I couldn't resist firing up the MP3 player to listen to that fine 70s Scottish band bashing out *Shang-a-Lang* and *Bye Bye Baby*. I've since learned that the "tartan teen sensations from Edinburgh" took their name by throwing a dart at a map of the USA and it hitting the rather larger Bay City in Michigan[27].

I stopped in Garibaldi for steak and beer then rode on to camp by the riverside just after Wheeler.

151 km today / 14,267 km since London

Wednesday 30th July

It was an early and brutal start at 06:10, straight into 600 metres of climbing in 34 kms, but amply rewarded by a great breakfast of meatloaf, eggs, hash browns, toast and coffee near the town of Seaside. Thence onward to Astoria on the Columbia River where I popped into the supermarket for milk and bread…and stumbled across the gun counter, just next to dairy produce – only in America! Fascinated, I struck up conversation with the

---

[27] http://en.wikipedia.org/wiki/Bay_City_Rollers

girl at the counter, Adria, who proudly showed me some of the guns in sizes and colours to suit everyone – for example this nice little pink number just for the ladies. Mind-boggling! I'd seen gun shops in several towns but hadn't expected to be able to pick one up quite so casually in a supermarket along with the groceries. I asked one or two basic questions about the provenance of the weapons, background checks, and could I buy one here and now if I wanted? Apologetically she replied that she didn't know very much about them because she was filling in temporarily for an absent colleague and usually worked at the fruit and veg counter. But she proudly informed me that Oregon is much better for buying guns, because background checks are much faster – just a day or two – than say California, where they can take up to a week. She seemed to intimate that that was deeply unconstitutional.

How about this pink one for the wife, Sir?

Astoria was the final town in Oregon, and it was a spectacular and somewhat unnerving exit, rising up to around 60 metres above the estuary of the Columbia River to cross the 6.5 km bridge into Washington State. It's a striking and mighty cantilevered feat of engineering built of intricate latticed steel, but rather narrow and exposed to a fresh sea breeze coming in off the Pacific which buffeted me hither and thither as trucks squeezed past in both directions. I was relieved to complete the crossing without incident, and stopped to recompose myself and eat lunch at a picnic site with a view back over the bridge.

A petite, sprightly and smartly dressed elderly lady approached, introduced herself as Sandy, and announced that she'd recently retired from the US Postal Service: "I'm good at retirement, shouldadunnit long ago" she said and told me how she now spends her days cruising up and down the highway meeting people at the picnic spots. She asked where I was going so I gave her my card and said I was heading to Vancouver, then across Canada and down to New York City, then I'd fly to Lisbon and ride back up to London (about 8,000 kms). There was little reaction. Where had I come from? Well, from London, the long way round via Asia and Australasia (about 15,000 kms). No response, blank expression. But how had I got right here? Well I'd ridden up from San Francisco (1,300 kms). She was open-mouthed in disbelief: "You cycled here from 'Frisco on that bike? Are you crazy?" She couldn't get over that!

A little further down the road I met Zach, a student cycling to Mexico. I warned him not to mention it if he met Sandy – she'd surely have a heart attack. He was carrying less luggage than some people I know take on a day ride. I felt a little patriotic surge of pride when I noticed that his smart and new-looking American-made Surly *Long Haul Trucker* bicycle was equipped with a British-made Brooks leather saddle.

On to South Bend which proclaimed itself to be the "oyster capital of the world", but sadly nothing was open, so on a little further to Raymond. The only place open to eat at was a fast food burger house on a big shopping estate with plenty of convenient nooks for rough sleepers, so I settled in for burgers and wifi till dark then got myself tucked up under an awning behind the hypermarket.

149 km today / 14,416 km since London

Thursday 31ˢᵗ July

I returned to the burger bar for breakfast at 05:30 and was away by 06:15. An easier day followed with fewer hills and less wind as Highway 101 led me eastwards, inland and past an RV park with a big sign outside: HEATED STORAGE UNITS. Oh my Lord, I'd seen it all now. Heated storage units for your RV motor palace – driving or parked, you can keep pumping out that CO_2 all year round!

At Elma I needed cash, so pedalled into the drive-thru cash-point, as one does in America, and met the rather corpulent James in his car, in the queue. The conversation went something like this:

Me: "So you don't have to get out of your car anymore?"

James: "Hell no! I can't believe you got no drive-thrus in Yerp! Why, you can drive-thru get married in Vegas!"

It was second breakfast time. The *Flippin' 50s Diner* fitted the bill admirably: a fantastic retro place with shiny red leatherette benches, old Chevy posters and hub caps bedecking the walls, and a life-size cardboard Elvis by the drum kit on the stage. The big ladies cooked me a mean Eggs Benedict while the Big Bopper pumped out of the speakers. Shame I hadn't arrived a couple of days later for a promising bill of Saturday Night Fever...rock on!

I soon stopped again, in Kamilche, for a picnic and some shopping and to take shade from the fierce heat, now nudging 35°C. Tommy pulled in on his laden touring bike, riding from San Diego to Seattle and back, some

4,000 km. He professed to be enjoying the heat, looked about 20 years old, and sported a baggy cotton t-shirt, football shorts and sneakers. Not a thread of lycra to be seen. I'd met a few American cycle tourists by now and they were all riding huge trans-continental distances – I guess that's the American way. We enjoyed a cold drink together and swapped a couple of route tips. I rode on another few kms but at 16:00 it was still uncomfortably hot so I pulled in under a bridge for a short siesta. At 16:30 the phone roused me from my slumbers – it was brother Antony bearing welcome titbits of news from the home front. The marvel of modern technology meant I rarely felt far from home.

My week on Highway 101, and my time in the USA for the time being, were coming to an end. 101 had been a spectacular roller-coaster of a ride, so much so that (sadly I now realise) it inspired me to twitter poetry. On re-reading these few lines I'm not sure they really do it justice:

Gettin' my kicks Havin' some fun
Writin' the lyrics Highway 101
It's bin a lot a fun, Highway 101
I'm nearly done on 101
Caught some sun on 101
Could'a bought a gun on 101
Sure had some fun
Dadoorunrun
US Highway 101

Antony's comment: "Don't give up the day job mate."

At 17:00 it was still hot but I was keen to get another 40 kms under my wheels, leaving an easy 120 kms for tomorrow to Port Angeles for the ferry to Canada. Further roadside snacks followed, and a burger in Hoodsport, before finding a nice quiet camp spot in the woods.

140 km today / 14,556 km since London

Friday 1st August

August already! Only two months left to finish this thing and still one and a half continents to go! It was an easy-going 125 kms to Port Angeles at the top of the Olympic peninsula, where I arrived by 16:00, with just one stop en route for a fabulous oyster, bacon and cheese omelette at the Halfway House in Brinnon. Enough fuel in that to get me to Canada.

MV Coho was an ancient and venerable vessel, named after the local silver salmon and built in 1959 – two years older than me! I rolled aboard for the 17:20 sailing to Victoria on Vancouver Island, British Columbia, and parked the Bacchetta on the foredeck where a bike rack made me feel welcome. Inside a cafeteria was doing a roaring trade serving fish, chips and beer. It was a smooth crossing and after 90 minutes we arrived at the quayside in Victoria where colonial colonnades basked resplendent in glorious golden evening sunshine. I disembarked and threaded my way through throngs of tourists to a cash-point for some Canadian dollars, then pottered northwards out of town on Highway 17 towards Sidney, from where I would take a morning ferry to Saltspring Island to avoid the more direct but busier multi-lane Highway 1, and to dodge a big climb.

I found a secluded copse to camp in just off the highway in the northern reaches of Victoria.

137 km today / 14,692 km since London

Saturday 2nd August

A bright sunny day of island-hopping began with a 20 km ride to Sidney and on to Swartz Bay for the 08:30 short ferry crossing to Saltspring Island, where I breakfasted in a café with the most idyllic views over Fulford Harbour and the pristine, sparkling estuary we'd just sailed into. Refuelling complete, I found some quiet lanes for ten or so hilly kilometres before joining the busy main road into the island's main town of Ganges, sadly choked up with crawling bumper-to-bumper traffic. Just ten kms further and I'd covered the length of Saltspring – why do they need so many cars on such a tiny island? From Vesuvius Bay it was another short ferry hop to Crofton, back on Vancouver Island, where I found a decent pub serving fine beers and soups. After that I was able to avoid Highway 1 for a further 20 kms of peaceful lanes before mixing in with heavy traffic for the final hour to Nanaimo and the final ferry of the day over to Gabriola Island, where I arrived at 16:00 – beer time! Fortunately there was a handy pub just a few yards up the road from the jetty.

Then it was a lumpy 6 kms to Terry and Becky's place up on the north coast, where I received the warmest of family welcomes, Terry being a cousin several times removed. They'd been following my progress via Twitter since London and had prepared a veritable feast for my arrival, the centrepiece of which was a whole local sockeye salmon. Two other cousins arrived to join the party: Lynne with her nationally famous folk-singer husband Gary Fjellgaard; and Art with his wife Judy and their friend Marie. The three cousins are all descendants of my great-great-grandmother who'd emigrated to Canada in the early years of the 20th century. I'd met them briefly in London many years previously, but this was the first time we'd properly spent time together. And what a wonderful evening it turned out to be, reminiscing almost as if we'd grown up together rather than continents apart. After the local salmon and prawns, a huge variety of salads appeared, followed by rhubarb pie and ice cream. We sat out on the patio until nearly midnight supping beer and wine, swapping family tales and attempting to establish just exactly how we were all related to each other, a most amusing mental challenge lubricated, if not entirely facilitated, by the copious supply of alcohol available.

My arrival could not have been better timed – Gary was expecting 120 fans to pour into his garden for an open-air folk concert the following day.

94 km today / 14,786 km since London

Sunday 3rd August

A fabulous, lazy day started with a luxurious lie-in till 08:00 followed by a large healthy fruity breakfast with Terry and Becky. Then over coffee I pored over my maps planning a 33-day ride schedule to arrive in New York City on 8th September. It looked like around 5,000 km on the route I'd chosen via Winnipeg and Niagara, so around 150 km/day – should be doable...with a fair wind. I wrote the dates across the map at 150 km intervals starting on 5th August from Vancouver through to 8th September in New York. Job done. Then we took the dogs for a walk down to the beach, had a swim and worked up a powerful thirst. As luck would have it, Becky knew of the perfect beachside bar serving beer and sandwiches.

Then it was time to head over to Gary and Lynne's place for the garden concert. Around 120 guests sat in deckchairs (I think they brought their own) and listened to Gary and two friends strumming their guitars and crooning old cowboy songs for a couple of wonderful warm hours in the afternoon sunshine. During the interval there was a touching moment when Gary invited Lynne up to the front to present her with a pair of earrings for their 58th wedding anniversary. I enjoyed the thigh-slapping music so much that I even bought the CD – well I tried, but Lynne wouldn't accept payment. Find Gary Fjellgaard[28] on YouTube and see what you think!

This idyllic day drew to a close with a dinner of local beers and leftovers from yesterday's feast followed by another walk with the dogs down to the beach, where we watched the sunset over Vancouver Island. If I ever wind up in Paradise, I hope it's like Gabriola!

0 km today / 14,786 km since London

---

[28] http://www.fjellgaard.bc.ca/

Monday 4th August

Georgi Georgiev is a sprightly 72 year-old Bulgarian bike inventor and builder who lives just round the corner from Terry and Becky. It would have been downright discourteous not to pay him a visit, so after breakfast I popped in. He's a well-known character on the island and revered to some extent within the tight-knit human-powered vehicle (HPV) community. HPVs are mostly laid-back bikes and trikes, but unlike mine, built for speed rather than touring. Some HPVs can be very fast indeed. In 2009 Georgi's *Varna Tempest* (named after his home town of Varna in Bulgaria) was ridden by his next-door neighbour Sam Whittingham to a new world speed of 82.8 mph[29] (this record subsequently broken in 2013 by 0.3 mph). I spent about 40 minutes with Georgi who, after inspecting the Bacchetta, delighted in providing a guided tour of his workshop and the wide variety of bikes he has produced over the years, including a step-through electric-assisted trike which he rode into town with me for coffee and cakes and a further hour swapping bikey stories.

I spent the rest of the day touring the island on my naked bike – much nimbler without the heavy panniers – stopping en route to swim in the idyllic Drumbeg Bay and for a *Salade Niçoise* and beer at Silva Bay.

Then it was back home to change, shower and pack for the morrow before heading out to Silva Bay again for a slap-up alfresco dinner with Terry, Becky, Lynne and Gary, who reduced us and diners at neighbouring tables to hysterics firstly trying to sort out a stubborn parasol, and then complaining about the small size of his fish portion (having ordered small), which he managed with such charm and aplomb that he scored a second helping…which ended up being a bit too much so I ate it for him. I urged him to write a song about this episode.

At sundown I went kayaking in the bay with Becky. We watched the sun set and the moon rise over the flat calm sea, a veritable millpond, in total silence – utterly sublime. Farewell beers were supped over family photo albums before retiring to bed and setting the alarm for a pre-dawn start.

41 km today / 14,827 km since London

---

[29] http://www.varnahandcycles.com/records.htm
http://www.ihpva.org/hpvarec3.htm#nom01

Tuesday 5ᵗʰ August

I was up at 04:45 for a quick snack and final kit packing before riding down to board the 06:30 ferry back to Nanaimo on Vancouver Island, then a short spin across town to a bigger ferry terminal for the 07:45 crossing to Horseshoe Bay on the mainland. This was a bright, sunny and spectacular cruise across the Strait of Georgia with fine views in all directions, and a

huge cooked breakfast in the ferry's cafeteria.

At Horseshoe Bay, effectively a suburb of North Vancouver, I met up with fellow low-life Bruce Gordon, also riding a Bacchetta funny bike. He has pedigree, having completed a 153-day global circumnavigation in 2011. I'd enjoyed following his progress through his blog and twitter feed at the time, and had made contact with him for various useful tips. He lived just up the coast from Horseshoe Bay and had accepted my invitation to ride with me on the first day of my trans-Canada ride, "shooting for Hope" (his words) which is a town at the foot of the Rockies.

Once we had escaped the dreary hinterland of Greater Vancouver, which sprawls for some 50 kms or so, it was an excellent fast day's ride in hot sunshine. We climbed around 1,300 metres, fairly gently: these were mere foothills – the serious climbing would start the following day. We feasted on a huge pasta lunch in Coquitlam then continued riding up Highway 7 by the Fraser River, enjoying a number of wildlife sightings including a black bear cub at the riverside and the awesome spectacle of an osprey hooking a fish in its talons and returning to its nest atop a pole in the river to feed its chick.

We made good time to Hope, where we checked into a motel at around 20:30. After a quick change into civvies we crossed the road for beers, clam chowder and a huge stir fry dinner, followed by a cooling dip in the motel pool before hitting the sack early in anticipation of the much harder day to follow.

180 km today / 15,007 km since London

Wednesday 6th August

Bruce is a busy man, running a roofing company, and regretfully couldn't take more than two days out of work. So after breakfast we set off in opposite directions – Bruce back towards Vancouver while I continued east, now on Highway 3, also known as the Crowsnest Highway. My entrance into the Rockies proper came just 3 kms after leaving Hope, and was sudden and brutal: a 5½-hour 60 km crawl up to the 1,500m Allison Pass. To follow, as the temperature rose to peak at 36°C, the road rolled up and down over a couple more high passes before plunging into a long fast descent to Princeton, where I arrived ravenous at 18:00 and found a Greek restaurant for a huge and delicious lamb dinner with beer.

After dinner I stocked up with provisions before riding out of town a further 20 kms to meet my daily 150 target. It felt good to be pointed east and homeward, getting closer now with every turn of the pedals. I made camp early at 20:15 in some long grass with the highway to one side and a sheer cliff to the other…hopefully safe from any wandering hungry bears.

153 km today / 15,160 km since London

Thursday 7th August

I was back on the road at 06:30 after a bowl of muesli, and enjoyed a second breakfast in the gold mining town of Hedley. Then there was a lovely gentle downhill run with a tailwind for most of the morning into Osoyoos, where I got a fast food lunch and took a dip in the lake to cool

off – it was 32°C in the shade. A monster climb was to follow so I found some shade under a tree for an hour's snooze before tackling the ascent to the Anarchist Pass.

I set off too early up this beast though; it was still scorching hot in the full sun (Garmin registered 44°C) as I twiddled up the early switchbacks in the low gears, pausing briefly each time a solitary tree offered respite from the furnace. During one of these intervals I met Paul Haizlip; clad in the scantiest of briefs and nothing else but running shoes and mirror shades, he was *running*

down from the summit, having run up there in the midday sun. Spiky bleached hair, a finely sculpted six-pack and various body piercings completed the picture. I couldn't help expressing a forthright and robust opinion on his sanity. He looked at the bike and me and returned the compliment, and we spent ten happy minutes together swapping stories and establishing our bonkers credentials. As for the heat, he was better acclimatized than me; he comes up to Canada for his summer holidays to cool down – he's from Arizona.

It took a further four hours, including a picnic stop, to reach the Anarchist Pass itself (1,233m) at 20:30 followed by a fast 20 kms down into Rock Creek, where I camped in woods behind the gas station.

151 km today / 15,312 km since London

Friday 8th August

I woke up to an overcast sky, which brought welcome relief from the heat, and the going was gently rolling to a relaxed coffee stop in Greenwood. It continued in similar vein to lunch in Grand Forks where, after several attempts, I got through to Pascale by phone for her birthday – phew! By then the clouds had dispersed and, inevitably, it was hot again for the day's main event – a 30 km slog up the 1,535m Paulson Pass, half-way up which I met Geordie cyclists Chris and Andy. They were riding from Newfoundland to Vancouver, and amazingly this was their first ever long bike tour, having flown into St John's and bought a couple of flat-bar utility bikes there. They were wearing cotton tee-shirts, baggy shorts and minimal bike specific clothing, but they were about 90% across the vast continent and still going strong.

I crested the Paulson Pass at 20:30 by which time darkness was descending, so 10 kms further on I turned off the highway into an official campsite by a lake and unrolled my bivi bag on a picnic table under a bright full moon.

144 km today / 15,456 km since London

Saturday 9th August

The mercury plummeted to 2°C overnight, making for a bone-chilling 27 km descent in little over half an hour into Castlegar, where I thawed out slowly over an excellent cooked breakfast and had a navigational decision to make: continue east on Highway 3 directly towards Creston, or take a longer northerly detour on 3A round Kootenay Lake to avoid two monster climbs. It wasn't a taxing choice – I'd done a good bit of high altitude work recently, so a flat day by the lake would make a change and sounded appealing.

And so the rest of the day was an easy going, gently rolling and utterly uplifting ride beside the Kootenay Lake and river. In Nelson I met Rob riding a recumbent trike on doctor's orders following a serious crash on his road bike, which had left him with a degree of back pain, and I felt a surge of patriotic pride when I spotted that his mount was a British-made ICE trike, built by Inspired Cycle Engineering in Cornwall.

At Balfour I took the longest free ferry ride in world, some 35 minutes across Lake Kootenay to Kootenay Bay, a service operated and funded by the BC Ministry of Transportation because it's more cost-effective than building and maintaining a road round the lake. I almost caused an international incident at disembarkation. As the only cyclist aboard I had filtered up to the front of the queue of RVs, trucks and Harleys and as the gate opened I began to roll but the ferryman held up a palm and told me to wait "until all the traffic is off…health and safety". How ironic! My heckles rose: "I AM TRAFFIC! Not safe to share this wide ramp? Don't be so bloody ridiculous! I have to share narrower roads with motors passing with inches to spare at far higher speeds – roads also operated and funded by the BC Ministry of Transportation" is what I wanted to shout at him. But in a moment of supreme self-control, I bit my tongue.

From Kootenay Bay I pootled southwards on a quiet 3A hugging the eastern shore of the lake. Traffic was scarce, the sun was warm, the views magnificent – these few essential elements combined to produce a perfect cycling moment, a sublime ride never to be forgotten. Indeed today's ride was so glorious that, sadly for you dear reader, it inspired me to poetry, and I made numerous stops to jot down the opening lines of what would eventually become my *Ode to Highway 3* – something for you to look forward to in the next few pages!

Shortly after passing a sign bearing the warning CONGESTED AREA (single cars were passing me every few minutes) I unrolled my bed in woods beside the lake.

168 km today / 15,624 km since London

Sunday 10th August

After a day like yesterday, anything was likely to be bland by comparison. And so it turned out – a pleasant ride but lacking jaw-dropping views at every turn, saving significant time on camera stops and enabling a record-breaking four breakfasts: one in the bivi bag before breaking camp, followed by stops in three cafés all of which were just simply too inviting to pass without stopping. The best of these was in Creston, where I rejoined Highway 3 and met local cyclist Neil, who recommended a great café, *A Break in Time*. Neil had been through the wars – a cancer survivor with a paralysed left arm. But he was still riding his bike with great verve and was full of good route and café advice – cyclists around the world always know where to find the best tea and cakes in their neck of the woods.

Shortly after a picnic lunch of tinned smoked clams and tomatoes I rode into mountain time zone and the GPS put itself forward another hour. Crossing time zone boundaries always felt significant – one hour closer to home and another 1/24th of the way round the planet. The mountains would end soon and I'd be down on the long flat prairie; the going would hopefully get easier, but would undoubtedly be less spectacular.

The temperature rose to a skin-scorching 40°C today, necessitating a couple of ice cream stops and an exquisitely soothing dip in an ice-cold stream in all my kit which, once back on the bike, provided about ten minutes of blissful air-conditioning before it all dried out again.

Numerous further stops ensued to jot down new stanzas for my *Ode to Highway 3* as they popped into my head, and there was a final halt for a giant pasta dinner in Cranbrook. 25 kms further down the road I pulled off the highway at 21:00 to set up camp in the lee of an electric substation.

155 km today / 15,778 km since London

Monday 11ᵗʰ August

Today was mostly spent climbing a gentle gradient up to the Crowsnest Pass (1,360m), a significant geographical feature, being the continental divide as well as marking the British Columbia/Alberta border. Rain falling to the west of the pass drains eventually into the Pacific Ocean, now some 600 km behind me as the crow flies, whereas precipitation on the eastern side flows 2,000-odd kms down into Hudson Bay. Strangely for a moment I felt on top of the world and that my ride should now be downhill all the way to New York City!

Other episodes today included my third puncture of the trip just after lunch in Fernie, caused by a 2cm thorn; another glorious mid-afternoon dip in an icy stream; and frequent stops to add verses to the lengthening Ode. After dinner and a spot of shopping in Sparwood I made camp in an industrial estate on the edge of small town Blairmore.

150 km today / 15,928 km since London

Tuesday 12ᵗʰ August

Today I emerged from the Rocky Mountains onto the Prairie. Awesome scenery gradually gave way to bland, and the first town I came to, Fort MacLeod, was a deathly quiet and nondescript grid of residential and light industrial development. The only open eatery to be found was a branch of the ubiquitous Tim Hortons fast food chain flogging tasteless burger pap. The scenic and culinary delights of British Columbia were already far behind me.

The morning's tailwind had turned when I began the afternoon shift – a 60 km push on a rolling road into the breeze, still at around 1,000m altitude, not quite onto the prairie proper just yet, where I'd been told I could expect tailwinds all the way across to Ontario.

At Lethbridge I sought a motel – I'd been riding mountains in a heatwave for a week since Vancouver so needed a thorough scrub-down. The cheapest room I could find in town was a hefty $79 but it did include breakfast and use of the computer room where, after a barbecue style dinner and a couple of pints of decent local stout, I did some electronic housekeeping, including backing up my photos and GPS files, and doubtless to the unbridled delight of friends and family following vicariously from afar, I updated my blog with my poetic scribblings of recent days:

Ode to Canada's Highway 3

Canada's Highway number 3
Yes siree, it's the 3 for me
Highway 3's the one I like
Cruisin' along on my bike
From the Pacific to the flat Prairie
Highway 3's the place to be

At dawn every day, back on the move
Mp3 pumping, I'm back in the groove
At dusk every day it's time to stop riding
Find a safe camp and go into hiding

Vancouver to Hope, rode with Bruce
Wind behind us, fast and loose
Highway 3, in the breeze
Up the Anarchist Pass it's a puff and a wheeze
Met crazy Paul running down – crazy way into town!

Highway 3, here we go
Up the hills I'm pretty slow
But once I'm on the other side
Hang on tight enjoy the ride

Who'd've known: Canada makes wine
Thousands of acres of grapes on the vine
Riding the Rockies, blimey it's hot!
Cycling these mountains takes all I've got

On the Paulson Pass met Chris 'n' Andy
Missing his wife, getting quite...hungry

At 20k an hour I see a lot more
Breath-taking scenery, wide-open jaw
Summits and lakes, torrents and streams
Roadside vendors selling fruit and ice-creams

At a hundred miles a day it's an eight-day ride
Over high passes and down the other side
20k an hour, enjoying the views
Detached from reality, missing the news

At noon if I can I jump in a stream
Rinse out my kit, get myself clean
At the end of the week I'll find a motel
Jump in the bathtub to soak out the smell

Maple syrup on my pancakes
Eggs and bacon, hash browns too
Sausage, ham, and tomato
Coffee please - and where's the loo?

Highway 3 for he who dares
Watch out for grizzly, black and brown bears
Highway 3, who dares wins
$2,000 for littering – use the bear-proof bins!

Half way up the mountain is the place that I stop
It's neither at the bottom nor at the top
Half way up the mountain is the place that I sit
There's no other place quite like it
[with apologies to A.A. Milne]

Highway 3, feel the heat
Crazy suntan on my feet
Wind's been kind I'm glad to say
When it blows it goes my way
Chevys and Harleys, RVs, the odd truck
Watch out for cyclists, please give a...fig

One-armed Neil, still awheel
Cracking jokes every line
Lives in Creston, hi-vis vest on
Even in the bright sunshine

For the eyes it's a feast
Going west or going east
For the cyclist it's a test
Going east or going west

Hope to Princeton and beyond
Of Highway 3 we're getting fond
Rock Creek, Greenwood, Castlegar
Highway 3's the best by far
Glad I'm not stuck in a car

Continental divide at the Crowsnest Pass
Downhill to New York from here?
You betcha sweet ass!
Out of the Rockies, onto the plains
Down on the Prairie, where it seldom rains

Gettin' my kicks, climbs not too steep
Route 66: watch and weep!
Also known as the Crowsnest
Highway 3. It's the best!

145 km today / 16,073 km since London

Wednesday 13ᵗʰ August

The motel did a good self-serve buffet breakfast so I ate everything I possibly could till I was stuffed, then filled my pockets with snacks for later and got out onto the flat road east over the prairie. Thus fuelled to the brim I rode for a non-stop stint of 84 kms to a roadside café in the small town of Grassy Lake, where I scored a stupendously good second breakfast served by some of the Mennonite Christians in traditional garb who have settled here in large numbers.

After some 4,000 kms of non-stop superlative scenery – the hills and mountains of New Zealand, the US pacific coast and the Canadian Rockies

– I was finally back on wide straight flat roads of the type last experienced across Australia some six weeks previously. Locals here say that it's so flat you can watch your dog run away for two days! I also had the benefit of a gentle tailwind so the miles flew by with moderate effort, though it was hot once again so I jumped into a handy canal in the early afternoon.

By 16:00 I'd covered 165 km and arrived in Medicine Hat – what a great name for a town that I'd last heard about in geography lessons at school – it's the English translation of the local word for the eagle tail feather headdress worn by traditional healers. I stopped for a burger and wifi and was joined by Doug, who announced that he is a regular cyclist on the Trans-Canadian Highway, which I was about to join (Medicine Hat marking the end of Highway 3). Doug's a friendly guy, lives just up the road (well 175 kms up the road) in Swift Current, and owns a Chinese restaurant to which he issued a free lunch invitation for tomorrow!

So I set off on the straight, flat, featureless four-lane Trans-Canadian Highway, a little doubtful that it was going to move me to any further poetry (a good thing as I wouldn't have to keep stopping to write new verses, and you won't have to read them). A continued tailwind blew me well past 200 km and pretty much up to the Saskatchewan border, where I found a handy camping spot just behind a tourist information place. Staff had handily left the wifi switched on, enabling me to log in and catch up with world news, emails and the twittersphere.

220 km today / 16,292 km since London

Thursday 14th August

I was up and away at 06:15 and was soon over the border into Saskatchewan, with the realisation that I was now into the last 50 days of the ride; just seven weeks to go to London! Normally a seven-week bike ride would look like a long ride; indeed I'd never done anything that long before. But in the current context, after 19 weeks on the road, seven more didn't seem very long and London was starting to feel pretty close. I unfolded the map for a reality check: there was still quite a long way to go – the ride wasn't over just yet.

It was another searing hot day on the prairie (average 30°C, peak 43°C) across the gently rolling Cypress Hills and into a moderate headwind – what a difference a day makes! The pretty and scenic tourist routes of British Columbia with eggs benedict aplenty were far behind me now, having given way to the vast interior provinces; a drier grittier working man's Canada featuring less wifi and more dust.

I stopped for a second breakfast at 1/21 (junction of Highways 1 and 21). There's a crossroads, a filling station and a small food store. And that's it. In the middle of nowhere, bereft of shade and semi-arid, I was effectively back in the desert.

A couple of hours later in the small village of Tompkins a local lady was serving burgers, hot dogs and perogies – deep fried dough balls – from a small shed just off the highway. She offered two varieties: with potato and cheese, or potato and bacon. Easy decision – both, with coke. Thence to the deserted local campsite where I took a cold shower and found a shady spot under a tree for forty winks.

Just 24 km further east I pulled into Gull Lake for another cold drink and a toastie. Today was proving to be hard work, and I emailed Doug not to expect me for lunch – hopefully I'd make it in time for dinner.

I finally made Swift Current by 19:30 and found Casey's Diner (Doug's restaurant) in the main street. He welcomed me in, found a safe haven for the bike, sat me down and brought me beer – nectar after a long, hard, hot day in the rolling deckchair. The restaurant was a self-service buffet – all I could eat for free. Doug sat with me and talked while I stuffed my face. He runs as well as cycles and does an iron distance triathlon every year, something I was thinking of doing one day, so we'd plenty to yap about. We exchanged marathon notes – his personal best is three hours and twenty seconds, so I got some kudos for my sub-three (by three seconds) at London in 2013, which never goes amiss! He was most apologetic about not being able to offer me a bed for the night at his house – he already had guests staying – but I'd be welcome to sleep on the deck under his flat on the other side of town. He walked me over there and put a rug out, I unrolled my sleeping bag and was asleep before my head hit the stuff-bag full of cycling kit that doubled as my pillow.

175 km today / 16,468 km since London

Friday 15th August

Another day into the wind and across rolling hills had me beginning to doubt numerous reassurances that the prairie would be pancake-flat with helpful tailwinds all the way across, forcing café and picnic stops for refuelling at 40, 80 and 120 kms. A great morale boosting moment came when Radio 4's poet in residence, Ian "Bard of Barnsley" McMillan, re-tweeted my *Ode to Highway 3* – that really made my day! I arrived in Moose Jaw at 19:30 and found a mediocre restaurant for soup, fish and beer before retiring to a sheltered spot behind a church to unroll the bivi bag and hopefully stay reasonably sheltered from the inclement weather that was forecast for the night.

175 km today / 16,643 km since London

Saturday 16th August

The night stayed dry but I woke up to overcast skies and a stiff easterly breeze, so it was a slow ride to Regina by 12:30, by which time the heavens were darkening and it was drizzling gently. I stopped for coffee and re-checked the forecast – a stormy afternoon and night looked in prospect, so I decided to abandon the ride, did some shopping and checked into a cheap motel.

As the weather deteriorated, a productive afternoon of bike tourist's chores followed: warmshowers hosts were booked up in Winnipeg, Thunder Bay and Sault Sainte Marie; European maps were marked up with target dates for the Lisbon-Bordeaux-London route; then a little bike checking and fettling; finally a long hot soak in the tub with dirty bike kit.

I dashed across the road between the raindrops to a Caribbean restaurant for an excellent beef curry with beer, concluding the day most satisfactorily.

77 km today / 16,719 km since London

Sunday 17th August

I made an early start at 06:15 under dark foreboding skies, back on the rather monotonous Trans-Canada Highway. However, the situation soon improved on both counts: the weather brightened and I turned off the TCH to the south onto Highway 48, a parallel but much smaller road carrying far less traffic. This road turned out to be a delight. A railway ran alongside and there were small villages every 13 kms because, I was told, that was the range of the early trains before they needed to stop to take on more coal and water.

Being a Sunday probably accounted for lower traffic levels, but it also meant that there were few shops and cafés open in the villages. At Odessa I peered into a closed shop and caught the eye of the kindly shopkeeper who came to the door and, upon hearing the plight of a weary and hungry traveller, opened up for me to buy my daily provisions. An hour or so later I arrived at Montmartre, "Paris of the Prairies", where locals have erected their own Eiffel Tower! Built of steel in 2009, and 8.5 metres tall, it's an exact replica of the original at 1/38th scale. "Every small town needs some sort of icon to be remembered by" according to its builder and local resident, Mr Englot.[30]

In the early evening I rolled into the village of Windthorst where Norm's Place was open and bustling. I joined dozens of locals to enjoy Norm's all-you-can-eat smorgasbord of salads with baked ham and lasagne. And beer – perfect! Thus fortified and replenished, I rode on to Kennedy by around 19:45 where I unrolled my bed on a picnic table in a large wooden spectator stand at the local rodeo ground, providing a useful sheltered camping spot as rain still threatened.

179 km today / 16,898 km since London

Monday 18th August

Rolling at 06:15 on Highway 48 after my daily muesli, early fog soon cleared and a helpful nor'-westerly pushed me through a series of small villages, none of which sported an open café until Maryfield at 10:00, by which time I'd covered 75 kms and was ravenous. I was directed to the Arlington Hotel, which served breakfast…from 11:00. But, there not being another soul around, the self-professed bored waitress was happy to open up early and cook me a gigantic top-notch full breakfast with coffee. Then she

---

[30] http://tinyurl.com/h9uzpjt

proudly set about displaying her extensive body-wide collection of tattoos and piercings …well, thankfully, not quite all of them. Most people in Saskatchewan have tats she contended, as her 17 year-old son appeared, himself bearing evidence of this assertion. Wasn't 17 a bit young to make such a momentous and irrevocable decision, I wondered? Totally legal, with parental permission, she assured me…so that's alright then! Her 55 year-old mother had to date, she lamented, consistently and stubbornly resisted family pressures to ink her body. She then recommended a great parlour down the road if I wanted to get started – it's never too late, she added.

Seven kms down the road from Maryfield I crossed the next provincial border into Manitoba, and the clocks went forward another hour. Highway 48 came to an end a little later, but I'd spotted another TCH avoidance option which entailed turning south for an hour on 83 then east again on 2, taking me directly to Winnipeg on smaller parallel roads. It was another sweltering day so I stopped for a picnic and rest in rare roadside shade at 14:00, and again a couple of hours later for cold drinks at Pipestone, followed by a final 50 km push to finish at Souris for a decent burger and chips, but sadly after such a long hot day, no beer.

I was beginning to tire of samey food across the prairie. There was much less variety on offer than back in BC and the three US states I'd crossed, and I was starting to look forward to Spanish and French cuisine – it didn't seem so far away now. As I unrolled my bed on a picnic table in the town campsite a couple of lads from one of the hundreds of behemoth-sized RVs demonstrated their impressive BMX biking skills.

205 km today / 17,103 km since London

Tuesday 19th August

The day began with two breakfasts in quick succession: muesli at the campsite then a sandwich and coffee in the local café, where I learnt that large numbers of British expat farmers have come to this part of Canada to farm wheat, canola and cattle and escape the tedium of EU regulations. Yet, after just a year or two, many of these new immigrants start getting nostalgic and saying how things were so much better back home…the grass always looks greener from the other side.

I hit the road at 08:00 and managed 80 kms to Glenboro in time for a Chinese lunch and some shopping before a shady snooze under a tree in the heat of the day. Then a cold beer in Holland, a small sleepy village with a windmill, where locals have erected a commendable road safety sign: DRIVE SLOW WE LOVE OUR CHILDREN – admirable message but deplorable grammar! An afternoon picnic comprised my habitual salad of chopped tomato, onion, apple, cheese, nuts, raisins and half a loaf of bread – my picnics were generally a lot healthier than the hot meal stops.

I then rode into the small town of Kipling, home of the world's largest red paperclip – it's a happening place! On 12th July 2005, I learnt, local man Kyle MacDonald posted a picture of a red paperclip on his blog and asked if anyone wanted to barter for something bigger or better. A few days later he traded the paperclip for a pen shaped like a fish. This he traded for a doorknob. And so it continued, each time trading up for something bigger or better. After 14 exchanges he had traded up to a house![31]

I camped outside an open barn in St Claude, ready to retreat inside at the first sight of rain.

148 km today / 17,252 km since London

Wednesday 20th August

Thinking back over the whole trip as I woke up: four months ago I'd just arrived in Russia; three, Thailand; two, Australia; one, New Zealand. And, looking forward, if all went to plan: in a month I'd be in Spain; and in six weeks, London! These sobering thoughts gave rise to mixed emotions – I was greatly looking forward to reunions with friends and family, but more than a little concerned about how I'd adjust and settle back into familiar and comfortable old routines. The nomadic lifestyle had become a way of life, with its own routines; I was enjoying it immensely and feared that I'd miss it terribly when it ended.

After muesli I was rolling at 07:00 on what I'd come to think of as budum roads. Built from concrete sections between which small gaps have emerged over the years, such roads cause the bike to go "budum" every few seconds – most maddening! I had to remind myself now and again, despite such occasional mild discomforts, how much better all roads had been since Russia and Kazakhstan; there really was no comparison. In the same vein, I faced another patience-testing and energy-sapping headwind, but nothing by comparison with those early weeks of the trip when I frequently couldn't even manage to stay upright on the bike.

At Elm Creek I stopped at a roadside snack caravan which wasn't yet open, so I began picnicking, whereupon the owner appeared and produced a free coffee for me. A truck driver pulled in – he was hauling a triple-deck trailer of pigs, 70 per deck, on a three-hour drive to Brandon, and cheerily explained that he'd stopped to check on their welfare – make sure they had enough water and weren't getting too hot. Within a few short hours, he

---

[31] http://oneredpaperclip.blogspot.co.uk/

added, they would all be pork chops. I felt somewhat uneasy as I peered in at the middle deck and met the reciprocated gaze of condemned porcine eyes staring out. Yet half an hour later I had little trouble managing an egg and bacon sandwich.

By early afternoon I arrived in Winnipeg, capital of Manitoba, a grand city boundary sign announcing its situation at the heart of the continent. I was half way across Canada in 15 days, bang on schedule for my planned arrival in New York City on 8th September. Daniel and Rachel were my fabulous warmshowers hosts in a suburb close to downtown Winnipeg.

I spent the afternoon doing a bike check and service, swapping the tyres around and replacing brake pads which had worn down on those long descents in the Rockies. Then we walked into town to the liquor store to procure a selection of ales for a jolly evening session with neighbours called in from both sides to share so there'd be no noise complaints.

105 km today / 17,357 km since London

Thursday 21st August

Dan did porridge and coffee for breakfast, after which I pedalled out of the big city into rain and headwind at 08:00 – so much for prevailing westerlies. A rather slow day was to follow at just 17 km/h average speed. In a café at Anola after 40 kms I ordered the "hungry man" full cooked breakfast, which tripled up on all ingredients, and got into some road safety banter with truckers who were taking a break from their work on a local construction site. As they settled up their bills, they paid mine too.

I spent most of the day on Highways 15 and 44, gradually climbing out of the prairies and into a new and pretty landscape of hills and lakes. Today was my fifth and last day away from the Trans-Canada Highway, which I finally re-joined towards the end of the day at West Hawk Lake, and was more than ready to stop after 160 tiring kms into the wind. But the next warmshowers was booked for the 24th in Thunder Bay, some 700 kms to the east, so I'd need to cover around 175 km/day to make that target, plus a bit more for three days if I was to arrive at any sort of sociable hour at my hosts'.

So I pushed on as night fell, crossed the border into Ontario, and finally pulled into a filling station near Clearwater Bay shortly before midnight. It was looking like rain so I found a sheltered spot under an overhanging roof, got settled down, and then realised there were staff members still inside. Dilemma: hide or not? I was likely to be spotted anyway so decided to make a clean breast of it and declared my intentions as they came out and locked up, preparing to leave. They were super friendly, chatted for a few minutes, gave me the password for the wifi, left me half a warm fried chicken and bade me good night.

195 km today / 17,552 km since London

Friday 22nd August

I was up at 05:00 and away at 06:15 after muesli and Twitter updates. It was 25 kms to a good second breakfast at Kenora where, at the cash point, I got into conversation with the next guy in the queue who offered me $10 for RoadPeace. Turning it down, I gave him my card and urged him to give online instead – the wrong decision as he never did. Always take cash for your charity when offered! Generosity of spirit continued: at a lakeside picnic area I was approached by a couple driving their RV across Canada *in two days* (and they thought I was crazy!) to give me a ham roll, a tub of macaroni salad, an apple and a banana, explaining that they'd packed too much food in their cooler.

The riding was up and down hills and beside lakes all day – lots of lakes and lots of hills, not steep or long but pretty constant with little respite so the going was again pretty slow. I got a good smoothie and cake at the bakery in Vermilion Bay, and later a burger in Dryden, before camping early behind a fire station at 21:00.

172 km today / 17,724 km since London

Saturday 23rd August

Determined to keep to the schedule, I was out of the sack at 05:00 and away at 05:45 on flatter roads but still into relentless headwinds, making for a long hard day at just 17 km/h once again. Towns and villages were few and far between, and I rode 100 kms to Ignace before finding a café for soup and a burger, and provisions for the seat bag. 50 kms further down the road I was rather hoping to find a decent dinner at English River, but it was pretty much a ghost town so I picnicked outside a closed pub and laboured on to Upsala by 22:30 and collapsed exhausted in a giant road-salt hangar.

There were several close passes by trucks today; driving standards had deteriorated sharply since crossing the Ontario border. And I crossed into the Eastern time zone – another hour closer to home!

203 km today / 17,927 km since London

Sunday 24th August

I timed my alarm to get up and into a café by 07:00 hoping that a) there would be a café in Upsala and b) it would open at 07:00...right on both counts, and serving a jolly decent breakfast to boot! A fellow diner, concerned for my welfare camping out in the wilds every night, cheerfully warned about wandering packs of hungry wolves – much more likely to attack me than bears, he said, advising that I should definitely be carrying bear spray. A little while later an adult black bear nearly did get me, but not in the way I'd imagined – he dashed out of the forest and across the road just a few yards ahead of me at top speed, around 50 km/h. Looking like he weighed well north of 100kgs, I doubt bear spray would have afforded much protection.

Just before midday I crossed another significant boundary, marked by a large sign reading: ATLANTIC WATERSHED. FROM HERE ALL STREAMS FLOW SOUTH INTO THE ATLANTIC OCEAN. It felt like another giant step closer to home.

Hills and headwind retarded progress as usual, as did a sightseeing visit to the spectacular Kakabeka Falls on my approach to Thunder Bay on Lake Superior, where I arrived at warmshowers hosts Frank and Marcie at 18:30. They had to pop out for a couple of hours and left me alone in their house to shower and help myself to dinner and beer – amazingly trusting. They reappeared on the scene with their daughter and her boyfriend at around 21:00 just as I was clearing up and about to get my head down. We played dice and word games and drank wine until well after midnight.

142 km today / 18,068 km since London

Monday 25th August

After a quick breakfast I left my warmshowers digs at 08:00, stopped for coffee and cakes as I was leaving the environs of Thunder Bay an hour later, then found a quiet laney route to keep me off the Trans-Canada Highway for a further hour. My midday snack was a full cooked breakfast at a remote gas station where I got chatting with a trucker who, I was rather alarmed to learn, was hauling uranium ore across thousands of kms east from a Saskatchewan mine to a processing plant in Ontario. That sounded a bit risky to me – we use special trains in the UK for radioactive cargoes to

Sellafield, I told him[32]. It wouldn't be safe enough by train he said, on account of the moose. Contradicting the advice I'd received only the day before, he counselled not worrying about bear or wolf...it was moose I really wanted to steer clear of. Weighing up to 2,000lbs, and with tiny brains, they have been known to ram trains and trucks, he said.

Today was somewhat overcast but I did enjoy the rare benefit of a tailwind for most of the day. The highway rolled up hill and down dale so the going was not much faster than previous days, but significantly easier at around 19 km/h. At Nipigon I found an excellent steak and Caesar salad for dinner, then the road took a more easterly trajectory – back into the wind and back into the hills. As I laboured up the final climb of the day I stopped to chat with a guy taking photos of the magnificent sunset over Lake Superior. He was on a driving holiday with his dog, and it turned out he was from Streatham in south London – small world! He dug out a bottle of amaretto and we clinked glasses as the sun slowly sank below the lake.

A short while later I set up camp between the Highway and the railway, right next to a signal gantry with handy escape ladder in case of any bear, wolf or moose visits during the night.

152 km today / 18,220 km since London

Tuesday 26th August

I slept pretty well; there were no nocturnal visits by hungry wild animals, but three brief interruptions as long slow freight trains creaked and rumbled past just a few feet away.

Two weeks and around 2,000 kms to go to New York City! I was up and away on muesli power by 06:45 with a good tailwind but a rollercoaster road all day. Parking my bike outside a diner in Schreiber I was approached by a couple of motorbikers – Jeannine Marinier and Lincoln McRae – who said they'd passed me no fewer than four times on the road since the Oregon coast. They invited me to share their table and paid for my triple egg and steak lunch, after which I finished their chips. Our progress eastwards together had been like the hare and the tortoise: I'd kept plodding slowly on while they'd spent extended periods camping in one or two spots and visiting relatives.

Driving standards continued to disappoint, and occasionally alarm – they were far worse in Ontario than other provinces I'd ridden across.

---

[32] Esteemed physicist and proof-reader Malcolm Dancy since informs me that uranium ore is not particularly radioactive; the waste transported to Sellafield is seriously more dangerous.

Drivers were less patient and careful, more hurried and aggressive, with particularly poor overtaking skills on regular display. At one point I had to veer right off the highway to avoid an oncoming van overtaking a long truck at high speed and coming straight at me, reviving scary memories of Russia's lawless highways. Frequent roadside signs reminding drivers of speeding fines appeared to be completely ineffective.

The weather was overcast and drizzling by the end of the day. At 19:00 I found soup and lasagne for dinner near Marathon before camping under the cover of the overhanging roof of a closed motel.

147 km today / 18,367 km since London

Wednesday 27th August

Marathon itself is actually some 5 kms downhill off the highway, but there was nowhere else for breakfast within 100 kms so I reluctantly made the detour for what turned out to be nothing special, but a cyclist needs to refuel! After the climb back up to the highway it was an easy going five-hour ride to White River, where I found good soup and a chicken wrap in the village café, then a small supermarket to stock up on various vital victuals.

An hour further on I stopped riding as a solitary cyclist approached from the opposite direction – fellow Trans-Canada rider Marie-Claude from Quebec City was riding coast to coast from St John's, Newfoundland to Victoria, British Columbia. We swapped useful tips about the routes we'd ridden and warmshowers hosts we'd visited.

At 18:30 I stopped early by Hammer Lake, lured into Fishing Moose Lodge where cheap but decent cabins were available for hire – this was timely as it was looking like rain again. After I'd scrubbed up the proprietor cooked me an excellent dinner of liver and bacon with onions, mash and gravy, followed by apple pie and ice cream. He apologetically explained that he didn't have a licence to serve alcohol with meals…but happily he did run a shop with off-licence, I was welcome to buy beer, and he could lend me a bottle opener and a glass. So it all came good in the end!

133 km today / 18,500 km since London

Thursday 28th August

A rude shock lay in store as I set off from my cosy, comfy cabin at 07:00 – freezing fog! This was the first time I'd ridden in severe cold since the New

Zealand winter. An hour later I pulled into a motel for a steaming mug of coffee and, as I gradually thawed out, I fell into conversation with vacationers who were in the region for the bear hunting season. They explained that they spent most of their time hiding quietly in trees with bait set beneath, which sounded about as exciting as watching paint dry, or fishing. Or cycling 100+ miles a day – every day – for six months, suggested brother Antony. Each to his own I suppose.

An hour later the sun had burned off the fog to reveal a beautiful crisp day with an early autumnal feel, and the going was easy to Wawa, where I found an excellent lunch of home-made vegetable soup followed by pitta stuffed with roast lamb. The afternoon was a hillier affair, heading south now beside the eastern shores of Lake Superior – the biggest lake in the world, which I'd been skirting for four days now. At around 18:00 I stopped at a picnic area with a vantage point over the lake and an information board where I read that this greatest of the Great Lakes has a 4,385 km shoreline and the capacity of the other four combined. It's 82,100 km², which sounded big, but just how big is that? Wales is always useful for such comparisons, so I looked it up: Lake Superior is four times bigger than Wales. No wonder it was taking so long to ride round.

I camped just off the Highway at 20:30.

156 km today / 18,656 km since London

Friday 29th August

Today was a properly grim day, summed up in three words: rain, headwind, hills. I stopped at every opportunity for coffee and cakes, chicken and chips, tea and sympathy, and at one point was reduced to finding

Lake Superior dumping itself on me

amusement in taking silly selfies. My target for the day had been Sault Ste. Marie, but at 16:00 with 40 kms to go I stopped for cakes and coffee in the general store at Havilland and bumped into 84 year-old Ken who had cycled across four continents. Inevitably we got yakking, an hour passed, it was still raining so he introduced me to the proprietors and helped me negotiate free dry accommodation in their garden shed for $25 including dinner and breakfast – an offer too good to refuse!

So I changed out of my wet kit and settled in a warm corner of the store to catch up with twitter and emails and send out messages to a number of potential warmshowers hosts since the forecast was not looking good for coming days. Dinner was duly served: good local fish and chips with salad and a cup of tea.

It was a loud and stormy night of heavy rain with added thunderclaps, making a fearsome racket amplified by the tin roof of the little shed where I was squashed in with my bike, garden tools and various other paraphernalia. Nonetheless I stayed cosy and dry and somehow managed to sleep pretty well.

97 km today / 18,752 km since London

Saturday 30th August

At 07:00 I went back into the general store and was served an excellent three-egg breakfast with ham, potatoes, toast and coffee, fortifying me nicely against the murk of another cold, grey and miserable day starting with a hilly 40 kms to Sault Ste. Marie, where I boosted morale with a second large breakfast. From there I remained on Highway 17 East, still the Trans-Canada, Lake Superior finally behind me, and the road flattening out now beside Lake Huron. Headwinds and drizzle persisted all day, punctuated by some further comforting stops at bakeries for lots of bread, cakes and coffee, and a picnic lunch near Thessalon during a rare brighter spell. I got well and truly drenched in an almighty downpour at around 18:00, and found a roofed area in an urban park for a dry camp just off the Highway in Blind River.

170 km today / 18,923 km since London

Sunday 31st August

Another vile day to be summed up in three words: wet wet wet! Lake Huron pretty much dumped itself on me today. Heavy rain all morning forced three breakfast stops in quick succession and I spent lengthy spells trawling the warmshowers website firing off hopeful messages to potential hosts right through to New York City, where I'd just learned Pascale would be joining me on 9th September for a short holiday – serious additional wifely pressure to meet my deadline!

At Espanola it was with some relief that I turned south off the Trans-Canada Highway for the final time. There had been more close passes by trucks today – about half of Ontario truckers needed to go back to driving school, I opined into the twittersphere.

After a gut-busting all-you-can-eat Chinese buffet in Espanola I was on Highway 6 which carried possibly a tenth of the traffic levels of the TCH and rolled across an empty scrubby landscape for 50 kms down to a swing-bridge and onto the world's largest freshwater island, Manitoulin, on Lake Huron. Thence a 12 km detour westbound on Highway 540 to my next warmshowers host, Justin, who met me at the door in his wheelchair.

Paralysed from the waist down following a mountain-biking crash in 1997, Justin has completely adapted to his predicament. Taking off at a remarkable lick in his lightweight, state-of-the-art wheelchair, he led me on a guided tour of his eclectic empire – an alternative self-sufficient community involving solar and wind power, extensive well-maintained vegetable beds and lots of chickens. In his spare time he goes cycle touring on a hand-cranked bike, towing a trailer with solar panel for electric assistance when needed. He's optimistic that advancing medical science will one day get him back on his feet, and back on his bike. Justin is an inspiration.

Another British cyclist, Matthew, was also warmshowering that night. He too was on a recumbent, but riding the length of the Americas, north to south, over three years, under no time pressures. Completing the happy hippy ensemble, a handful of other apparently semi-permanent residents welcomed me into a communal living space where I was served a variety of delicious home-grown vegan snacks and salads before being shown to a shower and bedroom.

165 km today / 19,087 km since London

Monday 1st September

I've been in Canada a whole month! Just one week to New York City now, and one month to London.

I left my warmshowers refuge at 07:00, found a café in Little Current for breakfast, and overheard a bunch of bearded, leather-clad, Harley-Davidson-insignia-sporting motorbikers bemoaning the fact that they had missed out on some riding in recent days on account of all the rain. You pussy-cats want to take a leaf out of my book and man up a bit, I mused. This was not an opinion I chose to share with them.

Waiting for the ferry

Highway 6 was serenely peaceful and with a good shoulder, but annoyingly of the budum tendency. Bright sunshine had degraded to foggy murk after the first hour but the rain held off for the morning ride to South Baymouth, where Manitoulin Island comes to an end. I had 90 minutes to kill before boarding the 13:30 ferry across Lake Huron to Tobermory, back on the mainland – just time for a relaxing pizza and beer. Sailing time was two hours, providing a further useful carbo-loading opportunity: pie and mash with beer did the trick nicely.

As I disembarked at Tobermory I spotted another laid-back rider in the traffic queue ahead and filtered up to say hi – it was fellow Brit, Matthew, who'd also been at Justin's retreat last night. We set off together heading south for some 20 kms on Highway 6 until BANG! his back tyre exploded in fine style. He had all the kit he needed to sort it out so we parted company – I needed to move on sharply as I had another warmshowers host booked in Owen Sound 100 kms further down the road. In the event, however, that turned out to be about 50 kms too far due to the stiffening headwind and an unwelcome reappearance of rain. I turned off the highway into a timber yard, found a cosy dry spot to camp in a brand new wooden display shed and texted an apology to my waiting host.

118 km today / 19,205 km since London

Tuesday 2nd September

I enjoyed a combination of a good road and good luck today, managing to dodge some torrential rainstorms which stayed a few hours ahead of me all day. I followed lightly flooded roads towards dark skies but stayed dry in sunny weather and with favourable winds for an easy 200 km blast down the arrow-straight and largely empty highway to Guelph near Toronto, where warmshowers host Jan was ready for me with a fabulous full roast dinner and beer followed by fresh fruit salad and ice cream. Jan had taken up cycling relatively recently on retirement, and hadn't been idle: her touring CV already included a crossing of the Canadian Rockies; Vancouver to the Arctic; Turkey, Colombia and Cuba; and a Nullarbor crossing from Perth to Melbourne. So much common ground we yakked till midnight.

202 km today / 19,407 km since London

Wednesday 3rd September

I woke to the alluring aroma of a full cooked breakfast sizzling in the pan. Downstairs in a flash, Jan was just plating it all up as I arrived in the kitchen – another stupendous five-star warmshowers result! In good cheer and with full belly I set off at 08:00 into glorious wall-to-wall sunshine – it was wonderful to see that golden orb again after a solid week of grey skies and heavy rain. I followed a lovely quiet route through shady forest for 50 kms bearing south to Burlington where, suddenly, I found myself in the big city. Effectively Greater Toronto, this was the first city since Winnipeg – quite a shock to the system after weeks of expansive prairie stretching to every horizon. I negotiated busy boulevards down to Lake Ontario and found a superb shared bike and skate route on the waterfront taking me around the western edge of the lake where I stopped briefly for a picnic before rolling on through St Catharines and up to Niagara. The falls are indeed spectacular, stunning and impressive. The town itself however, spoilt by intensive tourism, is a gaudy Disneyesque nightmare.

I crossed a high bridge over the Niagara River and back into the USA – New York State! The edge of the continent, the Big Apple and the end of

You know when you're back in the USA!

the North American road were now in plain view, just five days away. After clearing customs quickly I rode on to Lockport where yet another warmshowers host was booked but hadn't yet provided an address, so I stopped in a local bar to try for wifi or use the phone. Within moments the landlord had recruited most of the patrons on the case, divvying out the tasks most effectively. One lent me a phone, another bought me beer, a third advised directions; a fourth even offered to put my bike in his pickup truck and give me a lift out to my host's address because he thought it was rather a long way to cycle out of town. I declined gracefully, explaining that another three kms wasn't really that far compared to the 169 I'd already ridden that day, and rode to Nancy's place on the edge of town, arriving a little later than planned at 21:30. She was waiting patiently and provided a garage for the bike, snacks and a hot drink, and a bed in the basement.

172 km today / 19,578 km since London

Thursday 4th September

Armed by Nancy with a local cycling map and advice to use the excellent Erie canal bike route to bypass Rochester city centre, I set off in fine weather again heading inexorably Atlantic-wards. There were so many properties with flags fluttering outside, I began to wonder if not flying a giant stars and stripes on one's front lawn was tantamount to treason. Also on many front lawns, New Yorkers displayed prominent banners advocating that NY's SAFE act be repealed as a matter of urgency. These were so prolific that I eventually had to stop and google to find out what they could possibly be so worked up about. Of course, silly me, I might have guessed…it was about protecting their constitutional right to go on shooting each other.[33]

I rode a long day today to reach Syracuse, despite the heat peaking in the low 30s, rolling slowly into town just after 22:00, very much in the dark as the main front dynamo light had recently given up the ghost and I just had a couple of small back-up LEDs – useful to be seen by other road users, but no good for lighting up the road. Warmshowers hosts Jenny and Olin, both teachers, were dutifully waiting up for me with restorative beers at the ready.

240 km today / 19,818 km since London

Friday 5th September

After coffee and toast with Jenny and Olin I was away at 08:00 only to be tempted into a café on the way out of town 30 minutes later for a full cooked breakfast. A TV blared in the corner and the weatherman announced with some glee that it was going to be another triple-aitcher – a hot, humid and hazy day.

---

[33] http://tinyurl.com/n8dc7pe
http://www.scopeny.org/

I was riding Bike Route 5 on Highway 31 which runs parallel to the Erie Canal beside which there was an off road cycle route, but progress would have been too slow on that – not that the hazy humid heat permitted particularly rapid progress. A mid-afternoon break was forced by my fourth (and final as it turned out) puncture of the tour. I stopped under a bridge for shade and after digging out the offending sharp stone and replacing the tube I tried in vain to fix the front light, a normally reliable German dynamo-driven LED – an expensive bit of kit, not widely available. At home there was an identical one on my Roberts fixie, so I emailed Pascale to get our son Mark to remove it so she could bring it out to New York with her.

I used the canalside off-road bike route at dusk for the final 10 kms of the day to avoid a big hill just before Fort Plain where, after a giant pizza, I retired to a quiet spot to camp behind the medical centre.

150 km today / 19,967 km since London

Saturday 6th September

After my daily constitutional bowl of muesli at 05:30 I discovered the local corner store was already open and selling coffee and doughnuts – great fuel for powering me along a lovely smooth yet off-road route beside the Mohawk river for around 50 kms to Amsterdam, a quiet sleepy village where I was rather hoping to find more coffee and cakes, but everything looked closed and deathly quiet. I spotted a solitary elderly guy on the other side of the street, and went over to ask him if he knew of any local cafés that might be open. His reply was odd: "Do you like gardening?" I thought perhaps he hadn't heard or understood my request, so I repeated myself a little more slowly and loudly, lest he was hard of hearing. But he persisted with his line of questioning – did I like gardening? – adding that he was an antique dealer and would I like to go back to his place and see his lovely garden? The penny dropped and alarm bells rang – this was surely a euphemism for something else he had in mind. I declined with as much grace as I could muster, whereupon he indicated a bakery just a hundred yards up the street!

This turned out to be the most fabulous small independent Italian bakery I'd ever set foot in outside Italy, and I promptly made it my mission to sample the extensive range of bountiful Lisa's tempting delights (not a euphemism). There were fairy cakes and fruitcakes, banana breads and blueberry turnovers, raspberry pies and apple crumbles, pecan pies and gingerbread cookies, lemon cupcakes and chocolate peanut butter gourmet brownies. Not forgetting the Boston cream filled cupcakes with chocolate ganache frosting. All served with endless good coffee to wash them down while Lisa sat opposite me enthusing about my ride and her café and jumping up to attend energetically to the steady trickle of customers popping in for their daily bread. I ended up engrossed in conversation with three generations of a charming local family and was alarmed to see that I'd frittered away almost two hours consuming cakes and coffee. There was nothing to pay – Pat, Jennifer, Harper and Henry had paid my rather substantial bill.

I tore myself away from this cakey paradise and waddled back out to the bike to ride on to Albany, just another 50 kms or so, barely enough time to work up an appetite again, but it proved impossible to pass by an alluring little Greek restaurant with pork souvlakis on the menu.

As I rode out of Albany the heavens opened forcing me to take refuge at the first opportunity, a drive-thru Dunkin Donuts place. I couldn't face any more doughnuts or cakes, but I did enjoy a spot of people-watching from a bench seat at the window near the drive-through hatch. Some customers looked so large that perhaps getting out of the car to buy their doughnuts was impossible – were they physically wedged into their cars and needing careful prising out at the end of each journey, I wondered.

I crossed over the Hudson River and turned south onto Highway 9 – just 200-odd kms from New York City now. It was a lumpy and scenic 50 kms down the valley to the small town of Hudson, where another warmshowers host awaited: James and his two tiny kittens in their cosy Airstream caravan. We went into a town centre bar for a great dinner of onion soup, pot roast, and a variety of restorative local beers.

143 km today / 20,111 km since London

Sunday 7th September

After muesli in the caravan followed immediately by a full breakfast in town I was back on Highway 9, now signed as a cycle route, and very pretty, rolling gently through golden autumnal forest. Traffic was light for a few hours but got steadily busier from around midday with, I imagined, New Yorkers returning to their city after a weekend up state. It was a hot day again and, right across my path at one point, basking in the sun just like me, lounged a fellow low-life of the road, catching some rays on the shoulder of Highway 9: an eastern ribbon snake.

I arrived at 19:00 in Ossining, where my final warmshowers hosts, Peter and Loren, welcomed me into their rather grand detached house on Beach Road just above the Hudson River – the contrast with the previous night's caravan couldn't have been greater. After ablutions in a luxury bathroom, a

fine and copious pasta dinner was served with ample Sierra Nevada Pale Ale to wash it down before a guided tour of the house to admire their creativity: he's a cabinet maker and she's a potter.

149 km today / 20,259 km since London

How to ensure a warm welcome with warmshowers hosts

Monday 8th September

An email from my son Mark! I'd recently asked him, in exchange for a beer when I got home, to remove the front light from my Roberts fixie (hanging off a ceiling hook in the garage) for Pascale to bring out to me: *You forgot to mention that Roberts was chained up to another bike with what must be the most heavy duty chain in the entire universe, and didn't tell me where the key is! Had to take it off while Robbie was still hanging up. Two beers.*

Riding into New York City had been looming on the horizon for so long – and now the day was finally here. It was an exciting but also a moderately daunting prospect. As a daily commuter cyclist in big bad London town, I was steeled to the task; it would be a challenge but I know how to ride the city roads and use eye contact to control the traffic around me and would apply these long-practised principles of survival to reach my destination on the upper west side today. Essentially that means taking the lane and riding assertively because I have as much right to use the road as anyone else; arguably more so: pedestrians, cyclists and horse-riders use the roads as of right; motorists, operating potentially lethal machinery, must earn a licence which can be withdrawn in case of misuse. Discuss!

However, over a vat of porridge for breakfast, Peter explained that I wouldn't be needing my urban warrior tactics today – he would lead me into the Big Apple following an almost entirely car free route. He extricated a state-of-the-art Cruzbike front wheel drive recumbent from his cabinet-making workshop and we set off in brilliant autumn sunshine, at first through peaceful, lush forest on the South County Trailway (a disused railroad) for a couple of hours, then with an abrupt change of scenery, over the Harlem River on Broadway Bridge onto the manic streets of Manhattan.

But not for long! We soon diverted onto a peaceful segregated bike lane running right down the length of the west side beside the Hudson River to Battery Park at the southern end of the island with fine views over to the Statue of Liberty. A brilliant route, thanks to Peter – not at all the stressful entry into NYC that I had anticipated. New York, New York! If I could make it here, I could make it anywhere!

New York, New York! Cycling with Peter by the Hudson

We ate some sandwiches before Peter set off back home on the same route. I made my way to 77th Street on the upper west side, just a few yards off Broadway, and checked into the Hotel Belleclaire, where Pascale had reserved us a room. Staff were welcoming and helped me squeeze my bike and kit into the rather cramped lift up to the 9th floor.

I then went out in search of a bike box – there were four bike shops in the vicinity and I had one in my possession within a few minutes. Back in the hotel room I began taking the bike to bits again and packing it into the box ready for the flight to Europe. However, it was too tight a squeeze – this box, probably made for a skinny lightweight road bike, wasn't capacious enough for Bacchetta and all its peripherals, so I decided to try for a bigger one in another shop on the morrow.

I was of course spoilt for choice when it came to finding somewhere for dinner, but being tired I wanted something nearby. Hotel staff recommended an Italian place about a minute's walk away on Broadway/77th where I chose an excellent risotto cooked with champagne and truffle oil – well it's not every day that I ride into New York is it? On exactly the day I'd planned over a month previously, I'd reached the end of another continent.

78 km today / 20,338 km since London

Tuesday 9th September

Breakfast on Broadway! Eggs over easy on sourdough toast with unlimited coffee. I then found a bike shop with big boy's toys on display in the window – mountain bikes with 29-inch wheels. These must surely be shipped over from Taiwan or China in huge boxes – could they spare one for me? No problem! Bigger in all dimensions, Bacchetta fitted in comfortably.

My next urgent job was to tidy the room. There was bike kit sprawled and washing hanging everywhere, and Pascale about to arrive – it just wouldn't do! Once it was spotless I set off down Broadway, walked down to Times Square, had a Greek Salad and fruit smoothie in a diner with shiny red faux-leather seats, then took the subway from Penn Station out to JFK Airport to meet the Virgin flight from London. It landed early but clearing immigration and customs took an age. Pascale finally emerged in good spirits and we set off by subway back into the city, emerging at 50th Street for a stroll up 8th Avenue into Central Park, past the Strawberry Fields shrine to John Lennon and into the same Italian restaurant I'd eaten in the previous day for dinner – happy days!

0 km today / 20,338 km since London

Wednesday 10th September

Tourist time! After a great breakfast at a diner on Broadway we walked along 77th Street to the Hudson, turned south to walk by the river down to

Tourists in the Big Apple

42nd Street, and took the Circle Line three-hour boat tour around Manhattan Island. After that we visited Times Square, Grand Central Station, had another Italian dinner and watched a Broadway show – *The Gentleman's Guide to Love and Murder*. We'd been intrigued by the title, but never judge a book by its cover – it was nothing to write home about.

0 km today / 20,338 km since London

Thursday 11th September

A repeat breakfast at our favourite local diner, following which we spent the morning walking through Central Park up to Harlem, and back down to visit the Metropolitan Museum. We then made a very moving early evening visit to a packed Ground Zero on this 13th anniversary of the attacks on the Twin Towers of the World Trade Centre in 2001.

0 km today / 20,338 km since London

Friday 12th September

After eggs and smoked salmon at the usual place we took the subway to Brooklyn and walked back over the famous bridge to enjoy the splendid views of downtown Manhattan. It was a hot, sunny day spent largely meandering slowly northwards back towards our hotel through Chinatown, Washington Square, Greenwich Village, Madison Square Garden, Times Square and Broadway, finishing at a Greek restaurant for Moussaka and a bottle of Retsina.

0 km today / 20,338 km since London

Saturday 13th September

The weather broke overnight and we woke to cool grey skies. After a breakfast of fruit salad on French toast at the habitual place we took the subway and rail replacement bus(!) to Coney Island, a seaside resort in need of a lick of paint reminding me somewhat of Margate. We had good fun watching the rollercoaster riders and ate fish and chips with beer in the rain – I felt right at home.

Back on Manhattan we walked across Central Park to the Upper East Side to a recommended bar, but being small, loud and packed we took an immediate dislike, made a swift exit and found an excellent Mexican restaurant nearby where we recovered with Margaritas, a good bottle of Argentinian wine, and rib-eye steaks with refried beans.

0 km today / 20,338 km since London

Sunday 14th September

After a day off, the sun had made a reappearance by the time we emerged for our breakfast on Broadway – Eggs Benedict today with spinach and feta at the usual cheerful place which by this stage surely deserves a mention – the New Wave Café, 2210 Broadway. We then took the subway up to 138th Street in Harlem where we tried to get into the Abyssinian Baptist Church, famed for its gospel music and highly recommended to visitors of all faiths and none. However, they were not receiving visitors today, so we followed a walking route from our guide book through Harlem which took us past another church where the Hallelujahs were in full swing and resonating out into the street. We were welcomed in to participate in some tuneful and energetic praising of the Lord. Our walk continued through Marcus Garvey Park and down to Amy Ruth's Restaurant on 115th Street for a fabulous lunch of "Soul Food…Southern Comfort Cuisine"[34]. I chose chicken livers with okra and macaroni cheese, washed down with Harlem Brewing Company's Sugar Hill Golden Ale.

We meandered slowly back through Central Park in the warm afternoon sunshine to the hotel on 77th, Pascale picked up her bags, and we jumped on the subway out to JFK for her flight back to London. It was a sad moment after a lovely few days together, and I knew that the next time I'd see her, my adventure would be at an end.

I took the subway back into town and fetched up back at the New Wave Café for a rather lonely, simple pasta dinner. Back at the hotel I discovered that my GPS appeared to be missing the maps of Spain and Portugal, which I was sure I'd loaded months before the trip had begun, so I spent an hour in vain trying to download them in the hotel's computer room.

0 km today / 20,338 km since London

Monday 15th September

I packed up my bags ready to fly and after a final breakfast at the usual diner, went for a quick haircut and a short walk in Riverside Park by the Hudson. It was another perfect, warm and cloudless day. Back at the hotel waiting for my airport cab I checked the weather forecast for Lisbon – rain throughout the coming week.

A large cab was required for the airport transfer to JFK to fit the bike box, and the 20-mile journey took an hour due to heavy traffic, though my driver did shave off a few seconds by driving at high speed between the jams. Check-in was hassle-free and there was only $100 excess baggage charge to pay through to Lisbon via Dublin – the flight I'd panic-booked at Auckland airport almost two months previously before being allowed to fly into the USA. The security queue was long and tedious but decent beer was available once I got through to the departure lounge. My final flight of the tour took to the air at 17:30.

0 km today / 20,338 km since London

---

[34] http://amyruths.com/our-story/

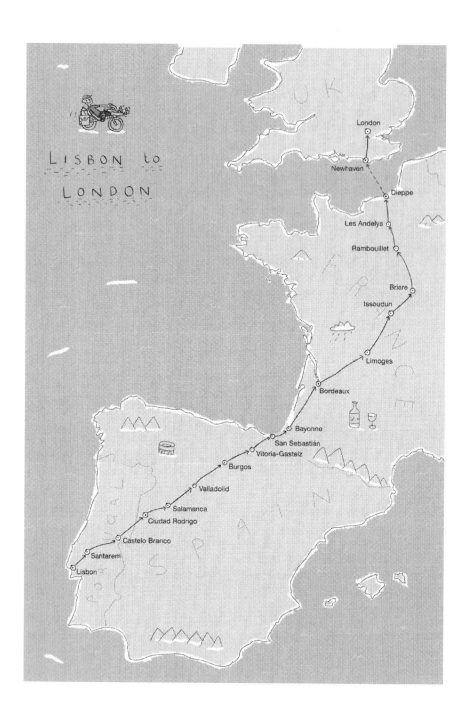

LISBON to
LONDON

London
Newhaven
Dieppe
Les Andelys
Rambouillet
Briare
Issoudun
Limoges
Bordeaux
Bayonne
San Sebastián
Vitoria-Gasteiz
Burgos
Valladolid
Salamanca
Ciudad Rodrigo
Castelo Branco
Santarem
Lisbon

LISBON TO LONDON

Tuesday 16ᵗʰ September

Read, ate, watched a movie, slept a bit, and landed 04:30 at Dublin, not feeling great. The only direct flight from JFK to Lisbon had been double the price. I found a quiet, dark, empty spot behind a fast food outlet to get a spot of shut-eye before laying into a mid-morning full Irish breakfast with Guinness, then spent a couple of hours reading the papers and dozing. The Lisbon flight took off 30 minutes late, at noon, and stormy weather delayed us further and resulted in a bouncy landing at Lisbon at around 15:10. My bike and bags appeared promptly on the carousel, I cleared customs by 16:00 and found a quiet corner in the car park to reassemble the bike. The job took quite a bit longer than usual because a) the new front light needed wiring in and the cables were too short so a bodge job was called for; and b) the bike box had evidently not been handled with kid gloves, so various bits like brake discs and bottle cages needed bending gently back into shape.

It was early evening when I finally pedalled out of the airport and pointed the bike vaguely northwards hoping I'd hit my intended route soon. Without a base map in the GPS it was tricky picking my way through unfamiliar suburbs, but the N10 north appeared soon enough. Then I realised I was famished and had almost no supplies, so stopped at a garage with a shop where cheerful staff made me a cheese and ham sandwich. There were cans of beer on the shelves and 5L flagons of water so I refilled all my bottles. Coffee and cakes were also available. An hour later I rode out into the night feeling much fortified and intending to get some serious distance under my wheels, but that plan was thwarted at 22:00 after just 25 kms: driving rain set in with a vicious intensity and I quickly retreated into a sheltered cove behind a superstore, rather thankful now for the accumulated delays of the day, without which I'd be right out of town with far less chance of finding decent roadside shelter. I looked at the weather app on the phone – a stormy week was forecast.

25 km today / 20,363 km since London

Wednesday 17ᵗʰ September

At 06:30 after muesli, I set off on a busy N3 as far as Santarem, then turned onto the quieter N118 up to Alpiarca, where I stopped off for great coffee and pastries and was surprised to see that they still smoke in the bars here – how quickly we got used to that ban in the UK, and how popular it has proved. Surely, if we were really bothered about air quality and public health, we could learn from that experience and ban cars, starting with diesels, in British town and city centres, where they're poisoning upwards of 50,000 people to death every year...but I'm not holding my breath.

The weather was sultry and storm clouds were threatening, but a helpful southerly wind pushed me up the Tejo valley to lunch in a *restaurante típico* near Chamusca. I was served a plate piled high with the freshest sardines I'd ever eaten, devoured them at speed with relish and good bread, and my plate was replenished before I could finish. Evidently I looked thin and hungry.

Bus shelter: a sign of civilisation

The rain came 20 kms into the afternoon shift, so I pulled into a useful audax hotel for a post prandial snooze – oh what joy to be back in a civilised land of bus shelters! I put my doziness and low energy levels down to jetlag; progress was slow but the scenery compensated as I climbed gently into the hilly Iberian interior. By 19:30 it was getting dark and I'd done the 150 kms required by the schedule to get to London on 1ˢᵗ October, so I stopped to camp under a convenient motorway bridge...just in time. At 20:00 the heavens opened while I was eating my luxurious feast of bread and Nutella. The plastic jar had survived since Australia and was almost empty; I had to cut it in half to wipe it clean with the bread to extract maximum calorific value. This was most definitely not glamping.

153 km today / 20,516 km since London

Thursday 18ᵗʰ September

As I prepared my breakfast at 06:00 I discovered that I'd managed to buy a box of baby cereal yesterday rather than muesli, which made for an interesting change! A decent second breakfast of coffee and cakes followed at Nisa, after which I faced a hilly 40 kms to Castelo Branco where I found burgers and wifi. An easier 50 kms to Penamacor came next but I was still rather jetlagged and energy levels were low so climbing was slow and laborious.

After a picnic lunch I made a navigational error taking the 233 north rather than the 569 east, and climbed for an hour before realising my mistake. Dilemma: to go back or go on? Continuing looked like it might involve 20 kms of *autostrada* tomorrow, but I couldn't face going back, so stayed on the 233, climbing towards Sabugal. It was brutally hilly and exhausting and I gave up at 19:30 on just 134 kms, tempted into a fully enclosed bus shelter which even sported its own fireplace and chimney – five stars! Sadly I had no matches or combustible materials. I went to bed wondering what had happened in the Scottish referendum – had they voted for independence? And more importantly still, had Jens Voigt broken the cycling hour record? I'd need to get hooked up to wifi the following day to find out.

134 km today / 20,650 km since London

Friday 19ᵗʰ September

It rained most of the night but I stayed cosy and dry in my five-star audax hotel, lying in bed for an extra hour hoping the rain would abate before I got going – it didn't, so I set off at 07:00 into heavy rain and was dripping wet by the time I found a village café 45 minutes later. The TV was on and I gleaned from the weather forecast that it had been wet for the past week and was set to rain all day. Furthermore it was looking similar over most of Western Europe. At least it wasn't cold, but I had rather been expecting any challenging weather conditions at this time of year on the Iberian peninsula to be heat-related. After the weather came the news – 55% of Scots had voted against independence, but Voigt's hour attempt was strangely omitted from the Portuguese headlines.

At 09:30 I crossed the border into Spain, took a photo and tweeted about the rain: "varying between light, heavy, torrential, and biblical. Going to ask for refund." Shortly after that I did manage to find a good route avoiding the *autovia*, and a great tapas lunch with beer in Ciudad Rodrigo. "Spain has redeemed itself" I tweeted.

The afternoon was spent on the N620 to Salamanca, stopping briefly for tapas snacks en route. As I approached the city a giant billboard outside a hotel announced room prices starting at €26, and I was too weak-willed to resist. I checked into a good clean ensuite room, took a shower and washed my kit, then went down to the bar for dinner – more tapas and beer. A number of guests were gathered in some excitement around the TV watching a bull fight. I joined them and forced myself to watch, trying to hide my distaste. How can anyone enjoy such a bloody terrible spectacle?

145 km today / 20,795 km since London

Saturday 20th September

I was up and away at 07:45, an hour later than planned, having forgotten to put my watch forward yesterday at the Spanish border. Away again into the rain, and still not feeling too energetic, but referring myself once again back to the tough early days of Russia and Kazakhstan – this was, by comparison, a walk in the park. The rain was warm, the roads and food were good, the wind was gentle and at my back, and I could understand something of what people were saying. Perhaps this would be a lesson for life – nothing would ever be very difficult again.

After coffee and cakes in Salamanca I was back on the N620, adjacent to the *Autovia de Castilla*, so traffic was light on this relatively minor but splendid diagonal route across Spain heading north-east towards the Pyrenees. All that was slowing my progress was too many tempting tapas bars.

After passing through the impressive medieval town of Tordesillas, the N620 finally let me down and led me directly onto the *autovia* – there was

Valladolid - the second antipodal point

no alternative showing on my paper map and still no Spanish map on the GPS. I rode a few kms on the motorway hard shoulder to Simancas then found a lovely quiet alternative route into the city of Valladolid, my second antipodal checkpoint (the first having been Wellington NZ back in July). Then the navigation got tricky: like all good things the N620 came to an end, and the GPS route I'd planned turned out to be on off-road tracks. I struggled to find a winding laney route through a series of small villages – Cabezon, Valoria, Duenas – but was losing great chunks of time. Then a sign: N620 Burgos, brilliant! I headed out, only to be dumped again onto the *autovia*. I made good time on the hard shoulder for about 10 kms until I spotted a flashing blue light in the rear view mirrors – uh-oh! The agent of the *Guardia Civil* was indeed very civil, but made it plain that I would have to leave the motorway at the next exit. There was no simple alternative route – it looked as though they'd built the motorway on top of the old road – and so I would have to zigzag on lanes all the way to Burgos, a tricky, time-consuming and frustrating business picking out a sensible route. I was really missing the Garmin maps – why weren't they showing up on the GPS?

I finally pitched up in the small town of Baltanas at 22:00 having covered just over 200 kms, but there were no signs onward to Quintana so I stopped to ask at a local bar, prompting a loud and animated discussion among half a dozen patrons who were evidently of several different opinions. Finally an entire family jumped into their car and beckoned me to follow them to (hopefully) the road I wanted. I camped by the roadside at the edge of town.

204 km today / 20,999 km since London

Sunday 21st September

There was a heavy dew when I awoke, damp and cold. I ate my muesli and then discovered that I hadn't been led to the Quintana road the night before, but it wasn't far away and much easier to find in daylight. I rode 40-odd kms on tiny, hilly, scenic lanes slowly to Villahoz by 11:00 where I partook of a second breakfast and lunch in one sitting: coffee, cakes, tapas and beer.

At 14:00 I finally arrived in Burgos, now enjoying weather much more in line with what I'd expected – bright warm sunshine – but it had taken me almost 24 hours to cover just 120 kms since Valladolid. I was a little on the back foot trying to keep on schedule, but nonetheless needed to make time to eat, so stopped at an enticing bakery for a cheese and ham pastry – so good that I went back in for a dessert pastry of peaches and cream. Then just a few metres further down the same street I discovered a café doing such a good deal on the *menu del día* involving pork cheek stew, flan and beer that riding past without stopping for an hour was never going to be within the realms of the possible.

Riding out of Burgos I could see mountains in the distance – the Pyrenees! France lay beyond: just 1,500 kms to go, nearly home! I took the N1 to Miranda de Ebro, stopping en route once more for refuelling in Rubena, where Ana the barmaid served me coke and snacks and gave €10 for RoadPeace. As the road tilted upwards into the mountains the sky blackened, the wind freshened, and the rain settled in. I arrived in Miranda de Ebro at 20:30 and dived straight into the first hotel just before it became torrential – phew! After hanging out various bits of damp kit I retreated to the bar to fortify myself with tortillas and beer.

160 km today / 21,159 km since London

Monday 22ⁿᵈ September

22ⁿᵈ September: European Car Free Day! This date always excites me because, in the dim and distant past I was the UK coordinator for this day and European Mobility Week[35]. The basic idea of these campaigns was to show how we could improve our towns and cities if only we could get rid of some of the motor traffic. What alternative uses we could find for our streets? Isolated successes included street markets, picnics, concerts, football, cycling and sand-castle competitions. Some years, over 60 British towns and cities participated, and legacies include a few permanently car-free streets – go and have a look at Museum Street in central London, one of my proudest achievements.[36] It's fair to say that these campaigns still have some way to run...

No space for cycling; riding the motorways can be safer

Somewhat perversely then, I celebrated Car Free Day by taking a ride on the *autovia* to Vitoria; it was nigh on impossible to find a sensible alternative for this 30 km stretch. The motorway was thick with traffic and it was raining to boot, but the hard shoulder was fine and smooth and I felt a good deal safer than on many

---

35 http://www.mobilityweek.eu/
36 https://en.wikipedia.org/wiki/Museum_Street

narrower roads where cycling is legal but there's no space. Perhaps cycle campaigners should argue the case for the right to ride on motorways – after all we pay for them out of our taxes too.

I made good time into Vitoria with no interference from the *Guardia Civil* and found a comfortable café for breakfast and a route planning session to look for roads I could use legally. But the strategic road network in that part of the world seems to be comprised mostly of motorways. I set off hopefully on the N240 north, but within a few kms it had morphed into another *autovia*. 13 kms later I managed to escape onto the 627 and found myself descending alongside the River Deba towards the coast, stopping en route for some excellent tapas and beer in Soraluze. After that it was an easy and pretty downhill ride to Deba on the coast, albeit narrow and twisty with no shoulder in places so, though legal, it was paradoxically rather more hazardous than the motorways. Fortunately traffic was not too heavy and most drivers were reasonably patient and well behaved.

At the seaside I turned east onto the undulating, scenic N634 with views reminiscent of the fantastic Oregon coast, stopping in Getaria, a lovely old seaside town, to find accommodation. A one-star hotel caught my eye, but rooms at €80 were a tad beyond my budget I explained to the helpful receptionist, showing her the magic letter. She directed me to a friend's house down a narrow lane for half the price – perfect!

I then had a rare bit of bike maintenance to attend to. For the past couple of days the rear hub had been getting noisy, which was mildly worrying. It's a pricey German 14-speed Rohloff hub gear, meant to be running silently in an oil bath, with a reputation of utter reliability and road-tested to 300,000 miles. It should never need attention apart from the occasional oil change, which was just as well since it is impossible to work on at the roadside – dismantling this baby is a job for a specialist engineer in the Rohloff workshop in Kassel. OK the oil change was a little overdue but surely that wouldn't be the source of the noise? I'd been speculating as I'd been riding and hoping it was not serious when really I should have just stopped and looked at it, because once I did it was pretty plain that the chain had stretched (understandably) and become slack, resulting in it rubbing against itself at the jockey wheels on the tensioner. I removed a link from the chain to shorten it and hey presto! the problem was sorted. I celebrated this minor engineering triumph in a local bar with tapas and beer.

132 km today / 21,291 km since London

Tuesday 23rd September

After pastries and coffee in a local café I hit the road north at 08:00 on a newly silenced bike. It was a short scenic coastal road to the glorious and cycle-friendly city of San Sebastián, which welcomed me onto its outstanding network of segregated cycle routes, all well used, with high

quality bike parking at every turn. Pedestrians too enjoyed space aplenty; indeed one road I used had evidently in a past life been a dual carriageway with now one entire side devoted exclusively for walking and cycling – hurrah! And yet, and yet…this beautiful historic city was still choked with car traffic.

San Sebastián - lots of space for cycling!

20 kms further up the road I crossed my penultimate international border: France! I immediately celebrated with a *croque monsieur* and beer at the first bistro in Hendaye. From there it was slow going on the spectacular D810 corniche through a succession of major holiday resorts: St Jean de Luz, Biarritz and Bayonne, all jammed up with traffic – what a sad way to spend a holiday!

In Bayonne I wheeled my steed into a bike shop hoping to borrow a track pump, but the grumpy salesman told me that bikes were not allowed inside and moreover he wasn't in the business of lending out pumps…*bienvenue en France*! I explained (in French) that I'd ridden round the world, stopping in the bike shops of twenty countries along the way to pump up my tyres, and this was the first time I'd been refused, but my appeal cut no mustard. As I was leaving I noticed there were no other customers in the shop… A few kms further down the road I tried again at another bike shop – *mais oui Monsieur, bien sûr, pas de problème*! My faith in French humanity, hospitality and generosity (not to mention liberty, equality and fraternity) was duly restored.

At Labenne I finally escaped the traffic-clogged D810 and continued northwards on the quieter D652 up into Les Landes; away too from the roller-coaster clifftop route and into a vast area of flat pine forest where I soon picked up the excellent *Vélodyssée* cycle route running between small towns. If a measure of a good bike route is how many others are using it, this was a five-star route – there were fast roadies, tourers, shoppers, mountain bikers, elderly users, kids, walkers and skaters. It was a carefree joy to ride and I pedalled on till dusk at 21:00, finally stopping to hang my hat in a roadside fruit stall just south of Mimizan.

165 km today / 21,456 km since London

Wednesday 24th September

I was on the road at 07:30 and stopped 30 minutes later for a huge café breakfast of croissant, pain au raisins, an entire baguette and three coffees, over which I met 60-something Thibault. White-bearded, in his t-shirt, baggy shorts, baseball cap, backpack, walking boots and poles, he was doing the long distance *Chemin de Compostelle*, also on my bucket list. How I admire such energetic and adventurous old crocks...oh hang on a minute... We exchanged notes and niceties before I excused myself to press on and make good time for a lunch date with family friends in Cestas near Bordeaux. But the wind blew against me on the long straight flat roads across Les Landes, sapping energy and necessitating a quick pit-stop in a boulangerie at Mios. I used some off-road cycle tracks which are fine for casual holidaymakers in no particular hurry, but not for the long distance cyclist on a mission to get to lunch – too much time is lost losing priority at side roads, meandering around the trees, and being sent on lengthy detours to avoid roundabouts. So I soon gave up and got back on the road.

Lunch in a Cestas café with Nicole and Jean-Jacques was great fun. Both retired English teachers, lovers of all things British and space-frame Moulton riders, they'd been following my progress on Twitter and were eager to have some of the gaps filled in. I did my best in the brief time available and told them to look out for the book, then it was time to move

With Catherine and Sylvie, les belles soeurs

swiftly on to the next social engagement: ten kms further up the road to my sister-in-law and hubbie, Sylvie and Denis, in Pessac – how wonderful to be back with family again! Sylvie's sister Catherine was also there, so it was party time! Beer, a shower, a quick dip in the pool and aperitifs succeeded each other in short order during which I took phone calls from my father-in-law, Jean, and a journalist, who together were plotting a media reception for me when I arrived with them on the Loire in a couple of days' time.

Dinner was *formidable*: *magret de canard* with sautéed potatoes, green beans and a rather splendid wine from just down the road – St Emilion Grand Cru 2006. In the natural order of things, fromage et dessert followed, necessitating the uncorking of another bottle. With some 800 kms still to go to London, the circumnavigation celebrations were already getting underway!

113 km today / 21,569 km since London

Thursday 25th September

A lie-in and a late start – I only needed 100 kms today. After breakfast with the in-laws I hit the road at 10:00 into the centre of Bordeaux and out onto the Bergerac road, where I found a good boulangerie for coffee and pastries at 11:15. Shortly after that refill I turned off the main road onto a blissfully peaceful lane through the vineyards of Entre-Deux-Mers to St Germain du Puch, where I partook of the *menu du jour* on a café terrace before pedalling into one of the most prestigious vineyards of them all – Pomerol. Amazingly the bike found its own way into Château Haut Goujon where, after sampling some recent and less recent wines, I selected a couple of the sumptuous 2001 vintage to donate to hosts further up route, only wishing I could fit a couple of cases into my panniers.

At St Aulaye I checked into a small hotel having ridden just 89 kms   I was becoming lazy and demob happy! There was no good reason not to camp but I just couldn't be bothered. I had a shower and went out for dinner, a pretty mediocre steak and chips, but there was only one place open in this small village. As I ate I realised that this would be my last night alone; I had arrangements in place now for every night back to London.

89 km today / 21,658 km since London

Friday 26th September

After a breakfast in the boulangerie and an entertaining chat with the jolly baker I was off at 08:00 and an hour later arrived in Riberac, a splendid old town with a lively street market just setting up. Several enticing hotels and restaurant blackboards with mouth-watering menus caught my eye – clearly this is where I should have stopped over last night. Oh well, *une bonne addresse* for next time I ride down this way. A few kms further down the road the whole village of Verteillac was *en fête*, entirely decked out with garlands of thousands of hand-made paper flowers spanning the streets and linking the church tower with the town hall. This was in aid of the *Félibrée fête occitane*, a festival celebrating the language, culture and traditions of the region, as I found out from a local woman who also told me that dozens of English expats had settled locally and were busy running local shops and businesses including bistros…rather a shame they couldn't cook, she lamented wistfully.

Today was altogether an easy-going and magnificent ride in perfect weather conditions across the Dordogne and into the Limousin on the D708, a quiet road of rolling hills under a cloudless deep blue sky – cycling doesn't get much better than this! At Chalus I turned onto the N21 into Isle, near Limoges, where I was warmly and generously welcomed by Jean and Monique, friends of my sister-in-law. The deal was similar to warmshowers: I regaled them with selected bikey anecdotes from around the world in return for dinner and wine – a very fair deal when the dinner turned out to be fish with ratatouille and a 2001 Pomerol. These were followed by an excellent local cheeseboard and mirabelle tart. Merci et bonne nuit!

134 km today / 21,792 km since London

Saturday 27th September

Jean and Monique set off at 05:45 on a day coach trip to Niort, leaving me free to devour the contents of their fridge before setting off north at 07:30. I headed into Limoges city centre and out onto the rolling and scenic D914 in warm sunshine through a series of sleepy villages, the prettiest of which was surely La Souterraine (would be lovelier still were its tiny streets not choked with fuming motor traffic). The roads flattened out after around 80 kms and I arrived in good time at the Issoudun Ibis hotel for my 17:30

Brothers reunited

rendezvous with brother Antony, aka @UprightTone. He'd come out by train with his bike to escort me home over the final four days and was sitting outside in the early evening sunshine reading his book, having ridden down from Vierzon, some 30 kms to the north. It was a grand reunion – I'd not seen him since leaving Harwich on April 5th, so following our traditional back-slapping routine there were some serious celebrations to be getting on with! After a quick shower and kit wash we ambled into town to enjoy a couple of Pastis before repairing to the sumptuous Trois Rois restaurant for a five-course gourmet dinner and a bottle of Burgundy; a 2009 Pommard, if you must know – when only the best will do!

168 km today / 21,960 km since London

Sunday 28th September

Our hotel provided an excellent value all-you-can-eat buffet breakfast, and we got away at around 08:15 in fine weather again and on flat quiet 'D' roads to Aubigny-sur-Nère, where we enjoyed a simple but fine menu du jour of *salade forestière* and meatballs with beer.

A few more kms down the road we were met in Autry-le-Châtel by Alain and Eric, two local club cyclists who led us to Briare and its famous *Pont Canal*, a spectacular 662m aqueduct built in 1896 to carry the Canal Latéral à la Loire over the River Loire on its journey to the River Seine.

Here a small crowd greeted us, including the Mayor of Briare and representatives of the local press. I'd not had such an official or grand reception since those heady early days in Eastern Europe. This one had been orchestrated by my father-in-law, Jean, and his wife, Michelle, who were also present with other family members

Grand reception at Briare-le-Canal

to enjoy a jolly half-hour photo-shoot and interviews and an impromptu Q&A session with a growing crowd of passers-by on this fine sunny Sunday. The thing that seemed to interest people most was my dog stick.

Alain and Eric then led us on to Ouzouer-sur-Trézée, the home village of their cycling club and of Jean and Michelle, who hosted a fabulous champagne garden party reception attended by various friends from the village, more local club cyclists and the Mayor and his wife – a great honour!

At around 19:00 the visitors all went home and the party continued in more intimate family fashion with an *épaule de sept heures* (slow-cooked lamb shoulder with beans) and a 2004 Pomerol. Bonne nuit!

121 km today / 22,081 km since London

Monday 29th September

We enjoyed a convivial and sumptuous breakfast of fresh croissants and pains au chocolat, home-made jams and coffee with Jean and Michelle before setting off at 08:30 under grey skies and light rain, but that cleared after an hour or so and we sped across a flat landscape towards Paris on good roads all day, stopping for an excellent menu du jour at the evidently popular *Côte et Port* bistrot in Pithiviers. A gregarious diner at the next table took it upon himself to introduce me to the editor of the local paper, a regular patron. A friendly chat morphed into an interview and photo-shoot of me shaking hands with the chef outside the front of the café, cementing the spirit of the *Entente Cordiale*.

At Dourdan we stopped for teatime drinks and cakes, finally arriving on somewhat busier roads – the suburbs of Paris – into Rambouillet at 18:30, where we checked into the Mercure hotel before finding an excellent dinner at the Cheval Rouge restaurant.

162 km today / 22,243 km since London

Tuesday 30th September

At €14 each we eschewed the hotel breakfast in favour of coffee and pastries at a local café, then hit the road at 08:00 for our final day in France, riding up to the coast for the ferry back to Blighty. It was another fine sunny day, and once we'd escaped the environs of Paris we were riding lovely quiet lanes all day with a lunch stop at Les Andeleys by the Seine and a couple of boulangerie stops to keep the carb levels topped up.

We rolled into Dieppe at around 19:00, checked into our hotel, then set out for the sea-front for a dinner which absolutely had to involve oysters. Fortunately these are not hard to find in Dieppe and we settled into a great harbourside place which also served a most splendidly scrumptious seafood sauerkraut. A couple of bottles of *Cidre de Normandie* lubricated the consumption of the menu gourmand, punctuated by the classic *Trou Normand* – an apple sorbet afloat in a bowl of Calvados. A short walk round the port afterwards helped with digestive matters, terminating in a small bar for a medicinal sleeping draught-sized Calvados.

184 km today / 22,427 km since London

Wednesday 1st October

We were up and out early from our hotel and on the 05:30 ferry, where we grabbed another couple of hours' kip before eating a particularly poor quality English breakfast prior to disembarking at Newhaven – welcome to England! Kingston Wheeler and laid-back logo designer Dominic Trevett met us off the ferry, having set off at 05:00 from his place in Morden (south London) and ridden down – great effort!

The three of us pottered gently northwards and upwards on horribly busy roads in light rain, though both traffic and drizzle gradually cleared once we'd reached the twisty lanes of the South Downs. It felt weirdly foreign to be back on British roads. Dominic led us on a moderately hilly route via Newick, where the Cottage Bakery did us good bacon sandwiches and coffee.

At The Bell in Outwood we were met for lunch by Dave Bradshaw (who'd ridden to Warsaw with me in April) and a work colleague, Andy. I supped my first English pint for six months; it barely touched the sides! The liver and bacon casserole was top-notch too, and Antony's plans for the day's *grande finale* could have gone horribly wrong at this stage had we succumbed to the temptation and British tradition of buying a round each...

And so we were five to roll together over the final miles of my world tour, crossing the North Downs into London via the delights of Coulsdon, Croydon and Mitcham. I'd tweeted and blogged that I was planning to arrive back at Bikefix at 17:00, and thought it would be rather good form to arrive on the dot, so when it looked as if we'd be getting in a few minutes early, Antony's encyclopaedic knowledge of London pubs came in handy and we grabbed a cheeky pint at the Rugby Tavern, just around the corner from Lamb's Conduit Street.

At 17:00 precisely we rolled around the corner and up to the bike shop for the warmest reception I could possibly have wished for. A sizeable crowd of friends, colleagues and family gave up a great cheer, a huge welcome home banner was unfurled, and Champagne corks popped. There were folk from RoadPeace, Kingston Wheelers, the London Cycling Campaign, parkrun, Audax UK, and Hammersmith & Fulham council. My entire UK-based family had also turned out for the occasion. To be honest it was a tiny bit overwhelming, but I just managed to control my emotions.

Lamb's Conduit Street is a characterful, car-free, convivial and carefree street where we spent a pleasant hour outside BikeFix necking Champagne, trying to speak with as many well-wishers as possible and posing for photos, one of the more popular being of my spectacularly-patterned tanned feet, thanks to my Shimano bike sandals.

Antony was Master of Ceremonies and kept us tightly on schedule: at 18:00 we moved a short way along the street to The Lamb for fine ales; and an hour later we parted from friends and colleagues to move over the road into Vats wine bar for a wonderfully intimate family dinner.

Then I rode home.

127 km today / 22,554 km since London

EPILOGUE

Five days after getting back home, I went back to work – a bit of a culture shock, for which I was under-prepared. It was good to be warmly welcomed back among old friends and colleagues, but the long-planned adventure of a lifetime was over and the return to routine a little hard to come to terms with. Some solace was found in giving a number of slide shows and writing this book, but living in the past wasn't going to cut the mustard for long. I needed new challenges!

I was pleased to return to some routines nonetheless, and parkrun was one of them. But all that cycling had done nothing for my running fitness and speed – quite the opposite in fact. I was down a couple of minutes on my PB (personal best) and to make matters worse, some of my chief rivals had joined a proper running club while I'd been away, and got faster! Well, if you can't beat them, join them – so I signed up to the *Hercules Wimbledon Athletics Club* and started going to training nights at the track. Gradually my running improved again and one thing led to another and before I knew it I'd started swimming lessons, bought a wetsuit, and signed up for an iron distance triathlon. Training for that took a good chunk of time out of 2015, but I did manage to squeeze in an audax SR series and a fourth appearance at Paris-Brest-Paris.

And so it was that at 07:15 one cold windswept September morning I ran down the beach with 430 other lunatics into the chilly waters of Weymouth Bay. An iron distance triathlon comprises a 3.8 km swim, a 180 km bike ride and a 42.2 km run (i.e. a full marathon). My key objective was to survive; finishing would be a bonus. I almost fell at the first hurdle – the sea was so choppy I got sea-sick on the second lap and had to stop and tread water for five minutes while regurgitating my breakfast. Luckily there weren't too many competitors behind me. I felt pretty awful after that but still had 700 metres to swim back to shore, so breast-stroked doggedly on until dragging myself onto the beach, exhausted. The swim had taken an hour and 45 minutes, about 15 minutes more than I'd hoped for. I'd been thinking about six hours on the bike and four on the run would get me across the finish line in something around 12 hours, give or take. But the inauspicious start had sapped my energy levels and dented my confidence and the cycling and the run each took an hour longer than expected, not helped by my taking a wrong turn on the bike adding 10 km to the ride. The cycle route followed a moderately hilly course to Wareham and back, twice;

then the run went back and forth along the promenade at Weymouth beach four times from one end to the other, with runners collecting different coloured wrist bands at the end of each lap. I ran more and more slowly and eventually finished in the dark and the rain at 21:14, over five hours behind the Polish winner. His official finish time was 8:42:32; mine was 13:59:10, which secured me 337th place out of 398 finishers. Not a brilliant result but I was absolutely ecstatic just to finish at all – job done!

In 2016 I decided with a small group of Wimbledon parkrun friends to have a crack at standard distance duathlon, which involves much shorter cycling and running distances and no swimming at all. Altogether much easier! A standard distance duathlon consists of a 10 km run, a 40 km bike ride, then a final 5 km run. This arrangement suited me much better and I managed to get myself qualified for Team GB (Old Codgers Division) and a place at the world championships at Avilés in Spain in June which was fantastic fun – like a mini-Olympics with opening and closing ceremonies and athletes from around the world, 45 of them in my 55-59 male age group, including 19 Britons. I was reasonably pleased with my debut international performance – despite having trouble finding my bike in the first transition and falling off it in the second, I managed to come 12th in our group, and third Brit, with a finishing time of 2:23:11, some 11 minutes behind the Dutch winner and new world champion, Henry Dullink. This has apparently pre-qualified me for entry into the 2017 world championships at Penticton, BC, in Canada – not a million miles from Gabriola, so another visit to Paradise island could be on the cards.

It's not easy fitting all of the above around a full-time job, so I'm increasingly looking forward to retirement and the time to train properly. My dad, who got me into all this in the first place, is now well into his eighties and still active, riding his bike most days and leading rides for the Dorset Cyclists' Network most weeks. A shining example still, he wonders these days how he ever found time to go to work. There are loads of oldies in audax and running, and now that our performances are measured against age-graded charts we can look forward to doing better as we get older!

A final shout out on behalf of RoadPeace – if you do drive, please go carefully and safely, and remember to give cyclists a wide berth. It's in the Highway Code you know[37]. And it might be me!

---

[37] http://www.highwaycode.info/rule/163

GUINNESS WORLD RECORD

The world ride was in my sights long before I became aware that there is actually a world record for this lunacy: *Fastest Circumnavigation by Bicycle*. I'd always planned a six-month ride – around 180 days. So when Scotsman Mark Beaumont set a new record of 195 days in 2008, I thought wahey! Might as well register a challenge at Guinness World Records (GWR) myself! However, thanks to a BBC documentary and a subsequent book, Mark's record attracted the attention of a lot of other riders who got the same idea…and it turned out that some of them could ride their bikes a lot faster than me. The record set by Mark has been broken a number of times, and now stands at just 106 days including transits[38] – that's an average of 320 km (200 miles) a day for over three months, just staggering! I neither had the ability, nor frankly any desire, to challenge that – I wanted to stop and see people and sights on the way. So I abandoned the record attempt, but not before an interesting exchange of emails with GWR.

When is a bike not a bike?

Shortly after registering my intended attempt with GWR in August 2008, I emailed to check that it would be acceptable to ride a recumbent bike. I probably shouldn't have done that! Between September and December 2008 the following bizarre correspondence ensued…

GWR: A recumbent bicycle is not acceptable for this attempt.

RE: This is a great disappointment, and begs the question: how do you define a bicycle? My bike is purely human-powered. It is simply a different shape. Please therefore reconsider your decision. If after reconsideration you still consider that a recumbent bicycle is not acceptable for this attempt, then I would like to establish a new world record category – Fastest Circumnavigation by Recumbent Bicycle.

GWR: One of the difficulties of this record is the physical demand imposed by using a regular bicycle. A recumbent bicycle removes some of that difficulty. Furthermore, accepting a recumbent bicycle would be unfair

---

[38] http://tinyurl.com/n36tztu

to our current and previous record holders who have already achieved this record. We will not be opening a new category for a recumbent bicycle.

RE: Thanks for your response…of course there will always be improvements made to "normal" bikes which will remove some of the difficulties that the current record holder had to face on his successful attempt. If you exclude my bike, what other bikes might not be acceptable, now or in the future? Where do you draw the line? Tricky business! Bikes come in all shapes and sizes… Human-powered should in my view be the one and only defining characteristic.

My preference therefore remains that you reconsider and permit me to attempt the existing record on my recumbent. Assuming pessimistically that you stick by your decision that "A recumbent bicycle is not acceptable for this attempt", I am disappointed that you will not be opening a new category for a recumbent bicycle. Please reconsider this.

I have read through all the documents you emailed me on 5th September and would be happy to be governed by similar guidelines. Therefore it should be relatively straightforward for you to open a new category. I am particularly keen to try this on a recumbent because indeed such a bike is more efficient, and I would like, if I succeed, to help achieve greater notoriety for these bikes among the wider population. It is partly because we recumbent enthusiasts are excluded from large numbers of amateur and professional events, and it now appears, GWR, that we remain side-lined and low-profile in more than one sense! This appears from our perspective to be a matter of prejudice. Surely GWR does not intend to be prejudiced against any minority community, simply on the grounds of the shape of their bike? Therefore please reconsider this decision. It would be a rather colourful record to achieve, and should result in good publicity both for GWR as well for recumbent bicycles, judging by the significant and hugely positive press interest and coverage obtained by the current record holder Mark Beaumont.

I should add here that I have no commercial or vested interest whatever in the promotion of recumbents or any other types of bikes. I hope you will be sympathetic, and take your time to consider this request with colleagues, and look forward to your response.

GWR: After having discussed your proposal with the rest of the Records Management Team, our decision still stands regarding recumbent bicycles. If any changes are made in the future regarding this, we will inform you of these.

RE: Thank you for having discussed my proposal with the rest of the Records Management Team. Obviously I am disappointed that your decision still stands regarding recumbent bicycles. Your emails to me are very brief…it would be good to know the reasoning behind your objection to my proposal. It strikes me that GWR accepts all kinds of bizarre record categories, and my proposal, compared to some you accept, looks pretty normal. Is there any kind of appeals procedure open to me? Could I come up to your offices to make my case and hear your objections to my proposal please?

GWR: As mentioned in one of the previous emails: "One of the difficulties of this record is the physical demand imposed by using a regular bicycle. A recumbent bicycle removes some of that difficulty. Furthermore, accepting a recumbent bicycle would be unfair to our current and previous record holders who have already achieved this record." If you would like to submit a rejection appeal you must do this via the website. We hope this solves your query.

RE: I am afraid this does not solve my query. I have already responded to the above point, in my message to you via the GWR website dated 16th September.

The two specific points which I feel you have not addressed are:

1. Why you will not consider setting up a new category for recumbent bicycle.

2. Can we not discuss this face to face please? Because having now sent several appeal messages via the website, I do not feel that I am getting a full or fair hearing.

GWR: We will not be opening a separate category for any other type of bicycle. In accepting a recumbent bicycle we would have to accept all other modifications – which we will not do. Unfortunately, due to the high volume of claims we deal with on an everyday basis, we are unable to invite any of our claimants to our offices.

RE: You just made one of my points for me. You said: "In accepting a recumbent bicycle we would have to accept all other modifications - which we will not do."

But you do accept other modifications!

In an earlier query I put to you that bikes obviously over time evolve, e.g. are made of newer improved lighter and stronger materials, such as carbon fibre, aluminium and titanium replacing steel. These are modifications which improve bikes and make them easier to ride around the world, or anywhere else.

Did you check that the current GWR holder Mark Beaumont's bike was exactly identical to the first person's bike used to set this record? Of course you did not! Of course Mark's bike was different, for example it had a relatively recently invented 14-speed Rohloff hub gear which may have given him a significant advantage over previous record holders who did not have this gearing system available to them.

Begging the question: where do you draw the line? Why can you not accept that a bike is an exclusively human-powered two-wheeled vehicle? Any other attempt to define it opens a can of worms. Would you for instance accept a semi-recumbent?

I have previously asked about your appeals procedure. You said "If you would like to submit a rejection appeal you must do this via the website." So in fact you are saying that the correspondence between us, on-going since 9th September, is my only channel of appeal – I send a message to you via the website and you reply very briefly by email. This is not a fair appeals procedure, because I cannot make my case to anyone other than you, or by any other means (eg a meeting at your offices, which you refused in your email dated 30th September). Please therefore let me have the details of the Managing Director so I can write in to him or her with my appeal.

GWR: As you have mentioned yourself, these modifications are the result of the evolution of the bicycle. They are performance modifications. A recumbent bicycle does not fall under these modifications as it is a completely different category – for which we will not be opening a category. I have passed on your details to our Director of Records. We hope this solves your query.

RE: I am afraid the query is not solved, however we are going round in circles now. I am most dissatisfied and surprised frankly at GWR response to this matter. The strangest aspect to me is the fact that you will not consider opening a new category, and give no explanation for that refusal. GWR lists hundreds of more bizarre exploits as records.

In an earlier message (17th September) you wrote "If any changes are made in the future regarding this, we will inform you of these." Please do inform me if/when the time comes that you take a more enlightened view. I am planning my attempt for 2014 so you have plenty of time to think again! I will follow to the letter the regulations that you have kindly provided me with – so you would even be able to change your mind during or after the attempt if you feel so inclined.

Please forward this message to the Director of Records.

RE: I'd be grateful if you could please acknowledge receipt of my message on 27th November (copy below) and confirm that you passed it onto the Director of Records as requested

GWR: We did receive your message and passed it on to our director of records as requested.

VITAL STATISTICS

- 22,554 km pedalled
- 4 continents traversed
- 18 countries visited
- 1,320 hours ridden
- 4,310 hours including all stops
- 17.3 km/h average speed
- 5.3 km/h including all down time
- 116,269 metres climbed (Everest x 13)
- 6,000,000 pedal revolutions
- 1,000,000 calories consumed
- 68 nights camping
- 59 hotels/motels
- 18 nights with family
- 17 warmshowers
- 11 nights with friends
- 3 night flights
- 3 nights in sheds
- 2 nights on ferries
- 0 days ill
- 650,000 more deaths on the road

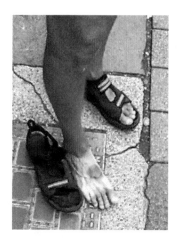

Made in the USA
Charleston, SC
07 August 2016